P9-DDM-635

Unelected Representatives

LIBRARY
BRYAN COLLEGE
DAYTON, TN. 37321

UNELECTED

REPRESENTATIVES

Congressional Staff and

the Future of

Representative Government

MICHAEL J. MALBIN

Basic Books, Inc., Publishers

NEW YORK

68673

The material quoted on pages 85–86 is reprinted from *Newsday*, March 23, 1979, pages 3 and 11. Copyright © 1979. Reprinted by permission.

Library of Congress Cataloging in Publication Data

Malbin, Michael J
   Unelected representatives.

   Includes bibliographical references and index.
   1. United States. Congress—Officials and employees. 2. Representative government and representation—United States. I. Title.
JK1083.M34   328.73'0761   79–3127
ISBN 0–465–08866–X

Copyright © 1980 by Michael J. Malbin
Printed in the United States of America
DESIGNED BY VINCENT TORRE
10 9 8 7 6 5 4 3 2 1

CONTENTS

v

PART 4
Conclusion

ACKNOWLEDGMENTS

THIS BOOK never could have been written without the cooperation and help of many people, most of whose names appear in the following chapters. In this space, I should like to thank some of the people who were not part of story but whose contribution helped me understand what the story was all about.

Irving Kristol, coeditor of *Public Interest,* gave me the idea for this study in 1976, when he asked me to write an article on congressional staffs. After that article appeared, he then encouraged me to apply to the American Enterprise Institute for Public Policy Research for a fellowship to write a book on the subject. AEI provided me with everything I needed—in fact, the atmosphere was so pleasant that I joined the regular staff after my two-year leave from *National Journal.*

Several people have read all or part of this book in draft form. The whole manuscript was read by Thomas Mann and Norman Ornstein, two of my colleagues in AEI's Congress Project, and by Leslie Lenkowsky. Individual chapters were read by Walter Berns, Paul Halpern, Richard Levy, Stephen Miller, Rudolph Penner, and David Price. These readers will recognize where their insights saved me from error or forced me to probe more deeply. They will also know where my stubbornness prevailed over what may have been their better judgment. Such are the friendly exchanges that lie behind the ritualized, but nonetheless accurate disclaimer that the responsibility for any mistakes in fact or judgment is mine.

Martin Kessler, president and copublisher of Basic Books, has been my most critical, and therefore most helpful reader. It has been a pleasure to work with him and with Kathleen Long, the Congress Project's secretary, who typed the manuscript.

Several sections in this book have appeared previously. The article mentioned earlier, "Congressional Committee Staffs: Who's in

Charge Here?" *The Public Interest,* Spring 1977, pp. 16–49, contains some material that reappears in these pages. Much of the chapter on the House Commerce Subcommittee on Oversight and Investigations (chapter 7) was in "The Bolling Committee Revisited: Energy Oversight On An Investigative Subcommittee," a paper delivered at the annual meeting of the American Political Science Association in September 1978. An abbreviated version of chapter 9, on Congress's use of policy analysis in the natural gas debate, was published in *Bureaucrats, Policy Analysts and Statesmen,* Robert Goldwin, ed. (Washington: American Enterprise Institute, 1980). The data for the appendix were collected as part of AEI's Congress Project and will also appear in book length, *Vital Statistics On Congress—1980,* John Bibby, Thomas E. Mann and Norman J. Ornstein, eds. (Washington: American Enterprise Institute, forthcoming, 1980).

PART 1

Congressional Staff:
Unelected Representatives

Chapter 1

The Problem

I WAS NERVOUS. Fresh from academe, on my first assignment as a journalist, I was in the middle of an article about a conference committee that was deadlocked over the use of highway trust fund money for mass transit. I had done all the easy interviews—staffers and lobbyists who filled me in on the issues and players. But sooner or later I knew I would have to interview some elected senators and representatives. The $23 billion authorization bill was the most significant one to come out of the House Public Works Subcommittee on Transportation that year (1973), so it seemed obvious to me that I ought to see the chairman. So there I was, waiting in the office of the late John Kluczynski (D-Ill.) with tape recorder clutched in hand, and, as I said, I was nervous. After all, this interview could be the one to give me the political insights I needed to impress my new editors.

When I first got to Kluczynski's office, the receptionist said the congressman would be glad to see me in a few minutes. Then, while I waited, she telephoned one of the committee staff professionals working on the bill. The chairman wanted him there, she said, in case I raised any technical issues. That seemed a reasonable enough request, until we reached the first "technical" question.

I began the interview with what I thought was a throwaway question. (My experienced colleagues said that was a good way to break the ice.) What makes this issue important, I asked?

"This is a tremendously important bill. It involves millions of dollars," Klucyznski began to answer, and then paused. "No—*billions,* isn't it?" he asked, turning to the staff aide.

That did it—the balloon was pricked and my case of nerves was over. The significance of that brief exchange was too clear to be missed, even by a newcomer. I was initially shocked, but quickly began realizing that to understand Congress, I had better start paying attention to the role of its staff.

That realization has only been confirmed by subsequent experience. Rarely do representatives or senators depend as totally on their staffs as Kluczynski did that day, particularly not on a major bill handled by a subcommittee they head. In fact, most members seem broadly to be in control of most of what their own staffs are doing with the authority delegated to them. Nevertheless, it is not unfair to suggest that Congress as a whole has become the institutional embodiment of Kluczynski's spirit. The members cannot begin to control the workload that their staffs collectively help to generate. Yet, Congress could not function in today's world without the staff on which it has come to depend.

This represents a revolutionary change in an institution that, as recently as 1945, saw no need for permanent professional committee staffs. The congressional budget is almost forty-five times as large as it was three decades ago. In that same time committee staffs, the most important element of the congressional bureaucracy in policy terms, have increased almost eightfold, personal staffs have increased fivefold, and support agencies* have taken on a new importance. The numbers only begin to tell the story of staff influence, however. More impressive are the kinds of tasks members of Congress have become willing to delegate to their staffs. This has reached the point where some members publicly ask whether they or their staffs are in charge.

In principle, of course, the members hire, fire, and therefore control their staffs. Nevertheless, the staff exercises a great deal of indirect influence over which the members' control is at best tenuous and imperfect. That influence arises from the simple fact the members have more to do than time in which to do it and it extends well beyond the housekeeping functions familiar to most of us. We all know that committee staffs arrange hearings, draft bills, and hold

---

*The four support agencies are the Library of Congress, General Accounting Office, Office of Technology Assessment, and Congressional Budget Office.

stacks of paper with reams of information for members during debates. But the way these staffs can substantively affect every step in the legislative process may be less familiar. For example, their ability to run committee investigations, the results of which they can skillfully leak to the media, gives them influence over the items members choose to put on the legislative agenda. Once a bill is on the agenda, the staff works to assemble a coalition behind it, arranging detailed amendments with other staff members and with interest group representatives to broaden support for the bill without sacrificing the goals the chairman, often at their urging, has adopted. When conflicts cannot be resolved, the members may then learn enough about the details to weigh the political costs of compromise. But even then, the role of the member is clearly limited. As former Senator Dick Clark (D-Iowa), once said: "There is no question about our enormous dependency and their influence. In all legislation, they're the ones that lay out the options."[1]

The system that leads staffs to have this kind of influence does have a rational basis. The reason for committee staffs, and the source of their influence, is an extension of the reason for having committees: the idea that Congress is best served if members become specialists, with the vast majority accepting the expertise of a few on most issues. Committee staffs grew when it became apparent that even specialized committee members needed help if Congress was to get the information required for making informed decisions. Congress needs staffs, just as it needs specialist members, to help it evaluate the flood of material from the outside and perhaps even come up with ideas of its own. The system clearly provides benefits. It seems no accident that Congress, the most powerful parliamentary body in the world, is also the one with the largest staff. Without its staff, Congress would quickly become the prisoner of its outside sources of information in the executive branch and interest groups.

Yet, the costs have been high. The staffs—individually well educated, hard working, and, in general, devoted to what they perceive to be the public good—collectively create a situation in which many of the elected members fear they are becoming insulated administrators in a bureaucratized organization that leaves them no better able to cope than they were when they did all the work themselves.[2] The seriousness of this situation would be difficult to overemphasize.

We all know from studies of public opinion that the policy messages conveyed by voters to their representatives are at best tenuous and ambiguous.[3] But this tenuous connection becomes stretched to the breaking point when the representatives delegate too much of their control to appointed staff aides. How much delegation is "too much" is open to debate, of course. But there can be no doubt that precisely what staffs do and how they do it are matters that relate to the basic principles underlying representative government—the very principles that give members, and through them their staffs, their reason for being.

The problem has arisen partly from the sheer size of today's congressional staffs and partly from the ways in which members have transformed the role of staff over the past few decades. Congress has been pursuing at least four somewhat conflicting aims as it has increased the size of its staff. Its aims have included: (1) a desire to be less dependent on the executive branch and outside interest groups for information; (2) a desire, especially among Republicans and junior Democrats, to put their own imprint on issues of national importance; (3) a desire on the part of an increasing number of members to devote their time and resources to gaining credit in the media for putting new issues on the legislative agenda instead of working quietly to impress their colleagues through committee specialization;[4] and (4) a desire on the part of almost everyone in Congress to gain some control over their expanding workloads and over the increasingly fragmented nature of their work. Of these different goals, the first suggests an increase in the size of Congress's professional staff but says nothing about the way the staff should be used or how it should be controlled, the second suggests that the staff should not only grow but that staff resources should be dispersed, and the third suggests giving the enlarged staff new kinds of things to do. All three of these objectives have more or less been attained in the years since World War II. However, the first three objectives are incompatible with the fourth—and that is the one that raises the basic question of democratic control.

Congress has failed utterly to cope with its workload. If anything, the growth of staff has made the situation worse. First, on the level of sheer numbers, more staff means more information coming in to each member's office, with more management problems as different staff aides compete for the member's time to present their own nuggets in a timely fashion. The member, under these conditions, is becoming more of a chief executive officer in charge of a medium-sized business than a person who personally deliberates with his colleagues about policy.* Second, the problems created by large numbers are exacerbated by the staffs' new roles. Increasingly, the members want aides who will dream up new bills and amendments bearing their bosses' names instead of helping the bosses understand what is already on the agenda. The result is that the new staff bureaucracy and the workload it helps create threaten to bury Congress under its own paperwork, just as surely as if the staff never existed.

But recognizing a problem is one thing, understanding it is another. Like a first-year medical student faced with a sick person, the beginning observer of politics has no difficulty recognizing that something is wrong with the way Congress is working. But just as the physician knows he can sometimes make a disease worse by reacting to obvious symptoms without first identifying their underlying cause, so must the student of politics be aware that the precise causes and effects of staff growth need careful analysis before one can begin to think of remedies.

The need to proceed with caution has dictated the approach followed in this book. The relationships between staff and members are highly personal and at first blush appear to be as varied as the people elected to Congress. Therefore, to understand the way any staff works, it is necessary to get close to it and observe it in action. It takes a knowledge of the detailed particulars, in this highly individualized world, to sort out what is general.

That is why the book's general arguments are inferred from the details of individual stories learned during hundreds of interviews I conducted in the Ninety-fourth and Ninety-fifth Congresses (1975–1978).† Yet, the stories should not be confused with a series of disparate "case studies." Each of the subsequent chapters is based on studies of different committee staffs to illustrate specific stages of the

---

*Former Representative Abner Mikva (D-Ill.) told me that his way of dealing with this problem was to go to a hideaway office where the staff could not find him. He said he needed a place where he could read and think without being interrupted by staff aides who constantly wanted to add to his pile of papers, but said that he was reluctant to close the door to his own office because it would discourage the aides from coming up with the new ideas and information that he wanted from them.

†Any direct or indirect quotation in this book unaccompanied by a footnoted source comes from these interviews. The interviews may have one problem about which the reader should be warned in advance. Staff people tend to overemphasize their importance by failing to mention direct conversations among members. I tried to check this wherever possible, especially in the chapter on the Sunset Bill, where I concluded that direct conversations were significant at only a few key junctures. I may well have missed some of the important conversations among the senators, but not enough, I believe, to affect the conclusion.

legislative process or specific analytical themes. Thus, we learn how staff members persuade their bosses to adopt their ideas by hearing an articulate staff director describe how he goes about the job and placing that description in the context of other examples of similar acts of persuasion (chapter 3 and the beginning of chapter 4). We get a sense of how staffs negotiate and act on behalf of their members in other stages of the legislative process through a detailed examination of two specific pieces of legislation (chapters 4 and 5). We learn, by examining the way two subcommittees do related investigations, how staffs responsible directly to their chairmen act on the chairmen's behalf to control the flow of information to other members, how the staff's judgment affects what gets to the chairmen themselves, and how some staffs act independently of their staff directors and chairmen to see that information in their possession becomes known to the press and to other committee staffs (chapters 6 and 7). We then, look at two nonpartisan staffs (chapter 8), and we discover that while nonpartisan staffs act more nearly as neutral information conduits than "chairmen's staffs" do, they have problems of their own that preclude Congress from adopting them as a universal remedy to the symptoms uncovered. Finally, by an examination of the members' use of staff-produced policy analyses on a politically divisive issue (natural gas deregulation) we learn how members actually use some of the information their staffs produce. Only after the individual stories have thus been dissected do we suggest remedies. First, however, let us see how we got to where we are.

Chapter 2

The Post-1947 Era: Ballooning Staff with New Roles

THE PROBLEM of congressional staffing relates both to staff numbers and to the kinds of jobs members are willing to delegate to the new-style young activists they increasingly tend to hire. The two issues are connected. As we mentioned earlier, congressional staffs, have grown partly because members wanted to decentralize power while pursuing the legislative strategies of issue entrepreneurs. To help them achieve these aims they have hired staffs whose skills and career objectives are far different from those of the aides of the 1940s and 1950s. The career objectives of the staffs, in turn, independently influence the legislative process, reinforcing and exacerbating the problem. To understand the importance of this independent influence, however, we first need to place it in context.

A New Era

The United States Congress today is an institution made up of 539 elected senators, representatives, and nonvoting delegates and 23,528 staff. In comparison, the second most heavily staffed legislature in the world is the Canadian Parliament, which manages to make do with a staff of only 3,300.

It was not always this way. Until only a few decades ago, most congressional committees did not have permanent professional staffs, personal staffs were miniscule and support staffs were not much larger. The elected representatives of the people debated, compromised, and reached decisions about the nation's legislative business on their own. The new era began, roughly, with the Legislative Reorganization Act of 1946. At that time, Congress was housed comfortably in six buildings, members worked directly with their colleagues, and people had reason to believe that their opinions, expressed in letters, would be read by the person they voted to put in office. This has all changed. Congress is now a vast enterprise crowded into fifteen buildings, with one more under construction and sixteen more in the planning stage.[1]

Of course, many of the 23,528 people do not work directly on legislation. Most of the 10,000 or so on personal staffs work on press releases and constituency-related casework, while many in the Library of Congress, General Accounting Office, and on the various service staffs do work that relates even less directly to the legislative process. The four kinds of staff with the greatest influence over legislation are committee staffs (the most important, and therefore the focus of this book), legislative aides on personal staffs, some support agency staff, and the staffs serving the leadership and ad hoc groups. All have grown over recent decades. Just as importantly, all have been hiring a different type of person than the Capitol Hill staffer of decades past, and all have tended to increase the workload while strengthening the forces of institutional decentralization in Congress.

Committee Staffs

Congressional committees began hiring part-time, temporary clerks in the 1840s. In 1856, the Senate Finance and House Ways and Means Committees started receiving regular appropriations for full-time clerks,[2] and the remaining committees all had full-time clerks by the end of the century.[3] According to one count,[4] committee staff in 1891 numbered sixty-two in the House and forty-one in the Senate by 1891.* But until well into the twentieth century these staff positions were treated as patronage appointments for political cronies. In fact, personal and committee staffs were thoroughly intermingled in practice in the House and by law in the Senate. For example, legislation during the 1920s specified that a new Senate chairman's three top clerks from personal staff were to become clerks of the committee and that committee staff was to help the chairman with the work of his personal office.[5]

Nonpartisan professional committee staffs began to be developed at about this time on the House and Senate appropriations committees and on the newly formed (1926) Joint Committee on Internal Revenue Taxation. It was the the the money committees' successful experience with professional staffs that led Congress to institutionalize the practice in the Legislative Reorganization Act of 1946.[6] As part of a general realignment and reduction in the number of congressional committees, the act permitted all committees to hire up to four professional and six clerical workers each. (Exceptions were made for the two appropriations committees, which were allowed to determine their own staffing needs.) The permanent professionals authorized by this act (who have since been designated "statutory staff") were expected to be nonpartisan. Additional people for specific investigations were to be hired as needed, supposedly on a temporary basis. But already during the act's first years, committees began to hire such additional people on a quasi-permanent basis, so that ultimately the distinction between statutory and investigative staffs has become one that is honored rather in technical job descriptions than in on-the-job responsibilities.

The aim of nonpartisan professionalism apparently was main-

---

*For tables detailing the growth of committee, personal and support agency staffs, see the appendixes.

tained during the first six years after reorganization. Kenneth Kofmehl's *Professional Staffs of Congress,* the first book-length treatment of staffs was based on research done in the three Congresses between 1947 and 1952 (Eightieth through Eighty-second). It described "the prevailingly nonpartisan operation of most committees"[7] with minority party subcommittee chairmen on many committees and the whole staff accessible to every committee member on two-thirds of the committees Kofmehl studied. However, even as Kofmehl did his research, the system was already beginning to break down. By the end of his six years, several committees were beginning to designate some staff members as majority and others as minority.[8] Still, the prevailing conception of staff permitted Kofmehl to describe such party designation as "erroneous":

> It is not the function of the committee aides to promote particular policies but rather to facilitate the work of the entire committee by procuring information, by arranging for the services of other elements of the legislative and executive branch staffs, by pointing up relevant factors the committee should take into account when considering certain problems, by incorporating the committee's decisions in bills and reports and by discharging the manifold other staff duties that conserve the committee members' time and render less difficult the performance of their vital office. The members of a committee themselves, not the staff, should take care of the majority and minority interests and presumbly, as politicians, should be well-qualified to do so.[9]

Today very few committee staffs even try to meet Kofmehl's standard. Most had already moved decisively away from the nonpartisan evenhandedness by the time the first edition of Kofmehl's book came out in 1962. By then, Representative Clem Miller's published letters to his constituents described committee staffs in terms that showed that he for one regarded them as employees of the chairmen of the full committees and, through them, of the committees' majorities.[10] In the Senate, Randall Ripley's 1965 research led him to conclude:

> On most of the committees, most of the professional staff members are directly responsible only to the chairman. He appoints them and they retain their jobs only so long as they please him with their efforts. They tend to share his political coloration as well as his formal party affiliation. A few of the staff members may not have this special relationship with the chairman; but they are likely to have a similar relationship with the ranking minority member or, in a few cases, another senior member of the committee, probably a member of the majority party.[11]

This control of staff by chairmen led Republicans in the late 1960s to agitate for professional minority staff on every committee. The Legislative Reorganization Act of 1970[12] appeared to give the Republicans what they wanted. It increased each committee's statutory professional staff from four to six, required that two of the six professionals and one of the six statutory clerical staff be selected by the minority, and said that no less than one-third of each committee's remaining funds should be used for minority staff.

But Democrats in both the Senate and House decided to ignore the one-third minority staff requirement in 1971 and in subsequent years. The provision was revived in House committee reforms adopted in 1974 (H. Res. 988), but the House Democratic Caucus trimmed the proposal back again in 1975 by dropping the one-third guarantee for investigative staff while granting the minority one-third of each committee's increased allotment of eighteen statutory professionals and twelve clerical staff. However, as part of its 1977 reform resolution (S. Res. 4) the Senate required committees to give the minority a full one-third of all statutory and investigative staff within four years and is well on its way toward achieving this goal.

At the time the Legislative Reorganization Act of 1970 was passed, House committee staffs were about four times as large as they had been in 1947 (702 versus 167), and Senate committee staffs were about three times as large (635 versus 232). These numbers kept going up during the 1970s. Senate committee staffs nearly doubled again between 1970 and 1979 (to 1,217) while those in the House increased tripled (to 2,073).

The steady growth of Senate committee staffs since the early 1950s has been a direct result of the dispersal of power to junior senators, a process that began under the majority leadership of Lyndon B. Johnson. The so-called "Johnson Rule" of the 1950s assured every Democratic senator of at least one good committee assignment. Over the years, as this worked itself out, most Democratic senators were able to become chairmen of subcommittees, each with its own staff.

In the House, too, staff growth and internal democratization have gone hand in hand. The staff increases on House committees in the 1970s resulted largely from the 1973 House Democratic Caucus's "Subcommittee Bill of Rights" that liberated subcommittee chairmen from the control of the chairmen of full committees.[13] As a result, most of the committee staff increases in the House during the 1970s have been at the subcommittee level. (The subcommittee staffs examined in chapters 6 and 7, for example, are each as large as most full committee staffs of the 1960s.)

Thus, in both the House and the Senate, the increases in staffing of the 1950s and early 1960s were accompanied by a shift away from nonpartisan professional staffs serving whole committees to a system of staffs working primarily for individual members, generally chairmen. Since then, the principle of individual control has not changed, but the distribution of staff resources has become more widespread. This broader distribution both results from and reinforces internal democratization, as more members have the staff resources to pursue their own legislative ends.

Personal Staffs

Other forms of staff growth also have tended to support the growing decentralization of Congress. In this connection the increased number of legislative aides on personal staffs is an obvious case in point.

Although members who were not chairmen were first allowed to hire staffs of their own in 1893,[14] most of the growth, has taken place since 1947. Since 1947, personal staffs have increased from 1,449 to 7,067 in the House and from 590 to 3,612 in the Senate.

Since most personal staff aides do not work on legislation, the growth in personal staff does not by itself say anything about the growth of legislative assistance. Unfortunately, it is impossible to know how many legislative aides there were in the House and Senate before 1970, when the Legislative Reorganization Act introduced formal professional titles for people on personal staffs. But it is possible to talk about growth in the 1970s. Since the increase in the number of legislative aides in both the House and the Senate has been fairly modest, going up from an average of 1.3 per House member in 1972 to 2.2 in 1979 and from an average of 3.9 per senator in 1973 to 5.5 in 1979. (For details, see appendix A-6.)

From the numbers, it seems obvious that most of the members' new personal staff aides do constituency-related work that may help an incumbent win reelection[15] but that has little to do with the legislative process. Still, an increase of even one legislative aide per member is enough to produce a large number of amendments for the floor—particularly since the increase in both chambers is greatest among Republicans and Southern Democrats, who are most likely to be opposed to the thrust of committee reported legislation. (Again, see the appendix for the figures by party and region.) Thus, for example, we saw junior Republicans such as David Stockman of Michigan and Richard Cheney of Wyoming having the resources to lead the unsuccessful 1979 floor fight against federal loan guarantees for the Chrysler Corporation, even though neither was on the committee that reported the bill. The increase in personal staff legislative aides for Republicans and southern Democrats in turn reflects changing conservative attitudes toward the use of staff. Liberal northern Democrats were far more likely than Republicans or southern Democrats to rely heavily on staff during the early 1970s, but the situation was evening up in the late 1970s. We shall see this in the subsequent chapters, where we shall observe some media conscious, new-style conservatives using staffs to develop national issues in a manner similar to that pioneered by the liberal Democrats of previous years.

Support Agencies

The support agencies have also grown in the 1970s. Although the connection between this and internal democratization may not be clear at first glance, the link comes through the growth of policy analysis and the way analysis is used by the members.

In 1970, the 332 people who worked for the Library of Congress's Legislative Reference Service performed largely bibliographic, speechwriting, and factual research chores. The role of the service was expanded significantly by the Legislative Reorganization Act of 1970 (Sec. 321), which changed the name to the Congressional Research Service (CRS) and gave it the job of analyzing and evaluating legislative proposals upon request from a committee.* Between 1970 and 1976, CRS's staff grew rapidly—from 332 to 806. With the increased staff has come more policy analysis and

---

*While the Legislative Reorganization Act of 1946 also gave the then forty-two-year-old service a mandate to evaluate upon request, the task remained peripheral to the job of the understaffed and overworked service until 1970.

research. By the end of fiscal 1975, one study estimated that 63 percent of CRS's staff and 71 percent of its budget were devoted to these activities,[16] although "quick and dirty" research done on a fast deadline still seems to outweigh more thoughtful analysis.[17]

The General Accounting Office (GAO), established by the Budget and Accounting Act of 1921, is seven years younger than CRS's forebear, the Legislative Reference Service. During the 1960s it began expanding its traditional auditing functions to include reviews designed to "measure the effectiveness of a wide variety of government programs."[18] Congress affirmed its support of this new emphasis in the 1970 Legislative Reorganization Act, which explicitly directed the GAO to do "cost benefit studies of government programs" (Sec. 204). In response to this mandate, the GAO began hiring a more diverse group of professionals. True, the GAO still considers itself the watchdog of the federal treasury and stations accountants and auditors in every executive branch agency. However, by 1975, only 2,701 (or 65 percent) of its 4,142 professional staff were members of the two traditionally dominant professions,[19] accountants and auditors. And, a 1976 study of the GAO reported that 35 percent of the GAO's workload and more than half of its self-initiated work can be described as program evaluation.[20] Most of these are retrospective analyses of programs already in existence, but a fair number are prospective evaluations of legislation under consideration, such as the energy studies mentioned in chapter 9.

The two small remaining support agencies, the Office of Technology Assessment (OTA) and Congressional Budget Office (CBO), were created by statutes passed in 1972 and 1974, respectively, and began operations in 1974 and 1975.[21] Staff levels at the CBO have been around 200 since its first year, while OTA has grown steadily to a 1978 complement of 164 staff. About one-third of the staff at CBO and all at OTA directly or indirectly analyze and evaluate the implications of future policy choices for the Congress. (The rest of the staff at CBO works on budget estimating and scorekeeping.)

All four support agencies are organized along bureaucratic lines much more akin to the traditional nonpartisan staffs than the recently ascendent individualistic staffs of most committees.* Despite

---

*OTA has had difficulties defining a distinct mission for itself and for a time was in danger of becoming almost like personalized professional committee staff aides for OTA's congressional board members. The latter difficulty may have eased somewhat, but not the former.[22]

this, the growth in support agency policy analysis helps reinforce the internal decentralizing forces responsible for the growth of personalized subcommittee staffs. While most support agency analysis is produced at the request of chairmen or ranking minority members, overlaps in subcommittee jurisdiction as well as the virtual autonomy of most subcommittee chairmen mean that requests for analyses can be placed on just about any controversial issue. Since support agency reports become available to all senators and representatives upon release, the net result is to destroy the monopoly of information once enjoyed by committee chairmen. Anyone willing to let a subcommittee staff member or legislative aide take the time to study these reports is in a position to challenge the judgments of committee chairmen and often will.

Leadership Staffs and Ad Hoc Groups

The 1970s have seen increases not only in the staffs that introduce, negotiate, and analyze bills and amendments for committee members and other specialists, but also in the staffs that process information so as to help build coalitions among nonspecialists in the last stages before floor votes. These staffs generally do little more than react to materials developed elsewhere. None of the subsequent chapters focus on them directly, but they play an important role and should not be ignored.

We already have encountered two kinds of staff that do this type of work. Most legislative assistants in the House and Senate spend their time preparing their members for floor votes on issues that do not vitally concern them. They ride the elevators with their bosses before the votes and, in the rush, their nuanced phrases may, unintentionally or intentionally, influence how a member votes. These quick briefings, always important in the Senate, have lately become a factor in the House as well, as the introduction in 1975 of electronic voting has cut the time allowed per roll call from thirty to fifteen minutes, thereby reducing the time available for conversation among members. True, CRS also helps inform nonspecialist members by nonpartisan "issue briefs" prepared for the House and Senate computer system. However, these briefs tend to be read not by the members but by legislative assistants who then brief the members verbally.

Two remaining kinds of staffs intervene between committees and the floor: leadership staffs and the staffs of ad hoc issue and regional caucuses. In general, they are in competition with each other.

The role of these staffs is very different in the House and in the Senate. As has often been observed, the Senate, with only 100 members, has much less need than the House for formal coordination and a highly structured leadership. The staffs reflect this. Thus, in 1978 the Senate majority leader and majority whip had a combined total staff of only nine while the role of formal issue groups and regional caucus was virtually nil. In the House, the leadership and caucus staffs are both more significant. In 1978, the Democratic leadership had a staff of forty-six and the Republicans, forty-three. Most of these aides help with whip counts, scheduling, press relations, and other tasks related to the leaders' verbal communications with members, but a few in each party add to the written information flow with whip notices and (on the Republican side only) summaries of major bills and amendments.

The Republicans got the idea for doing bill summaries from the oldest of the ad hoc groups in the House, the liberal Democratic Study Group (DSG), which was founded in 1959 and had a staff of fifteen in 1978. Although best known outside Congress for its work on congressional reform, the DSG's summaries of bills and amendments—generally presenting arguments for and against divisive proposals—are probably read more widely than any other single collection of congressionally produced written material about pending legislation. The small Democratic Research Organization (staff size: three) and the Republican Study Committee (staff size: ten) both were formed in the early 1970s to provide conservative alternatives to the written material produced by the DSG and Republican Conference.[23]

The 1970s has been a period of explosive growth for the ad hoc groups. DSG was the only such group in existence before 1960. Two others were formed during the 1960s, seven between 1970 and 1974, and thirty from 1975 to 1979.[24] While several of the new groups are little more than excuses for occasional press releases (such as the Congressional Roller and Ball Bearing Coalition), most permit a pooling of personal staff resources to create alternative sources of information for members. As such, they compete with committees and with the leadership. Their growth, in other words, has fed the same decentralizing forces that produced the personalization of committee staffs.

Career Goals and the Staffer's Life

As we suggested earlier, the shift toward personalized control of committee staff has gone hand in hand with a shift in the type of person hired for the job. Once a sinecure for patronage appointments and later a professional job for midcareer bureaucrats, congressional staffs increasingly have become filled with people who see their jobs in Congress as stepping stones to something else. Legislative aides on personal staffs and research staffs who work for ad hoc issue groups try to move to committee staffs. These staffs, in turn, seem to be positioning themselves for jobs elsewhere in the Washington political community. The question for this book is whether their work as staff members is affected by what they want to do after they leave Capitol Hill.

Recent research on staffs has highlighted the new career pattern clearly. Harrison Fox and Susan Hammond have found that legislative assistants in the House tend to be in their twenties, while Senate personal staff professionals and committee professionals in both chambers are generally in their thirties and forties.[25] Perhaps more important, they found that 50 percent of their sample of 302 committee staff aides had been on the job four years or less, another 33 percent for four to ten years, and only 17 percent for eleven years or more.[26]

Clearly, most personal and committee staff aides are not settling in as career civil servants working toward their retirements. There are important exceptions of course, and a few committees still hire people who view their jobs much the same way as do their counterparts in executive agencies.* The illustrative studies in this book

*Interestingly, the support agencies also seem to be peopled with "new style," young professionals—the policy analysts. While the future ambitions of the policy analysts may not affect policy as directly as the ambitions of the committee staff members, they are clearly part of the same set of Washington "issue networks" as the committee staffs and their training, if not their ambition, does affect policy. These analysts may not affect the legislative agenda as directly as new-style committee staff lawyers, but they do affect the way members think about and debate issues. (For more on this, see chapter 9.)

suggest that the different perspectives of the two types of staffs affect the way they approach their jobs. If so, this would suggest that a Congress in which members prefer one type of staff should function differently from one in which the other was preferred. We shall return to this question in the conclusion.

While there may still be two basically different types of professional staff people on Capitol Hill, young professionals on the move seem now, after three decades of staff growth, to dominate the positions from which staffs influence policy. The members seem to want it that way. Several have said in interviews that they "hire them young, burn them out, and send them on."

Moreover, the working conditions on Capitol Hill and the Washington setting in which they occur all contribute toward producing staffs who have this same perspective. The young lawyers on the staffs tend disproportionately to be highly sought after people from top-ranked schools. They are paid well (salaries of $40,000 and above are common for committee professionals) and they are allowed to exercise a great deal of power at a relatively young age. The experience is exhilarating for a while. Washington lawyer-lobbyist Harry McPherson described the feeling in a book about his years working for Lyndon Johnson in the Senate and White House. Explaining his decision to go straight from law school to Johnson's staff, McPherson wrote:

> Why did I choose this "experience" instead of beginning a law practice and finding a responsible place in a small community? Partly because I wanted to find out what goes on in the councils of power—very much as a subway straphanger wants to know about scandals among the famous. Partly because I want to "do good", and a decade after Roosevelt it still seems as if Washington is the grand arena for doing good. Partly —perhaps chiefly—because I want to cast a shadow, to feel, however vicariously, that I have affected significant events and therefore exist.[27]

But for most of the professionals the exhilaration does not last forever. For one thing, they quickly reach a salary level not far below the legal maximum and then stay put. Another factor may be the overcrowded and noisy offices and the unpredictable and sometimes incredibly long working hours, many of which are spent doing nothing, or dreaming up new things to do, while waiting for five minutes of the member's time at the end of the day. But the most basic factor, the one that ultimately starts to grate on so many staff people, is the knowledge that however powerful they may appear, or however often they may have turned their own opinions into laws, they will never be anything other than surrogates for someone else. One successful young staffer who was in the middle of looking for another job captured this in a comment that could have been echoed by hundreds of his colleagues: "I just don't want to spend the rest of my life carrying someone else's water."

Working for someone else does not bother most people, of course. But members of Congress go out of their way to hire people who are both bright and ambitious and let them exercise power in an environment in which they are constantly made aware of their lack of independence. If many of the aides appear arrogant to the outside world —and many do—these same people may be as deferential as the most humble of junior executives when it comes to dealing with the person they refer to as "The Senator," "The Congressman," or "The Chairman." (The capital letters are there, even in speech.) As committee staffs have become more like personal staffs, with each staff member directly under the control of a single person, the precariousness of the job becomes self-evident. Staff members all have friends whose chairman retired, switched committees, or was beaten, leaving them with a new chairman wanting to "clean house." They all know competent people who were fired without warning because the boss sensed a slight, or just felt it was time for a change.

This uncertainty is undoubtedly valuable from the members' point of view: It is their best lever for keeping some control over the situation. As we shall see, the members delegate enormous authority to their staffs. They cannot possibly keep track of all or even most of what goes on in their name. But one thing they can do is to react instantly when they hear of something they do not like. "The rule that applies here," one staff director said, "is that you can exceed your authority only once. Then you'll either be fired or you won't have much authority."

The relationship of dependence between staff and member (Fox and Hammond called it "feudal" and likened it to a royal "court") may not bother those who get McPherson's existential thrill out of casting a shadow. But it does get to others, who are told periodically by former classmates that sooner or later they ought to think about finding a "real job" if they do not want to be left "behind." They fear their friends may be right.

One staff director talked about his attempts to get into a law firm.

He was in his early thirties and wanted to go back home to the Midwest. It was not easy. The firms in his home town wanted to start him out at the bottom. Sure, he had six years of high powered, legislative experience, but what did that have to do with family or local corporate law? He had never even drawn up a pleading or drafted a contract, they pointed out. Neither were the local corporations much more open-armed to the returning native. They all knew he was bright and would love to have him come back—at two-thirds his congressional salary. About the only firms that would talk about a raise wanted him to lobby. But the young staff director thought that if he had to lobby he might as well stay put in Congress. His friends back home would not consider lobbying a "real job" either, and he still enjoyed what he was doing.

However, when the joy starts to fade, the difficulty of returning home and the potential rewards of the nation's capital leads many of them to think about jobs in the Washington community. Committee staffs are expected, as part of their job, to get to know the people who work in their policy areas.* These are the people to whom the staffers turn when they want to, or have to, change jobs. By cultivating and becoming part of their policy networks, they insulate themselves from the insecurities of feudal dependence on their bosses.

Of all the possible kinds of "network" jobs in Washington, two seem clearly to be preferred: political appointments in the executive branch and lawyer-lobbying. An article in *National Journal* which traced what happened to twenty-one professional majority staff members who left the Senate Commerce Committee from November 1976 to May 1978 found that three got other jobs on Capitol Hill (all with Warren Magnuson, D-Wash., the former chairman of the committee), twelve got political appointments elsewhere in the federal government (eight as commissioners, administrators, or political staff on agencies or regulatory commissions within the committee's jurisdiction), four became Washington lawyer-lobbyists, and two went back home to Seattle to work on issues they had handled in committee.[30]

Nor is the Commerce Committee's experience unusual. As of mid-1979, the chairmen of the Federal Communications Commission

---

*Hugh Heclo has referred to these clusters of people in public and private interest groups, congressional staffs, think tanks, and the executive branch as "issue networks."[28] Nicholas Lemann, thinking more in terms of careers than policies, called them "survival networks."[29]

(Charles Ferris), Federal Deposit Insurance Corporation (Irvine H. Sprague), Federal Energy Regulatory Commission (Charles Curtis), Federal Maritime Commission (Richard Dashback), Federal Trade Commission (Michael Pertschuk), Interstate Commerce Commission (A. Daniel O'Neal, Jr.), National Endowment for the Arts (Livingston Biddle), Tennessee Valley Authority (S. David Freeman), the Administrator of the Veteran's Administration (Max Cleland), and two of six commissioners on the Federal Election Commission (John McGarry and Max Friedersdorf), all came directly or almost directly from jobs on congressional staffs. (Pertschuk, Dashback, and O'Neal all worked for the Senate Commerce Committee.) Scores of others fill the middle-level ranks of the cabinet level agencies.

Staff members who do not go to the executive branch are perfectly content to make handsome livings as lawyer-lobbyists. Harry McPherson took what many would consider the ideal path: from congressional staff to White House to one of Washington's most sought after lawyers and perennial presidential advisors. But, just as there are those who skip the legislative branch before fitting into the Washington community,[31] so are there plenty of congressional aides who skip the executive branch and still do very well. Michael Lemov (whom we shall meet in chapter 7) failed to get an appointment to the Federal Trade or Consumer Product Safety Commission and went to a law firm where he handles consumer protection issues for private clients affected by the bill he drafted as a House Commerce Committee aide. S. Lynn Sutcliffe (Senate Commerce Committee), William Van Ness (Senate Interior Committee), Howard Feldman (Senate Government Operations Committee), and Charles Curtis (House Commerce Committee) formed a law firm in 1976 that has been thriving. (Curtis left the firm in 1977 to become chairman of FERC.) Also thriving is Blum, Parker and Nash, a new firm active on energy issues, which has seven former staff members as partners or associates.[32]

All of these successful young lawyers trade directly on the fact that they know the laws and regulations concerning their clients because they helped write them, and they know the senators, representatives, and agency personnel who can affect these laws and regulations. They rarely get involved in direct conflicts of interest (an example involving William Demarest recounted in chapter 6 probably is an exception), and they rarely go out and blatantly advertise the obvious. (One new consulting firm did precisely that in a memo advertising its services to prospective clients for a $200,000 retainer,[33] but that was unusual.) Successful former aides generally know they do not have to do this.

What happens to congressional staffs after they leave Capitol Hill is only of indirect importance in a book on the influence of staff in the legislative process. The real question for us is whether the behavior of people *presently* on congressional staffs is affected by the Washington community career models constantly before them. Given their need to protect themselves against the uncertainties of their jobs, staff members would have to be inhuman not to be affected. That does not mean the staffs have to trim corners for interest groups, but it does mean they have to feel comfortable operating within the issue networks and may have to imitate what their predecessors did to get head.

Summary

Thus, we shall be looking for several different things as we proceed through our studies of individual committees:

- The effect of *staff size* on the way members do their job
- The effect of *staff career goals* on the way staffs behave
- The influence different kinds of staffs have at different stages of the legislative process
- The effect of both staff size and staff career goals on the Congress's ability to manage its workload, respond to national needs, and act as a check on the executive branch—all in a manner consistent with democratic principles

To this end, we begin by following the influence of staff over the course of a bill's progress through Congress.

PART 2

From Idea
to Statute Book:
Staffs at Work

Chapter 3

Selling Members on an Idea: The Staff of the Senate Small Business Committee

THE STAFF'S INFLUENCE, we have said, pervades the legislative process. No stage in that process is more important than the first: determining Congress's agenda. And at no stage have the newer-style staffs had a greater impact on the way Congress works. It is the one point in the process where the interests of the members, the goals of the staff, and the position of staff in the Washington issue network come together to influence what Congress does.

The importance of this stage to Congress as an institution cannot be overemphasized. Despite the popular misperceptions about executive branch domination of Congress's agenda, the fact is that much important legislation gets its start in Congress.[1] Many items on the president's personal priority list get there only after congressional committees surface them and make them attractive, while others that seem to have their start in the bureaucracy are drafted in close cooperation with committee staffs. Still others originate in Congress and are enacted with only a perfunctory involvement by the executive branch.

Given its enormous workload, Congress is able to retain control over its agenda in these situations only by means of its staff. However, the manner and scope of legislative initiatives depends more on the way members use their staffs than on sheer numbers. Some members hold their staffs under tight rein. They like their staffs to limit themselves to sifting other people's ideas, explaining the options to the member and perhaps coming up with some original, but closely related alternatives. The staff of the Joint Committee on Taxation works this way. Other members loosen the reins somewhat, letting staffs use their technical expertise aggressively to criticize the approaches before the committee and suggest better ways to do the job. The House Armed Services Committee uses its staff in this way to rewrite the annual military procurement authorization bill on almost a line-by-line basis. But the loosest reins are held by those members who in effect let their staffs take the lead, while they "backstop" what the staff is doing.

These last have been dubbed "entrepreneurial" staffs by David Price, a Duke University political scientist.[2] The term is illuminating. It draws our attention to staffs who act as if they were merchants, buying "products" wholesale, sifting through them and then selling a few of the choicer items to favored retail "buyers"—the staff aides's bosses.*

The connection between the interests of members, the goals of staff entrepreneurs, and the legislative agenda is direct. Senators and representatives believe their standing with the electorate is advanced if they can claim credit for authoring important bills or amendments or instigating well-publicized hearings. At the same time, their reputation inside Congress is advanced by their being identified with well chosen issues they can make "their own." Thus, out of concern for their internal and external reputation, the members are led to tell their staffs to look for "new ideas" for hearings, bills, or amendments. The staffers improve their position with the boss if they come up with ideas that have a practical chance of going somewhere in Congress and in the press. Such activity also enhances their position in the Washington community. The aide then becomes known to insiders as the person "really" responsible for such and such a program. Furthermore, as the aide becomes accepted and

---

*Price's "entrepreneurs" seem to correspond roughly to the people I have been labeling less precisely as "new-style" staffs. I will occasionally revert to the more general term, because the differences between newer and older staff styles relate to a great deal more than their entrepreneurial activities.

trusted by the member, he becomes known in Washington as someone worth cultivating as a "middle man": a person with an institutional stake in listening to new ideas from friendly interest groups
and then actively selling the members on the ideas the aide finds
most promising.

The Classic Model

Senator Warren G. Magnuson's twenty-three-year tenure as chairman of the Senate Commerce Committee (1955–1978) is an almost
ideal illustration of the relationship between members' interests,
staff goals, and committee agendas on a committee with an entrepreneurial staff.* During the senator's first eight years, he had used
the committee as a forum for interest group brokering among the
established industries and labor unions that had business before the
regulatory commissions under the committee's jurisdiction. Since
that jurisdiction included much that affected the maritime, fishing,
and transportation interests of his home state (Washington) the opportunities for gaining benefits seemed enough, under the political
wisdom then prevailing, to insure Magnuson's reelection indefinitely. But the people of Washington were not satisfied with Magnuson's conventional bread and butter concentration on local issues
and, in 1962, they almost rejected his bid for a fourth term against a
weak candidate. Everyone around the senator knew that if he spent
the next six years doing more of the same, he would be sure to attract
stronger opposition in 1968.

Gerald Grinstein, a young activist on the committee's staff, was
convinced even before the election that his boss would be better off
politically if he became active as a liberal legislative leader on major
national issues. Such a conversion, David Price noted, would also
mesh nicely with Grinstein's own politics.[3] After the election, Magnuson decided to listen to Grinstein, eventually making him the
committee's chief counsel.

Grinstein was allowed to hire young activists like himself who

---

*Price used this committee as his illustration of an entrepreneurial staff in the article
in which he introduced the distinction between "entrepreneurs" and "professionals."

were given the mission of finding issues that would refurbish Magnuson's reputation. His first appointment was Michael Pertschuk, an aide to Senator Maureen Neuberger (D–Ore.), who later succeeded Grinstein as chief counsel of the committee and in 1977 became chairman of the Federal Trade Commission. Pertschuk's work on the committee centered on "consumer" issues, broadly defined. One of these was a 1965 bill giving the federal government the authority to set mandatory safety standards for automobiles.

Grinstein and Perschuk saw the traffic safety issue then being publicized by Senator Abraham Ribicoff (D–Conn.) in the Government Operations Committee as a perfect vehicle for the "new" Magnuson.[4] They had to fight for jurisdiction with the Public Works Committee, which normally handled highway issues, but such fighting is often part of the job of the entrepreneurial staffer. New issues rarely fit neatly into old patterns.

The traffic safety bill helped forge a close working relationship between Pertschuk and Ralph Nader (the "star witness" uncovered by Ribicoff) that was to last throughout Pertschuk's twelve years on the committee. Those years are looked on by consumer movement activists as the committee's "golden years." Project after project was funneled from the public interest groups through Pertschuk to Magnuson.

The new approach worked for Magnuson—he was reelected easily in 1968. It also worked for his aides. Magnuson was persuaded to let their policy inclinations become his own (as long as they did not affect Washington adversely), and he delegated enormous tactical authority to translate those inclinations into laws.* In the process, the staff developed reputations within the Washington networks that helped them gain top political appointments on, or lucrative legal practices before, the commissions they had worked with and sometimes helped create.

---

*Harley M. Dirks, the chief staff person on the Labor-HEW Appropriations Subcommittee, also chaired by Magnuson, went so far at one point as to create transcripts for twelve days of hearings that never took place in 1976. He was fired when the incident was reported in the press[5], but Dirks clearly got the idea from somewhere that he had great leeway to operate outside normal bounds, on his own instigation.

The Senate Small Business Committee

While the entrepreneurialism of Magnuson's Commerce Committee staff may be unsurpassed, it is far from unique. In some ways, the importance of staff entrepreneurs to the agenda-setting process may be understood even better by examining in detail the Senate Select Committee on Small Business. Granted almost no legislative jurisdiction under the Senate's rules, very little comes the committee's way automatically. If the staff does look for topics on its own, the committee (a third and distinctly minor committee for most of its busy members) could easily find itself moribund.

Indeed, that nearly was its condition from 1969 through 1974, under the chairmanship of Senator Alan Bible. For six years, the Small Business Committee averaged only twenty-five days of hearings per year.[6] Moreover, many of those were held by Wisconsin Senator Gaylord Nelson's Monopoly Subcommittee, which conducted a running probe of competition in the drug industry. When Nelson succeeded Bible as chairman in 1975, the committee seemed as if it were reborn. From 1975 through 1978, it averaged fifty-seven days of hearings per year,[7] exceeding even the level of Bible's active predecessor, Senator George Smathers of Florida. Instead of a few sporadic hearings on unrelated, specialized subjects, the committee watched closely the effect of tax policy on small business, capital formation, minority-owned business, the family farm, energy research, and other similarly wide reaching subjects.

Remarkably, the committee's burst of activity under Nelson took place without a major turnover in the staff. Bible had twenty-one people on the committee's staff—the same number as Nelson. More importantly, two-thirds of the staff from Bible's last year, when the committee held only seventeen days of hearings and other meetings, stayed on to work for Nelson the next year, preparing sixty-two days of hearings in 1975. Thus, the staff's new activism was accomplished with many of the same old people. What changed were the chairman, the staff director, and, most importantly, the staff's marching orders.

The new staff director, William B. Cherkasky, made it clear to the staff that Nelson wanted the committee to be more active and was willing to give them a lot of running room. There was no lack of possible grounds for committee activity: Everything affecting the economy affects small business. Moreover, the committee's natural client group, small businesses and their trade associations, consists of some of the people who have been hurt most seriously by the regulatory statutes drafted in the late 1960s and early 1970s by the Commerce Committee and others. Yet, the committee is not made up of antigovernment conservatives. On the whole, committee members are on the lookout for ways to sponsor government programs and tax expenditures that help small business, to attack the anticompetitive activities of large corporations, and to add small business exceptions to regulations they otherwise support. With the potential subject matter of the committee virtually limitless and the policy inclinations of the members favorable to congressional action, all the staff needed was a green light from the chairman. When Nelson gave them one, they responded as he had hoped—confirming our point that the new role of the staff results from the interests of the members and does not initiate, *ex nihilo,* from the staff itself.

The Staff Director

Bill Cherkasky, the man to whom Nelson has given the job of running the staff of the newly rejuvenated committee, is in his fifties and had been president of a Wisconsin dairy firm and an officer in a realty company before a 1966 stint in the Commerce Department's Economic Development Administration. He joined Nelson's staff as legislative assistant in 1967 and served as his administrative assistant from 1969 until 1975, when he was named the Small Business Committee's staff director. He got the job, in other words, both because he knew about small business from personal experience and because he had earned Nelson's trust. Although older than most "new-style" staffers on Capitol Hill, he emphatically is a "chairman's man" who on the committee has become identified with the Washington network of people who specialize in issues of concern to small businesses.

The committee's rejuvenation obviously revolved around the staff's ability to sell the senators on their ideas and the senators' eagerness to listen. Cherkasky has played a pivotal role in the trans-

mission belt on this committee, because of his enthusiasm, his understanding of the chairman's interests and political needs, and the trust
the chairman places in his judgment. Because these are the same
factors associated with staff entrepreneurialism on any committee, I
talked with Cherkasky to probe exactly how he and others on the
staff go about getting items on the committee's working agenda.

The Entrepreneur as Middleman: Some Examples

Cherkasky described two specific issues on which the staff persuaded
Nelson to put something on the agenda—product liability and venture capital. The first, product liability, grew out of a judicial interpretation of the worker's compensation law under which an employee who is injured by machinery, but believes he was not
sufficiently compensated, must sue the original manufacturer of the
machinery, instead of his employer—no matter how old the equip-
ment, or whether it had been altered or resold. The decision resulted
in an incredible insurance premium increase for manufacturers. One
small company's annual bill, for example, went from $500 to $65,000
over a four-year span, with no offsetting increase in business.[8] "My
interest in the subject was stimulated in the summer of 1976," Cherkasky said, "by a National Small Business Association (NSB) newslet-
ter, *The Voice of Small Business.* I read about the subject, talked with
Herb Liebman (from the NSB) about it, and then raised it with
Nelson. When he said go ahead, I assigned a staff member to look into
it."

The venture capital issue got started in the committee during the
summer of 1977, when a person who specializes in helping new firms
raise money visited Herbert L. Spira, the committee's chief counsel.
(Spira, a forty-eight-year-old tax attorney, has been on the staff since
1963). In the past decade, this country's stock markets have become
dominated by pension funds and insurance companies (a development Peter Drucker referred to as "pension fund socialism"[9]). The
problem for small firms trying to break new ground, the visitor explained to Spira, was that the Pension Reform Act's "prudent man
rule" prevents most pension fund managers from investing in ven-
turesome companies. As a result, he and others in his position were

compelled to raise money abroad for American firms that could have been capitalized domestically with little trouble in the early 1970s, before the Pension Reform Act and a related rule promulgated by the Securities Exchange Commission. Spira and Cherkasky, convinced the subject was worth a hearing, went to see Nelson to sell him on the idea and Nelson bought it.

In both instances, Cherkasky and Spira were acting as middlemen. People affected by a policy told the staff that something was wrong; the staff saw that the issue could produce a good hearing and convinced Nelson to let them go ahead. The role of entrepreneur as middleman is essentially the same as the one Grinstein and Pertschuk played between Ralph Nader and Senator Magnuson on traffic safety and other issues. In each case, the staff got an idea from a lobbyist or some other interested party and passed it on. There was nothing venal about the staffs' relationships with lobbyists, of course; the staff simply used them as sources of information about issues they wanted to bring to their boss's attention.

And lobbyists are not the only sources. Many senators and representatives are known for cultivating academic specialists and for having their staffs look over the leading journals in their field. Senator Edward M. Kennedy's relationship with the Harvard faculty is a case in point. Much of what his staff does is to act as entrepreneurial middlemen between the academic world and the senator. In an article in the *Washington Post,* Spencer Rich gave the following example of the process at work:

> Cary Parker, a top aide to Senator Edward M. Kennedy (D–Mass.), was reading through some literature on the 18-year-old vote, which at that time was not allowed. He discovered to his delight that two top legal scholars, Archibald Cox and Paul Freund of Harvard Law School, had come to the conclusion that Congress could give the vote to 18-year-olds in federal elections merely by passing a law, rather than by constitutional amendment, as had always been thought necessary.
>
> Kennedy had always been interested in the subject, and Parker excitedly took the material to Kennedy and worked up the amendment to tack on to the Voting Rights Act extension bill. Civil rights groups begged Kennedy not to do it, for fear voting rights extension might be endangered. He hesitated, but then Majority Leader Mike Mansfield (D–Mont.) didn't. He introduced the amendment for himself, Kennedy and Warren G. Magnuson (D–Wash.) and rammed it through Congress —and that's how the 18-year-olds got the vote.[10]

Similarly, as we shall see in chapter 8, the Republican push in 1978 for major income tax cuts was inspired by the economic theories of Arthur Laffer, which had been brought to the attention of the Senate and House largely through the efforts of one middleman outside Congress (*Wall Street Journal* editorialist Jude Wanniski) and another one inside (Republican House Budget Committee economist Paul Craig Roberts). Cherkasky and Spira's role on product liability and venture capital, in other words, were typical examples of a widespread phenomenon.

The Member and His Time

Nelson had given the staff the green light to do more work on product liability and venture capital, but that took care of only the first hurdle on the way to a committee hearing. Getting a member to agree to let a staff go to work is hard enough, since even staff resources have their limits. But it is even more difficult to persuade a person on a minor committee, with no legislative jurisdiction, to put that subject on his own personal working agenda: first, to prepare for and chair hearings and, then, to gain the attention and support of colleagues on committees with legislative jurisdiction. To achieve this, Nelson (or some other senator willing to chair the hearings) would have to be shown that the effort was worth their while.

According to Cherkasky senators generally have to be shown two things before they will go ahead. First, the issue has to "make the senator look good." Thus the product liability hearings ended up being chaired by Senator John Culver (D–Iowa) because, said Cherkasky, Culver's administrative assistant "was looking for Main Street issues that would sell in Des Moines." The second thing the senators want to hear is that the issue raises a problem Congress can correct. According to Cherkasky, they tend not to be interested in issues, however serious, that they cannot connect to a legislative solution:

> There is always a problem with raising an issue and then finding out later on that it is insoluble. You have done a disservice because you have raised people's hopes and they think Congress is going to do something.

Nothing comes of it and you are embarrassed because you are criticized at the end of it all.*

Only when Cherkasky had satisfied himself that he had an idea that was susceptible to legislative solution, that fit with Nelson's general concerns, and that would make him look good, did he feel confident about bringing it to his chairman. Even then, despite Cherkasky's ability generally to know how Nelson would react, he did not always guess correctly. When that happened, he apparently had his chairman's support to look for other senators interested in his ideas.†

> I thought that Nelson ought to be involved with women in business because a lot of women vote, and I had a good issue. I wanted to create an associate administrator in the Small Business Administration (SBA) for women's business. I took the issue to him, and told him he ought to be on the thing, and he rejected it.
>
> I was flabbergasted. I said, "Here's a winner for you," And then I said, "OK, all right," and I talked to [Oklahoma Republican] Senator [Dewey] Bartlett's staff. They took it, right away. Bartlett introduced the bill, got a hearing on it and passed the bill.
>
> So, after a while, before they passed the bill, I went to see Nelson. I said, "Bartlett wants to hold a hearing on women in business and that's okay, isn't it?" He said, "Yes, it's a good issue."
>
> So I began to wonder why I had misfired on that one. I guess it was because he had just had five losing fights on the floor and I just hit him at the wrong time.

The moral: never underestimate the importance of a persistent staff salesman.

---

*Richard Harris made a point related to Cherkasky's in his book *Decision*, about the Senate's 1970 rejection of G. Harrold Carswell's nomination for the U.S. Supreme Court (New York: Ballantine Books, 1972). Although dismayed by Carswell's nomination, none of the leading liberal Democrats on the Senate Judiciary Committee seemed to have the will to fight it on the heels of the Senate's defeat of President Nixon's previous candidate for the same vacancy in the high court, Judge Clement Haynesworth. Only after a series of memoranda by Kennedy aide James Flug showed there was a chance to beat Carswell did the senators begin to think the effort might be worth their time.

†This is unusual. Other staff people are forced to do covertly what Nelson lets Cherkasky do openly. See chapter 6 for examples.

The Working Agenda

The Small Business Committee's agenda is the result of a collection of examples like these. To whatever extent the staff's entrepreneurialism is controlled by the senators, these controls come into force at the point when someone decides whether to chair a hearing proposed by the staff. The one other point at which the senators ostensibly take charge is at the beginning of each year when the committee meets to decide on its working agenda. To an outsider at these meetings, however, it looks more as if the staff tells the senators what it is doing than the senators telling the staff what they would like to have done. Cherkasky described the meetings in this way:

> We have a written work program that we discuss at the committee's annual meeting at the start of every year. The question we always have to answer to the senators is who put the list together, and I always have to say it doesn't come out of a whole cloth. We don't make it up out of a whole cloth and try to sell you on it; the fact is that we talk to aides in all the Small Business Committee senators' offices to see what their senators are interested in. Then we also get mail from lots of people and the associations. We check with them and say, "What do you think we ought to have on our agenda?"
>
> Then, every year in February the staff has a meeting with the associations, and a lot of small business people and professors, and just discuss informally, in a four-hour meeting sometimes, what are the issues facing small businessmen, what are the critical issues.
>
> Last year we had that meeting on February 7th. That exposed lots of the issues, most of which we were conversant with already. Out of all of this input, we put together the work program proposed at the annual meeting, and we have to defend ourselves at the annual meeting as to what the issues are.
>
> That doesn't take very long. Everybody says, "Well, this is just a working paper, isn't it?" We'll use this to initiate new hearings, and if something comes along during the year that ought to be exposed, we'll do that, too. It's nothing that we are set in concrete on, but it's a working paper and becomes a useful document. The product liability issue was not on the working agenda in early 1976, it became a part of the committee work after we discovered the issue in the summer of 1976.

Asked to comment on the scrutiny given staff proposals in these meetings, Cherkasky said:

Nelson always asks me, point blank, "How do you get these issues and what are they and what do they mean? Is there interest or are you just fishing around for something to do?"

We might get a letter from a staff aide, saying, "Here is a good issue you ought to have on your working agenda." But we may not go any further than just putting that on the agenda, and saying "Senator Culver requested this" or "Senator [Floyd] Haskell [D-Colo.] said it ought to be raised." For "Senator Haskell" read, "Senator Haskell's staff aide." We just assume that the senator is involved, but we know he isn't in most cases. And when Nelson says, "Where did you get this idea?" We say, "Well, out of Haskell's office," and he's not going to dispute it. If Haskell's office wants to raise it, why should he dispute it? It may never give birth to a hearing, but at least it's in there, in case somebody wants to work it. Of course, they don't all come from senators' offices. We dream a lot of them up ourselves.

Once it has been dreamed up, the idea is almost sure to get on the working agenda. Once there, it is just a question of persuading someone to hold a hearing.

The Small Business Committee may be somewhat more open to this form of staff influence than most legislative committees, but entrepreneurial staffs on legislative committees get many of their ideas on to their agendas in a manner that is not too far different from this. Senate Commerce Committee staff members said in interviews, for example, that Michael Pertschuk had a private ten-year plan for the committee when he became chief counsel in 1967 and saw the committee act on most of it before he left to become chairman of the Federal Trade Commission in 1977.

New Staff, Old Staff, and the Agenda

Since most of the Small Business Committee's agenda originates in the entrepreneurial middleman activities of the staff, the effect of staff turnover on the committee's agenda is a good test of the staff's importance. To the extent that staffs do nothing but pass on the ideas of the prominent and obvious lobbyists and academics in their field, it would be wrong to describe them as having an independent effect on the process. But if in fact the agenda changes when the staff changes, we get a different picture.

Selling Members on an Idea

We know from other committees that new staff often does result in new policy ideas. For example, Senator Estes Kefauver's investigations in the late 1950s of pricing patterns in the drug industry (the forerunners of Nelson's hearings on the same subject in the 1970s) resulted directly from his hiring Irene Till, a Federal Trade Commission economist, in 1957. When Till started working for Kefauver's Judiciary Subcommittee on Antitrust and Monopoly, the staff director asked her for new subjects that would fit with the themes Kefauver had developed in previous hearings on economic concentration in the automobile and steel industries. Till immediately suggested the pharmaceutical industry because of an experience her husband had some years before. The idea was set aside at first, but Till was given a green light in 1958 and the televised results became nationally famous a year later.[11]

Similarly, a recent article by Burton Hersh dates Senator Edward M. Kennedy's supposed turnaround on crime with his hiring of a new staff aide:

> Those who follow Kennedy identify the hardening of his attitude with the appearance on his staff of the owlishly intent Ken Feinberg in 1975. Feinberg arrived fresh from years of frustration as assistant U.S. attorney for the Southern District of New York, and he was still seething over the way the court system worked: "When I came down here to work for Kennedy I told him: 'I'm a liberal and I'm in favor of housing and all the rest of that but as for crime, Senator—crime can't wait!'" Kennedy now agreed, unreservedly. "I think that he found that he had always been uncomfortable with his liberal stance on criminal justice," Feinberg says. "Jim Flug and those people set the senator back on this stuff. Since when have the Kennedys been so permissive in the civil liberties field? Besides—" Feinberg hesitates—"there was a tremendous vacuum opening politically on the right."[12]

Changes in the quality of the Senate Small Business Committee have had similar effects on policy. As Cherkasky observed, Nelson's constant desire for new ideas that would keep the committee active required a much higher rate of turnover among the staff than we find on committees with older-style, less entrepreneurial staffs.*

> The trick around here is (1) hiring good people and (2) unleashing them. When I came to the committee here two and a half years ago, the

*See chapter 8.

people here had been hamstrung for six years by Bible and couldn't do anything, so it was a matter of unleashing them. Well, it was like all young men first coming up here. You know—they are all anxious to do things and they uncork a lot of work the first year, with a certain amount of urging. They are a pretty solid staff for a while until you burn them out and then you've got to replace them, turn them out on the ash heap and get some others. It is not an easy life, but it pays well.

The need for new ideas also dictated the kind of person Cherkasky looked for when he hired new staff:

> We always have a tax specialist because that's an important issue; the most important issue we face in this committee, I think, because it touches on everything else, and it is a very esoteric subject. You can't become an instant tax specialist, but that's an exception for us.
>
> There are people who are experts in regulatory problems and everything else that comes along, and it would be nice to have a specialist on every issue that a small business guy is going to have to face this year, but we just can't afford it. We have a very small staff, so we hire broadguage people who have the intelligence to grab one issue today and another one tomorrow and another one Friday, and Monday and to be able to carry all three or four balls at the same time.
>
> I also like to get experienced people. I'm sort of a [football coach] George Allen type: "The future is now." If you get a guy up here who can handle himself and knows, at least, the Senate or the House, or both, he will at least know what the rules are, because we don't have much time for a learning period; you've really got to jump in and start acting right away.
>
> For instance, Nelson agreed to do some hearings on economic concentration, and how the tax laws help to create that concentration. Nelson agreed to do that, but the guy who raised the issue was an economist whom we just hired from the Joint Economic Committee who is concerned about concentration. He raised the issue with Nelson and Nelson agreed to do it. He had talked to me about it and I said, "It's an issue I've been interested in for a long time and nobody has done any work on it. You do the work, raise it with him, and see what he does." And then he sold Nelson on it.

The example of a staff person coming in with an idea on which the committee eventually acts—much as when Irene Till joined Kefauver—has an interesting corollary. Many issues listed in the Small Business Committee's annual working agenda are in that publication only because of a staff member's interest. When the staff member leaves, the issue may well be dropped from the agenda. Cherkasky described the difference between issues that die when a staff member leaves and those that live on:

> Some issues never are very successful. Even though a staff person may be a zealot on them, he may never make the issue sing. He may not be able to get it off to the point where it goes from the private agenda to the public agenda. What we are looking for are public agenda issues. When some staff aides leave, their issues do not go on with anybody else around here. Nobody may be interested in them, and you really can't force a person to do a job around here on an issue he's not interested in or wants to learn something about, unless we've got to, like SBA, where you've really got to do it. So, I say certain issues will die when a staffer leaves because I'm not interested in it, I don't think it is going to go anywhere, and they are questions about which, in my own opinion, most senators don't give a damn.
>
> But with other issues, where I think we've got a crack at something that's good, anybody who is on the committee should have enough innate intelligence to learn about that issue pretty quickly and pick it up from a departing staffer. Most of the people around here are supposed to be instant authorities, including the senators who vote on those issues.

In other words, issues identified with a particular staff member will not die, if the staff director decides he does not want them to.

Jurisdictional Imperialism

The efforts of staffs to find new issues for their bosses often lead them to subjects that do not fall precisely within existing jurisdictional boundaries. Thus when the Senate Commerce Committee decided to push the traffic safety bill, it had to fight the Public Works Committee for jurisdiction. Similarly, Senator Kennedy's efforts on behalf of airline deregulation in his Judiciary Subcommittee on Administrative Practices and Procedures provoked a jurisdictional conflict with Senator Howard Cannon (D-Nev.), chairman of the Commerce Committee's Aviation Subcommittee.

Even when the boundaries seem clear, aggressive staffs will look for ways to fuzz them over to grab some new turf for themselves and their bosses. The Small Business Committee's staff is no exception to this almost universal pattern among entrepreneurial staffs. One example given by Cherkasky indicates the relish with which staffs go about expanding their jurisdictional boundaries:

> You know, we have broad investigative authority. The legislative authority we have isn't that wide, but there are a lot of things you can do with even our legislative authority. We didn't have any legislative authority until last year. When we finally got it, I said the only thing that can stop us now from doing what we want to do is the other committees not realizing what we're up to, because we can swipe from them very rapidly.
>
> In fact, we have a bill in now which would take from the Department of Commerce the Office of Minority Business Enterprise and stick it into SBA (Small Business Administration), because that would have two offices in one and it would be the SBA that would run the program. And it really created a lot of excitement around here. We've got the undersecretary of commerce coming down to see me tomorrow; Juanita Kreps [then secretary of commerce] is all excited and wants to know what is coming off.
>
> As a matter of fact, I presented this to the Commerce Committee first of all and they said, "take it, it isn't worth a damn. Run away with it. It ought to be abolished, but if you want it, take it." So Magnuson doesn't care. We've got Bennett Johnson, a southerner, [and Commerce Committee member] who agreed to sponsor legislation. He's got a black guy on his staff who has gotten the Congressional black caucus behind us, and so on. So we've got it pretty well wired. We're liable to steal that jurisdiction away from the Commerce Committee, with their blessing stick it in SBA, and before you know it, that's more jurisdiction.

The bill did not pass the Ninety-fifth Congress, but Cherkasky jokingly suggested he was likely to try to catch some bigger fish:

> Actually I'd like to figure out some way to get the Defense Department in SBA, because we could make it the biggest agency in the country if we keep going this way. But seriously, we have broad-guaged investigative authority to deal with small business problems, and just about everything affects small business. I mean, just about anything you can think of has some kind of a handle on it for small business, so that the only thing we lack is more staff and more Senators with time and interest.

Of course, other staff directors may object to seeing some of their own turf invaded. Jurisdiction is a *very* serious matter to staffers, even more serious than it is for senators. Senators serve on three committees, have more issues urged on them by staff than they can possibly handle, and can always find issues worth their time in one of their committees' jurisdictions, however revised or redefined. In contrast, the essence of the staff member's position in the Washington community is defined by the relationships he establishes with the issue networks surrounding his fields of specialization. For a staff member, loss of jurisdiction means losing a part of his life support system. The policy consequences of the staff's interest in gaining jurisdiction varies with the issue. On some issues, the staff may give needed publicity to a problem that was being ignored elsewhere. On others, the staff's interest may excite jealousies that affect the flow of legislative business for reasons that have nothing to do with an issue's external politics. In either case, the staff for its own reasons clearly makes a difference to Congress's work.

This role of staff has shown up with particular clarity in congressional reform resolutions, where jurisdiction has become the issue itself, instead of the means of getting at some other issue. For example, a recent book about the 1974 House Committee reform proposals led by Representative Richard Bolling (D-Mo.), dealt with the effort made by the staff of the House Post Office and Civil Service Committee (marked for extinction by the Bolling plan) to work with outside interest groups to defeat the committee realignment proposal.[13] Similarly, some Senate Small Business Committee staff members were said by staff people who worked on Senate committee reorganization in 1977 to have activated small business groups to lobby for the committee's continued existence, despite Senator Nelson's public support of a proposal that would have abolished it. (Nelson was a member of the select committee that proposed the committee reforms.) Asked if he did this, Cherkasky said:

> Absolutely. I cleared it with Nelson. I asked him if he had any objection to the small business community pillorying the Rules Committee with letters, and he said no. The staff was involved with this, and I was as deeply involved as anybody, I guess. I felt my job was to help make sure the small business community had a voice in Congress. Nelson said he couldn't help, but he didn't tell me not to do it.

It seems no accident that the staff should have felt a responsibility to see that the Small Business Committee maintained its separate, institutionalized voice in Congress—with staff, of course.

Conclusion

The indirect impact on jurisdictional conflict is only one of several ways in which staff entrepreneurial activities systematically affect Congress's performance. More important are the results that flow from the members' constant desire for "new ideas." In practice, as we have seen, this means that the staff should discover "problems" amenable to legislative fixes. If no "problem" can be found, a "crisis" might do; but the last thing the staff needs are a set of intractable "conditions." At one time, the institutional incentives leading staffs torward new issues resulted in an unmistakable partisan bias; the problems discovered tended to be social ones to be remedied by governmental action. Now, as the government has gotten more active, the problem might just as easily be governmental (such as the "prudent man rule" affecting venture capital that was mentioned earlier) and the remedy a corrective amendment instead of a new program. In both cases, however, the approach tends to lead staff—with their own time frameworks already shortened by their desire to gain credit in the Washington job network—to exaggerate the members' politically natural, but nevertheless unfortunate, tendency to avoid thinking of the long-range impacts of the policies before them.

The atmosphere in which staff entrepreneurialism flourishes also creates a bias in favor of issues that look good in the press. Cherkasky noted that members want to "look good" and to do so they need issues that "sing." There is a two-way relationship here: Publicity may move an issue forward; issues may be put forward for the sake of publicity. Senator Magnuson's new staff and legislative style grew directly out of his desire for publicity that would help him get reelected in 1968. Other senators may react less abruptly, but no less directly. Thus, the staff looks not only for issues the press will like, but a good entrepreneurial staffer is expected to know how to "package" what he has in a way the press will find interesting. To date, this side of the work of the entrepreneurial staff remains largely a Senate phenomenon. But in recent years House members have also begun using the legislative resources of their Chamber to impress statewide media in anticipation of future Senate campaigns in much the same ways that senators try to impress on the national media the idea that they are "presidential timber."

The self-interest of members and their entrepreneurial staffs may motivate a great deal of what the staffs are asked to do, but the institutional consequences extend beyond the electoral aims that set the activities in motion. By creating incentives for finding new legislative issues, the Congress helps enhance its role as an independent body able to influence the national agenda in broad terms. At least some of this activity clearly helps Congress maintain its position as a coequal branch of government. But as we saw, Congress, in the process, has given up much of its control over the agenda to the staff. Moreover, we saw that the Small Business Committee doubled its activity immediately after unleashing the staff. It seems clear, therefore, that as more and more of Congress's 250-plus committees and subcommittees adopt this staff style, the effect will be—indeed, to a large extent already has been—to turn its staffs into a mechanism for generating more work for Congress instead of helping it manage the existing workload. Our concerns about Congress's independence and about its inability to manage an increasingly fractionalized workload pull us in different directions. Both will have to be weighed carefully before we can achieve a balanced assessment of the effect of Congress's new use of staff on the legislative branch's ability to do its job.

Chapter 4

Shepherding a Bill Through the Senate: The Sunset Bill

WHAT IS the staff's role once an idea makes it to a member's personal legislative agenda? Part of the staff's job is to drum up publicity, both for the legislation itself and for his senator or representative. (How they do this will be discussed in our subsequent chapters on oversight.) If a member has adopted an idea solely for its symbolic value, as they often do,[1] publicity may be the end of it. But if a member is serious about getting a bill passed, he will have to start thinking about building a majority coalition.

First, the staff and member line up the initial sponsors. Then, as the leading sponsors try to gain more supporters in committee, before floor action or during a conference, they may be forced to modify their original proposal—either by adding new ideas or by softening the impact of something another member may find troublesome. In the Senate, this process of "massaging" a bill's language almost always takes place at the staff level, with direct negotiations among senators limited to a few rare instances in which items are too politically sensitive to be handled solely by staff. In the House, the members still tend to talk to each other directly about detailed legislative language, but less than they used to.

In this chapter and the next, we shall look at two instances of staff to staff negotiation to see how the process works. This chapter takes us through the full process leading to the Senate's adoption of "Sunset" legislation in 1978. The next is about the late-1977 phantom conference on the differing House and Senate Veterans' Educational Benefits bills.

The Sunset Bill provides us with an excellent example of the role of staff in the Senate. From its initial stages in late 1975 until Senate adoption in 1978, the Sunset Bill went through a succession of detailed staff negotiations to which the senators paid little direct attention. Yet, in the end, the senators retained clear control over those aspects of the process that affected them politically by the way they chose the participants and set the ground rules for the staff negotiations.

The principal sponsor of Sunset in the Senate was Edmund S. Muskie of Maine. Known through the 1960s and early 1970s as a leading liberal Democrat of fairly conventional views, Muskie became convinced after 1972 that the country could not long afford the programs he supported unless the Congress got better control over the federal budget. In 1973–1974 he and his staff were instrumental in developing and passing the Budget Reform Act in the Senate.[2] In 1975, as an alternative to the 1970s liberal Democratic creation of permanent spending programs to fight temporary recessions, they developed a "countercyclical aid" plan that would give direct cash grants to state and local governments during a recession, when their tax revenues were down, and would end automatically when the unemployment rate receded. Then, in 1976, as a capstone to his effort to bring the budget under control, Muskie and his staff began working on a Sunset Bill that would force periodic reauthorization of all federal spending programs, including those not presently reauthorized, according to a schedule that would allow better direct comparisons between programs with related objectives that were competing for the same federal dollars.

Intergovernmental Relations Subcommittee

The Sunset Bill was developed by the staff of Senator Muskie's Intergovernmental Relations (IGR) Subcommittee on the Committee on Government Operations. The subcommittee's staff director was Alvin From.

From, Muskie's key staff person on budget reform and countercyclical aid as well as Sunset, came to Washington in 1966 as an intern from the Northwestern University School of Journalism. In an interview with Bernard Asbell (whose 1978 book about Muskie, *The Senate Nobody Knows,* is a perceptive account of the way the institution works) From talked about why he stayed in Washington after his internship:

> Down here I ran into Ed May, whom I'd met when he spoke at Northwestern. Ed was going with the Office of Economic Opportunity. I mentioned that I was going back to take a job with *The Chicago Daily News,* and he said, "You don't want to do that. I've been in the journalism business and you'll have more fun if you come here."[3]

So, From worked for OEO from 1966 to 1969, and then he got a job with Senator Joseph Tydings' District of Columbia Committee. Then in the 1970 election:

> Tydings got beat by [J. Glenn] Beall, then John McEvoy, our staff director, moved over to become Muskie's A.A. [Administrative Assistant] and brought me onto this subcommittee in April of '71. I guess I've been staff director since November of '71.[4]

Muskie, a former governor, had the IGR Subcommittee created for him in 1962 and chaired it until 1978, when he left Governmental Affairs (as Government Operations was renamed in 1977) to go on Foreign Relations. Before From came, the subcommittee worked almost solely on issues directly related to federal-state-local government relations. Afterwards, IGR turned decisively toward considering the major "process" issues that Muskie saw dominating the future liberal agenda. Whether From's arrival in 1971 or Muskie's own experiences up to and through the disappointing presidential race in 1972 did more to turn Muskie to his new agenda must be left to speculation. When Asbell asked From who was following whom on Sunset, From said,

> Oh, Muskie first introduced something like the Sunset Bill in 1965, when I was still in college. So he's not new to it. That first idea was part of the original Intergovernmental Cooperation Act. Just before the Act's passage, the "sunset" part got knocked out. Then Muskie and Brock [Bill Brock, R-Tenn., a former IGR member] tried again, pushing for a provision in the budget bill to limit major program authorizations to three years. That got knocked out. What we've done since then is to take a raw idea and develop it, refine it into a very sophisticated process. . . .
>
> Sure, I presented the Senator the idea of this bill, but he took it and ran with it. And it wasn't an original idea on my part. I don't think there are many original ideas around this town. I think the way you make something go in Washington is through timing, having a sense of the right moment to run with an idea, when to avoid sticking your chin out and getting a good idea clipped before it is ready.
>
> Muskie once said—it was either his sixtieth or sixty-first birthday party in his office—that there were three stages in a political life. One is when you're young and you're brimming with new ideas. The second is when you have fewer, but you're better at recognizing good ideas when they come to you, and you're in a position to run with them. The third is when you reject out of hand any idea that's new. And he said, "I'm in the second stage." It was his roundabout way of expressing his appreciation to his staff. And as you know from being around Muskie, he's not the kind of guy who says things he doesn't want to say. He tried that at one point in his life, the '72 campaign, and he's not about to do it again.[5]

From was talking to Asbell essentially about his role in proposing new ideas for Muskie's consideration. When I asked him to focus instead on the extent to which Muskie gives his staff the leeway to develop and negotiate the details once he has agreed to the basic idea, From was more expansive about the role of the staff:

> We have an awful lot of authority as we deal with other staffs. We have a good idea of our limits, but within those limits, we're free. That puts us in a good position to negotiate, because we know a lot of Senators do not give their staffs that kind of authority. Part of it is that we've all been around for a while. Almost every one of the things we have done—the budget act, countercyclical aid, sunset—has been worked out extensively by staff. . . .
>
> There's no question about who's in charge, though. Muskie is unusual among the members of this body. His mind is amazing. In the middle

of a discussion, he'll start spouting off something from a memo of two years ago.

In these comments, From identified two things that may make the Sunset example somewhat atypical: the leeway Muskie gives the staff and the extent of Muskie's grasp of the detailed substance of material on which he chooses to take a lead. Many other senators, such as Warren Magnuson and Alan Cranston, give their staff at least as much leeway as Muskie does without having the same understanding of the material being negotiated in their name. Still others, such as Russell Long and Howard Cannon, pride themselves on their detailed knowledge and would never give their highly capable staffs the authority Muskie gave From. These differences in the way senators use their staffs will become apparent in the course of the discussion of Sunset, as From and others on the IGR staff negotiate with the staffs of the other committee chairmen.

What follows is a chronological account of the Sunset Bill from its conception in September 1975 until Senate passage in October 1978, presented in the form of a diary. The perspective will be largely that of the IGR staff and as such may at times appear to be biased in favor of the bill. If so, this is not because I am trying to argue in favor of its passage, but because Senator Muskie kindly agreed to let me have full access to all of the IGR staff's memos on the subject. I did not start following the bill personally until 1977, when I was able to devote full time to this book and supplement the IGR memos with personal observation and interviews. Thus, the diary is not even a full account of everything that all Senate staffs did on Sunset. Instead, it tries to use the Sunset Bill as a vehicle for giving the reader a feeling for the responsibilities one subcommittee staff took on as it negotiated with others on one bill.

1975

September. The new congressional budget process is about to finish its first trial run. People who are anxious for the reform to work seem, on the whole, to be happy that the Congress has managed to get through a cycle roughly on schedule, without questioning whether

Shepherding a Bill through the Senate

Congress made all that much difference to the end result. Unlike most of his supporters, however, Muskie is decidedly uneasy about the future of the new process. He is particularly concerned about the "uncontrollable" items in the budget—items that cannot be changed without first changing underlying substantive law. Congressional budget experts say that roughly 75 percent of the budget is uncontrollable in any given fiscal year but Muskie's staff thinks that realistically the figure is close to about 92 percent, since the salaries of federal employees who work in supposedly "controllable" programs are themselves all but uncontrollable. Moreover, Muskie is impressed by the fact that the supposedly fast-growing federal expenditures for education, all of which are controllable, have grown only half as quickly as the uncontrollable items in the budget. He has become convinced, therefore, that if congressional budget reform is ever going to mean anything, Congress has to be better able to control larger portions of the budget.

Muskie has been deeply concerned about this for months, but he is not sure how best to proceed. He is scheduled to give a dinner speech to the Liberal party of New York on October 9 and everyone around him recognizes the importance of the event for someone whose national ambitions are not entirely squelched. Robert Rackleff of the IGR staff, who will write the speech, said that he has "known since June it was coming up and knew it was important. Unlike normal speeches, interest in this one spread wider than IGR."[6] The Budget Committee staff, veterans of the 1968 and 1972 campaigns and academic friends all have been sending in ideas. "Over the summer," Rackleff said, "I did a great deal of reading and thinking and research, and we talked within the IGR staff right here, particularly with Al From, about what kind of theme we wanted. That was continuous. . . . The problem was how you express a liberal's concern for the plight of government today. How do you take what has been an orgy of breast beating about the failure of liberalism, the junking of the ideals of the New Deal, and turn them positive and affirmative."[7] By the end of the month, however, Rackleff had still not found the way to express the theme.

September 26. Memo from From to Muskie: "When you meet with Jim Lynn [the director of the Office of Management and Budget] this afternoon, you ought to be aware that as part of our anti-big government theme in IGR, we are developing legislation . . . [that would] automatically terminate all grant-in-aid programs at the end of three or five years, thereby forcing the reauthorization of those programs and hopefully the elimination of many. A similar provision was in Title VII of the Budget Bill . . . but was knocked out." The language of the memo seems to indicate that this is the first Muskie knows of the automatic termination bill the staff has been preparing. It is not very far along at this stage, however, and still seems to be limited to a small portion of the budget—grants-in-aid.

October 9. With the Senate staying in session into the night on the Israeli-Egyptian Sinai Agreements, Muskie is unable to deliver his Liberal party speech in New York. He has a friend deliver the speech for him and has it distributed widely to the press. The speech excites much favorable comment with its call for liberals to concern themselves with fiscal responsibility, productivity, regulatory simplification, and government efficiency. Muskie is pleased with the results and uses variations of the speech in almost every major address he delivers through his 1976 reelection campaign. He also asks his staff to think about concrete ways to follow up the speech's themes.

October 21. In a memo to Muskie, From suggests two opportunities to implement the theme: by acting as a fiscal watchdog on the Budget Committee and by pushing legislation "to reduce the size of government by eliminating wasteful programs." The IGR staff, he says, had been talking with the Budget Committee staff, the General Accounting Office, the Advisory Commission on Intergovernmental Relations, Charles Schultze (then of the Brookings Institution), and pollster Lou Harris and others about ideas that within the next month should lead to an automatic termination bill.

November 7. Muskie meets with From, Rackleff, and Allen Schick, a senior specialist with the Congressional Research Service who had helped develop the budget reform and who was to become Muskie's most important "academic" advisor on Sunset. The day before, From had sent Muskie a memo from Schick on the design of a system that would combine a zero-based review of the budget with automatic termination on a revolving four-year cycle. Schick urged that termination not be limited to grants-in-aid. "It is especially important that permanent programs such as entitlements be incorporated in the process because these often escape serious review."

The meeting goes well from From's point of view. Muskie pushes From on why he thinks the idea would fly when similar proposals had been defeated in the past. From replies that the times were different. Muskie then says, go ahead. Commenting on the meeting afterwards,

From says that the staff work that had preceded this meeting "was not just an investment of staff time with the Member uncommitted. I don't like to waste my time either. Part of the relationship between senators and staff is reading each other. Anyone who has been around here for some time doesn't go in to a senator with an idea without thinking the Senator would be interested."

This may be particularly important for an aide to Senator Muskie. Unlike many politicians, who learn primarily from verbal briefings, Muskie prefers to read. Except for some quick discussions during committee meetings and before the floor vote, this meeting was one of only about a half dozen Muskie held with his staff on Sunset in the three years between the bill's introduction and Senate passage.

So, the meeting on Sunset was both an unusual and a successful experience for the staff. From remarked on another occasion that he thought IGR could do justice to only one major new idea per Congress. Sunset was to be the staff's major project for the next three years.

December. James H. Davidson is put in charge of writing a draft bill along with the help of Lee Lockwood and others. Davidson is thirty-four years old with a 1966 bachelors degree in journalism and a 1969 law degree, both from the University of Missouri, and like From, his entire working life so far has been spent in government. (Before joining the IGR staff, he worked for the Missouri Secretary of State in 1969–1970 and for Senator Stuart Symington in 1971–1974.) Throughout the development of the Sunset Bill, Davidson will act as the lawyer who handles the technical details while From will be more of a political and tactical advisor.

Davidson initially speaks with the Legislative Counsel's office to get ideas about mechanisms available to put the staff's concepts into practice. (The Legislative Counsel's office employs twenty-one people in the Senate and forty-one in the House who are specialists in drafting legislative language.) Davidson is not satisfied with the specific suggestions he receives, so he closets himself to work on his own version. By December 21, he has finished a summary and explanation of "The Government Economy and Spending Reform Act of 1976," along lines laid out in Schick's November memorandum. The staff by this time has agreed that a workable bill would need four basic elements: (1) an action-forcing termination mechanism, (2) a schedule for reviewing programs, (3) an inventory of programs to be reviewed, and (4) some suggested means of evaluating the programs up for review.

1976

January 23. In a memo to Muskie From reports that the staff finally has resolved two key issues having to do with (1) exemptions for social security, other retirement programs, and interest on the debt and, (2) working out a schedule so programs in the same functional budget categories would come up for review together. He also reports that Senators John Glenn (R-Ohio) and IGR ranking minority member William Roth (R-Del.) have declared themselves ready to be among the initial cosponsors. Glenn is important because he would be willing to chair some hearings. From says that he will meet with the full committee's chief counsel, Richard Wegman, to make sure the bill is referred to IGR.

February 3. The bill is introduced as S.2925 and makes an immediate splash. Colleagues approach Muskie on the floor to ask to go on the bill as cosponsors (there eventually were fifty-eight cosponsors in 1976 and sixty in 1977), and Eric Sevareid praises the bill on his television news commentary.

February 6. A companion bill is introduced in the House.

March. IGR hearings are held on March 17, 18, 19, 24, and 25. The staff's preparations are fairly typical for a committee meeting in the Senate. All senators, when they enter the hearing room, find a folder of background material at their place including the bill, advance copies of testimony, and a brief staff memo discussing the issues and the witnesses. The staff prepares a much more detailed briefing book for Muskie. Such briefing books generally contain a series of memos discussing strategy, the issues, the witnesses, and an analysis of testimony submitted in advance. On Sunset, the books also contained memos with tables on the budgetary impact of those federal programs that did and those that did not come up for periodic reauthorization. The staff writes out questions Muskie might want to ask witnesses who have submitted advance testimony. But, since Government Operations witnesses are not always conscientious about sending in their testimony early, the staff sits behind the senator during the hearing to suggest questions to him. However, since Muskie is a careful reader of his briefing books, he tends to rely on whispered staff advice less than most of his colleagues.

There can be no doubt in the mind of anyone watching the hearing that the staff works for the chairman and not the subcommittee as a whole. And the few times Senators Glenn or James Sasser of Tennessee chair a Sunset hearing in Muskie's absence, the staff sits directly behind them making their suggestions only to the person in the chair. Senator Roth, who attended many of the Sunset hearings, relied on his own staff to do the same work for him. The procedure contrasts sharply with what happens on the House Armed Services or House Public Works Committees, where every member's folder contains a list of staff prepared questions for the witnesses, and it contrasts with the House Ways and Means and Senate Finance Committee, where the nonpartisan staff of the Joint Committee on Taxation supplies all members with technical information of the sort found in Muskie's briefing books (see Chapter 8).

Attendance at the hearings is poor, as is to be expected. In most Senate hearings, leading administration witnesses (or the combination of an important private witness and television cameras) may get the senators to turn out, but little else will. Generally, witnesses are heard by only one or two senators, with a covey of aides taking notes as they sit behind the empty chairs of the absent members. If a senator is particularly interested in the hearing, he may drop in for fifteen minutes or so to get his questions on the record. A staff member will lean over to give his own senator a quick, whispered briefing of what has happened so far, the Senator will ask his questions and leave. Except for the few senators who actually attend the hearing for an extended period, the witnesses are there essentially to get their positions on the public record and to inform the staff of potential trouble spots for their negotiations ahead.

April 5. A memo from From to Muskie before the last day of IGR hearings (April 7) identifies workload as a key issue about Sunset bothering senators and committee staff. Conversations with other staff indicate that at least two important amendments will be offered in subcommittee markup: (1) Roth wants to create a new "Hoover Commission" to study the organization of the executive branch and (2) Glenn wants Sunset to apply to tax expenditures. The staff also has been talking to Peter Pyrhh, who originated the concept of zero-based budgeting (ZBB) and helped Jimmy Carter set it up in Georgia.

(Carter by this time is the front runner for the Democratic presidential nomination.) Pyrhh urges that the bulk of the work on ZBB be done by the executive branch and From agrees.

April 26. A memo from From to Muskie says that the staff, in consultation with OMB, Pyrhh, Schultze and Schick, is making progress on a new draft of spending reform that would answer the major criticisms. Muskie *is informed* that the review cycle will be changed from four to five years and most ZBB work will be done by the executive branch.

April 27. A memo from From to the other senators on IGR lets them know that markups have been scheduled for May 13 and 14. The memo, unlike the one to Muskie, gives no more than the vaguest sketch of the bill. If the other senators want more information, they can ask their own staff.

April 28. Memo from From to Muskie says that he thinks the bill seems likely to be a major presidential campaign issue in 1976.

May 6. Five-page memo from From to Muskie, "Progress on Spending Reform," contains this sentence: "I believe we are now getting, for the first time, a reasonable picture of what we can and cannot expect to accomplish with the spending reform bill and what our principal objective should be in writing it."

May 12. Memo from From to Muskie the day before the IGR markup: "I have had two meetings so far with staff members of the other Senators on the subcommittee, and I see no one who opposes the bill at this point. . . . We may make a few minor changes to take into account the views of other Senators. . . . Every staff person representing a subcommittee member agreed that the proper strategy for handling this bill is for the subcommittee to push it up quickly to the full committee, for it is only that way that we can make the full committee chairmen and other potential opponents of the bill take it seriously."

May 13. The subcommittee behaves exactly according to the script laid out by the staff. The bill, with Glenn's tax expenditure and Roth's "Hoover Commission" provisions added, is approved in one day with little debate or detailed discussion.

June 3. In a memo to Muskie, From says he and Davidson have been speaking to the chief staff people of the standing committees. As on many issues affecting internal operations or jurisdiction, these staff people are to become key actors on Sunset during the next two years—clearly more important than most senators. From also has initiated discussions with lobbyists representing organized labor to see if he can soften labor's opposition to Sunset by amending the bill. Labor and civil rights organizations are opposed to Sunset; Common Cause and the Chamber of Commerce are for it. The opposition is based on some very significant concerns. First, the government is set up deliberately to make it easier to kill a bill than to pass it. This bias toward the *status quo* works against both the passage of new programs and the repeal of old ones. Civil rights organizations and their allies in organized labor feel they had to struggle for decades before the civil rights and Great Society programs of the 1960s were enacted. They fear that automatic termination will force them to reconstruct coalitions in favor of these programs every five years, and that the coalitions would have to be large enough to defeat new filibusters. The filibuster issue will be subject to extensive negotiations throughout the next three years, but the direct intervention of lobbyists never becomes particularly important to the development of the bill. Representatives from the Labor and Public Welfare Committee (later called Labor and Human Resources) will look after labor and civil rights interests, Veterans Committee staff will look after veterans' interests, and so forth. In this respect, Sunset is not a "typical" bill, on which lobbyists and staff would have worked much more closely than they did on Sunset.

June 4. In a memo, From alerts Muskie that Senator Abraham Ribicoff (D-Conn.), the chairman of the Government Operations Committee, will try to speak to him and to Charles Percy (R-Ill.), the committee's ranking minority member. Percy is cosponsor with Majority Whip (and future Majority Leader) Robert C. Byrd (D-W.Va.) of a regulatory reform bill he would like to schedule for full committee markup at the same time as Sunset. The staff has not been able to resolve the scheduling issue on its own. (From thinks the Percy-Byrd bill would be an albatross around Sunset's neck.)

The Ford administration starts getting into the act at this time as well, offering deals to From that would trade the administration's support of Sunset for Muskie's support of regulatory reform. The offer, which was turned aside, is remarkable less for its content than for the way it is made. Bill Brock, the ranking Republican senator on Government Operations, conveyed the administration's message not to Muskie but to From, who in turn put it in one of his memos to his boss. According to several Senate aides on other committees, this has become standard operating procedure in the Senate. One former staff director said that at least half of the deals proposed by other senators to his boss were made by the other senator to him.

Summer. The scheduling issue delays the full committee's consideration of Sunset. The markup, tentatively planned for mid-June, before the national political conventions, has to be put off until August 3 and 4, effectively killing the bill for the year. The full committee reports the bill, but the Committee on Rules and Administration asserts its own jurisdiction over the issue. The bill is re-referred to Rules, with an agreement that Rules would report the bill by September 30. The committee, chaired by Howard Cannon (D-Nev.), has both Byrd and Minority Whip Robert Griffin (R-Mich.) as members. On procedural issues, it has long been considered a place where the interests of full committee chairmen would get a sympathetic hearing.

September 14. Memo from From to Muskie: "The slumbering opposition to the Sunset Bill, which we always anticipated would eventually awaken, has, indeed, arisen. The staffs of two committees—Labor and Public Welfare and Finance—are launching an all out effort to torpedo the bill. And while those committee staffs are in the lead, it seems clear to me that the staffs of other authorizing committees may soon join the opposition. Last Friday morning, they discussed the Sunset Bill at the weekly breakfast meeting of full committee staff directors,* and their hostility was apparent. The key question is whether the hostility toward Sunset of the top committee staff will really carry over to their bosses. . . . If, in fact, the staff hostility turns into committee chairman opposition, it will have an impact on the future of the bill both in the Rules Committee and on the floor."

September 15. The Rules Committee votes to report Sunset without endorsing it, and its written report recommends against floor action in 1976. Since it is too late in the session to expect any House action, From recommends against forcing a floor debate that may solidify opposition and prejudice the issue for the following year. From is hopeful that Jimmy Carter's support of Sunset during the campaign may help, if he is elected.

October 2. The Ninety-fourth Congress adjourns without a floor vote on Sunset.

---

*Staff directors of all Senate committees breakfast together every week. Former staff directors—many of whom work for the administration or as lobbyists—are invited to attend and administration officials often address the meeting. As From's comment suggests, a lot of cross-committee business is conducted at these meetings.

1977

January. In an effort to meet objections of the standing committee chairmen, Davidson and others on the staff have been working since adjournment on a new draft of the Sunset Bill. The staff has dropped all "zero-based budgeting" language from the draft because it feels ZBB is more appropriate to the executive branch budget process.

January 10. By memorandum, the staff informs Muskie of its changes in the bill. On the same day, Muskie reintroduces the re-named "Program Evaluation Act of 1977" as S.2. (The low number had been reserved by the staff in advance.)

March 1. In a memo to Muskie From says that whether or not to join Sunset with the Percy-Byrd Regulatory Reform Bill (S.600) is again going to be a major political issue, as it was in 1976. While the two bills can both be considered "Sunset" Bills, From considers S.600 to raise many complex problems and strongly urges Muskie to resist Percy's likely efforts to consider them together. After consultation with the full approval of Roth's staff (Theodore Farfaglia and Douglas Barrett), From outlines a strategy that calls for: (1) five days of the IGR hearings on S.2 in late March, (2) IGR markup of S.2 in late April (3) separate IGR hearings on S.600 in late May, (4) full committee approval of S.2 by the end of June and (5) a sixty to ninety-day time agreement from the Rules Committee. Governmental Affairs Committee senators will end up following the script faithfully through the fourth step, but the Rules Committee is another story, as we shall see.

March 22, 23, 24, 28, 29, 30. IGR hearings on S.2.

April 28. IGR marks up S.2 and orders it reported to the full committee. Since all nine senators in IGR are cosponsors of S.2, the markup is without incident.

June 9. With a full committee meeting set for June 14, From suggests and then arranges a June 13th meeting between the principal IGR sponsors of S.2—Muskie, Roth, Glenn, and Lawton Chiles (D-Fla.)—to discuss strategy.

June 13. From briefs the sponsors on his discussions with people in the administration and with Tom Hart of Senator Byrd's staff. In a memo to Muskie, written before the meeting, From: (1) urges Muskie to push hard for immediate consideration of S.2, with S.600 to follow separately, (2) warns him that Glenn might be susceptible to the idea of a Sunset pilot project, and (3) suggests Roth may not support the tax expenditure title. From recommends that Muskie remain strongly committed to both the tax expenditure title (Glenn's main concern) and to Roth's Hoover Commission as a way to keep both senators firmly with him in opposition to a pilot project and to joining S.2 and S.600. What From is doing here is telling Muskie in advance about how other staff members read the exact concerns of the other core members of the coalition Muskie is trying to build. Muskie presumably could have done this on his own, in direct conversations with other senators, as Russell Long does on any major tax bill. But that would have been much more time consuming than letting the staff do the advance work.

June 14. The full Governmental Affairs Committee meets. Normally, chairman Abraham Ribicoff likes to run what political scientists would describe as a "consensus committee". He prefers not to bring issues up in full committee meetings until after the staff has worked out agreements on behalf of their senators. Since many of the issues considered by the committee have to do with reforming governmental procedures, and since the full Senate, the parallel House committee and the full House are all considerably less reform-minded than this committee, he knows that a bill stands little chance of becoming law unless it comes out of Governmental Affairs with an overwhelming bipartisan majority. As a result, the committee that has given us "government in the Sunshine" prefers having the staff "work things out" in private meetings rather than reaching a decision after public debate, particularly if the debate might lead to a divisive vote. Even on those few occasions when close votes occur, they tend to be on isolated, politically controversial amendments that become sharpened as the staff tries to work out a consensus on the overall bill.[8]

The meeting on Sunset fits Ribicoff's style exactly. Percy argues for S.600, Muskie presses the need for quick action on S.2, and others (such as Jackson and Alaska's Ted Stevens) offer some very broad criticism of the concept. Then, with virtually no discussion of the bill's substantive provisions, Ribicoff adjourns the meeting and asks the staff to see what they can work out before the July 4 recess.

Over the next two weeks, there are daily staff meetings among people representing Ribicoff (Matthew Schneider and sometimes Richard Wegman), Muskie (From, Davidson, and others), Roth (Doug Barrett), Glenn (Len Bickwit, who was on Glenn's personal staff payroll) Percy (Stuart Statler), and Javits (Brian Conboy). Alan Schick also attends many of the meetings. Jackson is kept informed, but his staff does not participate. In some respects, this is the real Governmental Affairs "committee." At least, it is the one setting in which people deliberate as a group in which the committee's different interests are present. This is to be the first of four staff level "committees" that each redrafted S.2 in 1977–1978.

Senator Percy agrees quickly to let the committee move ahead with S.2 as long as IGR promises to proceed expeditiously with S.600. (IGR in fact did nothing more with S.600 for the rest of the Ninty-fifth Congress.) The staff then redrafts a version of S.2 that contains a series of compromises to satisfy most of the objections those present have with the bill.

Although most of the closed group's meetings are self-contained, the staff does meet on June 23 with representatives from Common Cause, the American Bar Association's Commission on Law and the Economy, and Ralph Nader's Congress Watch. (On a normal bill, there would be many more meetings with interest group representatives, with staff telling the groups which senators need to be lobbied and in what way.) The meeting is a strange affair. Although those present think they are there to be heard, the IGR staff sees the meeting as more cosmetic than substantive. Muskie's staff for some reason has had a decidedly uneasy relationship with Common Cause, even though it and the Chamber of Commerce are the only groups pushing Sunset in public. Part of it may have to do with claiming credit: Muskie has been interested in automatic termination for years, but the idea took off in the press in early 1976 when, at roughly the same time, Muskie introduced his bill and Common Cause of Colorado persuaded the state legislature to adopt a law that had the word "sunset" in the title. As long as the bill was in IGR, From and Davidson felt little need to call on Common Cause. Ribicoff's staff, in contrast, has been feasting on Common Cause bills since Ribicoff became chairman in 1975. As a result, Common Cause is able, at this crucial redrafting stage, to press their case successfully in private talks with Wegman and Schneider.

In Common Cause's view, Sunset should combine program evaluation procedures with a mechanism that would force a vote. Muskie sees the vote as being more important than formal evaluation, while Senator Cannon would be willing to evaluate without threatening to terminate. Common Cause gets its way when Schneider insists on including a separate "program evaluation" title in the bill. Muskie later is to take the first available opportunity away from the Governmental Affairs Committee, in testimony before the Rules Committee in September, to downplay the importance of program evaluation and say that it was stuck in the act at the "last minute." However, the fact is that this "last minute" is the first good opportunity for Common Cause to present its case to a staff member open to its point of view. Once that view is adopted, it stays in the bill.

While lobbyists may not have played a particularly important or active role on this bill, there is a lesson here that applies to other bills in very different situations. Successful lobbyists in Washington today are people who know how to work with the staffs. They know which particular members of a personal or committee staff are most likely to listen to them. And they know the importance of timing—of making their pitch at just the moment that staff member is likely to have his best chance to influence the bill. The staff of the full Governmental Affairs Committee will stay out of the picture for the rest of 1977 and 1978, but these two weeks of negotiations are enough for the staff (and through it, Common Cause) to have an important impact on the bill.

June 28. The committee meets to mark up the bill. The one issue too divisive for the staff to resolve is whether to apply the Sunset mechanism to tax expenditures (tax credits and deductions worth about $150 billion per year.[9]) The committee takes two votes on the issue. First, in the morning it turns back a motion offered by Roth to strike the entire tax expenditure title from the bill. Then in the afternoon, it votes seven to six to adopt an amendment offered by Senator John Danforth (R-Mo.) to eliminate the termination mechanism for tax expenditures. The majority of seven is made up of six Republicans plus Ribicoff. Ribicoff and three of the Republicans serve on the Finance Committee and invariably support Russell Long in conflicts between Governmental Affairs and Finance.

After the vote, Muskie says he would rather have the bill say nothing about tax expenditures than to call for review without the threat of termination. His motion is accepted, although many think he is acting in a fit of pique. In fact, however, From has known about the proposal for at least three weeks and has advised Muskie that keeping review without termination for tax expenditures would make it more likely that the same fall-back position would be adopted for all programs. Glenn is bitter about the vote,[10] and vows to fight for a floor amendment. Muskie say he will support Glenn.[11]

July. If the Senate wants to send S.2 to the House in time to get the other chamber moving, Muskie almost has to reach a time agreement with Senator Cannon, chairman of the Rules Committee, to report the bill within thirty or sixty days. Although Cannon had agreed to a time limit in 1976 near the end of a Congress, he is reluctant to agree to one this time, with more than a year left in the Ninety-fifth Congress. Byrd lets Cannon have his way.

August. Recess.

September 16. Cannon sends a "Dear Colleague" letter to other senators about S.2. It is a bland, basically conciliatory letter. But Cannon has attached a harsh nine-page Rules Committee "staff working paper" to the letter that: (1) questions the necessity of automatic termination, (2) claims the workload required by "Sunset" would produce meaningless paper "reviews" for most programs, and (3) suggests dropping the termination mechanism.

September 28. Muskie and Roth testify as the lead-off witnesses before the Rules Committee, and Muskie spends most of his time criticizing the staff working paper.[12] His exchanges with Cannon are heated, and it becomes clear to Muskie that he is not going to get anything out of the Rules Committee unless he does something dramatic. Without discussing what he is about to do with his staff, Muskie makes the following proposal at the end of his testimony:

> The Chairman will remember, and I think Senator Hatfield [Ranking Minority Member Mark O. Hatfield of Oregon] will remember, that when we developed the Budget Reform Act, the last and most constructive step was the cooperative work that the staffs of the two Committees did following the Rules Committee's hearings. . . . If we could get the same kind of work and commitment to develop this legislation I think that we can produce something of which both Committees can be proud.[13]

Cannon picks up Muskie's suggestion and expands it to set up a staff working group with representation from the various authorizing committees as well as Rules and Governmental Affairs.[14] (The staff working group on the budget reform act also included representatives from the other committees, contrary to what Muskie said.)[15] The working group set up by Cannon will obviously be weighted against Muskie's position, since the authorizing committee chairmen are the people most likely to oppose Sunset. But in Muskie's eyes, anything that moves the bill to the floor, where he could try to add strengthening amendments, would be preferable to having it languish in the Rules Committee. Muskie agrees, and Cannon directs the staff to work during the recess so the committee can hold no more than one day of additional hearings after the first of the year.

November 4. This is the last full meeting of Congress in 1977.

November 10. The staff working group meets for the first time. Twenty-seven people have been invited to represent all the standing committees and one individual Senator (Joseph Biden of Delaware, whose own "Sunset" Bill is also being considered by the Rules Committee[16]). The leaders of the group are:

- William M. Cochrane, staff director of the Rules Committee since 1973, when Cannon became chairman. Prior to becoming the formal staff director of the committee, Cochrane served from 1958–1972 as administrative assistant to Leverett B. Jordan (D-N.C.). Jordan became chairman of the committee in 1963 and used Cochrane as if he were on the committee staff.
- Ronald L. Hicks, a technical analyst on the Rules Committee staff. Hicks took a lot of heat from Senator Muskie for his work on Sunset, but most observers believe Hicks was a "good soldier" carrying out Cochrane's and/or Cannon's orders.
- Jonathan Steinberg, staff director of the Veterans' Affairs Committee, about whom we shall learn more in our discussion of the GI bill.
- Michael Stern, staff director of the Finance Commitee. Stern is respected by the many people who have had to work with or against him as a bright and forceful servant of his chairman, Russell Long. He worked for Wilbur Cohen when Cohen was Undersecretary and then Secretary of Health, Education, and Welfare in the Johnson administration, and was thought by many in the "welfare establishment" to be one of "their own" when Long hired him. But Stern did not see himself as an advocate for outside groups to Senator Long. Once it became clear to him that Long and ranking minority member John J. Williams (R–Del.) were opposed to President Nixon's guaranteed annual income plan, Stern played an important role in its defeat. With his good political sense of timing and his detailed knowledge of the issue, Stern put together a series of charts on work incentives that one close observer called politically "devastating." He did

so well, in fact, that Long made him the Finance Committee's staff director in 1973 when he was in his mid-thirties. However, Stern's competence does not mean he has the authority to negotiate a bargain in Russell Long's name. Unlike From, Steinberg, or many others at these meetings, Stern can never be sure he has clinched an agreement until his chairman says so himself.

Joseph R. Humphreys of the Finance Committee's staff attended many of the meetings in Stern's place, after the crucial first ones. He served as a "detail" person, similar to Hicks.

Others who play important roles include George Travers from the Armed Services Committee, Michael Glennon from Foreign Relations, Karen Schubeck from Agriculture, Frank Zweig and Michael Shoor from Human Resources, John McEvoy and Karen Williams of Muskie's Budget Committee and, of course, IGR's Davidson. All except Davidson, McEvoy, and Williams oppose Muskie's bill. Together, these are the key actors in a series of meetings that take most of the afternoon every Monday and Thursday during the recess.

The first meeting is nothing but a sparring match. The opponents, led by Stern and Steinberg, begin by trying to heap ridicule on the statement of the bill's purpose in the report of the Governmental Affairs Committee ("to establish a systematic and orderly procedure for reconsideration by Congress of its past program enactments . . .," etc.). The opponents also propose considering the bill line by line from beginning to end. Davidson objects to this as a stalling tactic and proposes in a November 14 memo to the group that it discuss the major controversial issues first. The group agrees and the rest of November is spent arguing about the merits of the termination mechanism.

November 28. John McLellan, the eighty-one-year-old chairman of the Appropriations Committee, dies in his sleep. Warren Magnuson is sure to become the new chairman of Appropriations when Congress reconvenes in January, in turn giving Cannon the chance to chair Commerce. The new chairman of the Rules Committee will be Claiborne Pell of Rhode Island. While Cannon and Pell both are among the sixty nominal sponsors of S.2, Cannon is a determined opponent of termination while Pell has not yet focused on the issue. Instinctively, however, Pell is certain of one thing: he is up for reelection in 1978 and does not want to get caught in a political crossfire with Muskie. Aware of this, Common Cause of Rhode Island makes sure over the next few months that Pell knows there are people in his state who care about Sunset.

December 1. As the staff meetings continue, Davidson, Steinberg, and Zweig begin to explore whether there are alternatives to termination. Uncertain about his authority here, Davidson feels he had better check with Muskie.

December 2 (Friday). Memo from From to Muskie: "We have come to a point in our negotiations with other committee staffs where we have to make a fundamental substantive decision. That is whether we are willing to compromise the comprehensive termination feature of the bill. The negotiations have reached a stalemate. . . . If we hold out and indicate no willingness to compromise termination, the staff group will either write a bill without us or just stand and not produce a bill at all. . . . While I don't particularly relish the thought of having to do it, I recommend that you give us the authority to compromise."

December 3 or 4. From and Davidson visit Muskie at his home, where he is recuperating from a disc operation. Muskie thinks termination is the key to Sunset and does not give them the authority to compromise. He says that his two highest priorities for 1978 are getting a Senate vote on Sunset and forcing the Senate to confront a serious test of the budget process.

December 5. Davidson informs the working group of Muskie's decision. Steinberg says that since the group was set up at Muskie's request, the Rules Committee staff should check with Cannon to see if the group should go on meeting.

December 8. Cochrane and Hicks have not talked to Cannon since the last meeting but Hicks tells the group that it is important to develop an alternative. Hicks and Cochrane are thinking of using the committee funding resolutions to get committees to do evaluations. Steinberg thinks there has to be some response specifically to the termination mechanism, a way for senators to force a vote on a program if they want one (a sort of "reverse Sunset"). Cochrane and Steinberg both are concerned that if the group does not have a concrete alternative to offer, senators may, if forced to choose, vote for Sunset rather than appear to be against efficiency. If given a choice between two proposals, however, they feel confident the Senate will prefer the milder one written by the working group.

December 19. Cochrane's and Steinberg's ideas are joined and circulated in draft form. This is the last meeting of the group for the year.

1978

January. The staff working group continues its four-hour Monday and Thursday afternoon sessions. Representatives of the Veterans (Steinberg) and Finance Committees (Stern, Humphreys) argue strongly for an alternative to termination that will allow twenty-five senators to circulate a petition and demand a vote on continuing a program. The Foreign Relations and Armed Services staffs are distrubed at even this, but give in. By the end of the month, the group has reached agreement on the basic issues and the drafting process begins in earnest.

February 15. The draft containing the working group's alternative to S.2 is being circulated in the form of a Senate resolution.

February 21. Muskie sends a letter to Pell predictably disagreeing with the substance of the staff's proposal and complaining that the use of a resolution could prevent the Senate from choosing between his approach and the staff's. (It would be out of order to substitute a bill for a resolution on the floor.)

April 19. The Rules Committee meets again on Sunset. Virtually nothing has happened in the two months since the staff prepared its first drafts. Hicks says there were several redrafts with technical changes, but the committee in fact has put the issue on a back burner while Pell handles his first round of committee funding resolutions. Pell's passive acceptance of the committee's staff's timing costs valuable weeks and will prove important later.

William Young, a member of Pell's personal staff, is following the issue for the new chairman. By the time the Rules Committee meets on April 19, Young knows the details of the staff working group's product and Pell knows enough to realize he is being put in a box he does not like. At the start of the hearing, Pell stresses that the staff group's written report was a report *to* and not a report *of* the committee. He assures Muskie that whatever the committee reports, Muskie will have a chance for a clear vote on S.2.

After the principal sponsors of S.2 criticize the working group's report, Comptroller General Elmer B. Staats takes his turn on the stand. Staats makes it clear that while he does not "really quarrel" with the idea of automatic termination, he likes the staff working group's emphasis on giving committees flexibility for program evaluation. Pell seizes upon the apparent moderation of Staats' statement. Faced with a clear impasse between Muskie and the staff working group, the GAO seems to be giving him a way out. With no staff of his own to work up an alternative, Pell asks the support agency if it "could give us a memorandum which would incorporate the best of all the different features that have been discussed."[17] When Young is asked later whether Pell had planned before the hearing to ask this of the GAO, Young says he had not: "He did it at that meeting with no advance discussion. I had no idea he was going to do that. There was a disagreement and it was clear that it wasn't going to do any good to ask the two principal staffs to have another go at it." Thus, Pell has used a neutral staff to buy himself some breathing room. He does not yet know the details of the material, but he senses instinctively that his political interests will be best served by avoiding a decision and getting some more advice.

June 8. The GAO's 100-page memorandum on Sunset is presented in the third, and final, Rules Committee hearing on S.2. It recommends: (1) that all programs be reviewed on an eight- instead of five-year cycle, and (2) that programs not reviewed be *considered for* termination (thus requiring an affirmative vote for termination instead of S.2's reversed procedure). After Harry Havens, the director of GAO's Program Analysis Division, has explained these recommendations on behalf of the absent Staats, Pell asks From to join Havens at the witness table and engages in a three-way discussion of the merits of Havens' statement. Asserting that the GAO has come up with "a good deal more than half a loaf, perhaps a three-quarter loaf,"[18] Pell asks Havens, From, and Biden aide Dick Andrews to work together over the next week to see if they can draft specific legislative language covering the points on which they agree and offering alternative proposals expressing their irreconcilable differences. The Rules Committee staff is not included in the redrafting process.

It seems obvious to anyone at the meeting that Pell has been shaken by the overwhelming approval of Proposition 13 in California just two days before. With almost 65 percent of the voters adopting a referendum to cut back state property taxes sharply, Pell—to quote from Al From's memo to Muskie written after the hearing—"talked over and over again about the necessity of following the people's will and terminating some on-going programs. He has never talked that way before."[19]

In a June 8 memo to Muskie, From says that "as usual" the key differences between S.2 and the GAO were over the termination mechanism, but adds that compromise may be possible this time.

June 12. In a memo to Muskie, From says the GAO has agreed to support a bill containing all of the important features of S.2, including automatic termination, with two qualifications. But, since one of the two qualifications involves a compromise on the length of the review cycle that Muskie has rejected once before, From asks Muskie to agree to it explicitly. Muskie agrees to the compromise.

June 21. The Rules Committee meets to consider the bill worked out by Muskie's staff and the GAO. Pell is solidly behind the compromise, but Cannon's continued opposition and Pell's deference to him have given the staff a mandate to prepare some thirty-two amendments to the bill. From tells Pell that twenty-six are acceptable technical amendments. After a lengthy private huddle around Pell during the markup to settle on procedure, the committee accepts the technical amendments in a bloc, rejects five of six controversial amendments, and adopts one adding military retirement and veteran's benefits to the list of exemptions. The committee reports the bill by a vote of 6 to 1.

July 14. The report of the Rules Committee is filed. (S. Rept. 95-981).

August 16. Muskie is getting little satisfaction from Majority Leader Robert Byrd about scheduling S.2 for floor action. An eleven-page, August 8 letter to Byrd answering the major criticisms of Sunset had produced no response. On the 16th Muskie decides to talk about S.2 at a meeting of the Democratic Policy Committee, chaired by Byrd. The committee, made up of nine senior Democratic senators including Muskie, is responsible for setting scheduling priorities for the floor. Muskie fails to get a commitment at the meeting, but Byrd asks Muskie to have his staff meet with Thomas D. Hart, Byrd's chief counsel for the policy committee, to see if they can work on the items in S.2 that concern him.

August 22. From and Davidson go to a meeting called by Hart. Besides Hart, they expect to see Dennis Thelan of Byrd's staff and Jon

Steinberg, the Veteran's Committee chief counsel who represents Cranston, the majority whip, on a wide variety of issues. When they get there, they find those three, joined by Mike Stern of the Finance Committee, Ron Hicks of Rules, Edwin K. Hall, who had been hired by Cannon away from Rules to be General Counsel of the Commerce, Science and Transportation Committee, and Stephen J. Paradise, staff director of Williams's Human Resources Committee. This meeting turns out to be the basis for the fourth and politically most significant staff redrafting of the Sunset Bill in 1977–1978. By the time the group is to finish a month later, all of the key opponents will have influenced the bill's contents.

Byrd's problems relate to the technical procedures to be followed on the floor in assuring privileged status to Sunset resolutions. Obviously important to him as a floor leader, they make little difference to the substance of S.2 and are easily compromised. The major work of the next month takes place in meetings between Steinberg, Stern (or sometimes Humphreys), From, Davidson, and occasionally Thelan. The first meeting with eveyone present starts out with a general discussion and seems to From as if it is a replay of Cannon's staff working group. It soon becomes evident, however, that 1978 is to be a lot different from 1977: in the wake of Proposition 13, Steinberg and Stern are now willing to agree to periodic reauthorizations for all permanently authorized programs. "Once they agreed to that," From said, "the rest was academic."

After the group reworks the bill, Cranston and Byrd sign on as cosponsors. None of the orginal core cosponsors have been lost because From and Davidson, in the course of protecting Muskie's interests, have seen to it that they do not bargain away anything that another person in Muskie's basic coalition considers crucial. On tax expenditures, From reiterates Muskie's promise to support a Glenn amendment on the floor while Stern says that, except for the tax issue, Long will not oppose the bill if the leadership accepts it. (Stern at one point suggested that Long might become a cosponsor. He did not, but he did vote for the bill in the end.)

September 26. The new version of S.2 is introduced. For the next two weeks, the question is whether Muskie can get the bill on the floor while keeping his word to Glenn. The Ninety-fifth Congress is in its closing weeks.[20] A major tax bill, an omnibus energy bill, the Humphrey-Hawkins Full Employment Bill and the Export-Import (Ex-Im) Bank Reauthorization Bill are all ahead of Sunset on the calendar, and are all open to threatened filibusters. There is literally no way Sunset is going to be considered unless the Senate agrees unanimously to do so. From the day the new version of S.2 is introduced, it is made clear to Muskie and his staff that they can get a unanimous consent agreement with no difficulty if Muskie will agree not to allow a vote on the Glenn amendment. Muskie refuses to agree to the deal until Glenn has a chance to try to get the bill on the floor with his amendment in order. At first (September 29 and 30, October 2), Muskie and Glenn try to attach S.2 as an amendment to the Ex-Im Bank Bill. When it becomes clear that the Ex-Im Bank Bill will not pass, they try adding it as an amendment to the tax bill and filing a cloture motion that will permit a vote on the Glenn amendment. At one point, after some procedural motions a Franz Kafka might have written, Sunset, hospital cost containment, and Humphrey-Hawkins all are riding on each other's backs as potential amendments to the tax bill.

After a series of procedural defeats in which neither Muskie nor Glenn get the clear votes they want, From writes a memo to Muskie on October 9 suggesting that he talk to Glenn about separating the Sunset bill from his tax expenditure amendment. "You've gone above and beyond for his amendment—to the point of jeopardizing a bill you've worked on for three years." From says Glenn can get a vote on his amendment by offering it separately as an amendment to the tax bill, while S.2 should have little trouble getting to the floor with the Glenn amendment off of it. Muskie shows the memo to Glenn and Glenn agrees to go along.

October 10. Glenn's separate amendment to the tax bill, imposing a termination mechanism on tax expenditures, is defeated by a surprisingly narrow vote of fifty to forty-one. Satisfied that this outcome bodes well for the Ninety-sixth Congress, Glenn tells the leadership he will not try to amend S.2. Long withdraws his objections to a unanimous consent agreement, thus allowing Sunset to come up by itself.

October 11. S.2 passes the Senate by a vote of eighty-seven to one. The margin may be inflated somewhat by the knowledge that House action is all but out of the question, but Muskie thinks that getting the Senate on record should make passing the bill easier in the Ninety-sixth Congress.

October 15. The Ninety-fifth Congress adjourns without the House considering Sunset.

Aftermath

After the elections in November, Muskie let it be known that he would give up his seat on Governmental Affairs in favor of one on Foreign Relations.* His IGR staff immediately began job hunting. From decided he wanted to leave Capitol Hill. "After ten years up here, I think I have learned all I can for now," he said. After exploring possibilities in the private sector (in Washington and elsewhere) and in the executive branch, he finally became an assistant to Alfred Kahn on the Council on Wage and Price Stability. Lee Lockwood and David Johnson went to work for From. Bob Rackleff, the author of the "Liberal Party Speech," became a speechwriter for Secretary of Labor Ray Marshall. Jim Davidson went back home to St. Louis for awhile, where he tried to start a magazine. When that did not work out, he became chief counsel for Senator Culver's Judiciary Subcommittee on Administrative Practices and Procedures, where he followed Sunset in spare moments but was compelled to devote the bulk of the time to other matters.

It is impossible at this writing to predict what may happen to the Sunset Bill in the Ninety-sixth Congress (let alone to predict whether its passage would actually lead to serious, substantive "Sunset" reviews by future Congresses). The vote at the end of the Ninety-fifth Congress built up a lot of momentum, but much of that was dissipated when Muskie switched committees and the staff dispersed. A new staff, working for a different chairman (James Sasser, D-Tenn.) with different priorities is handling the Senate bill in the Ninety-sixth Congress. The House Rules Committee did hold its first set of hearings on Sunset in 1979, but interest group opposition to the bill was getting stronger in both chambers as passage seemed a real possibility and as Proposition 13 faded into the background. Indeed it seems possible, as of this writing, that no bill will pass in 1980 or, if a bill does pass, it may well be without automatic termination.[21] But with all of the possibilities for both slippage and quick action that we saw in the Ninety-fourth and Ninety-fifth Congresses, it would be foolish to predict the outcome here.

*Muskie became Secretary of State on May 8, 1980.

Conclusion

For our purposes, however, what happens to the Sunset Bill does not matter to the story we are telling here. All the new staff can really do is repeat, in a more or less successful fashion, the kinds of processes the IGR staff went through between 1975 and 1978. To avoid losing sight of these, therefore, it would be worth recounting what they were:

1. The IGR staff picked up an idea Muskie had tried in earlier bills that fit in with a general political theme he was developing. The staff decided the time was ripe for a major legislative push and convinced Muskie to let them work on it.
2. The IGR staff worked on getting the general ideas into legislative language. It *informed* Muskie of what it had done and, hearing no objections, it went on ahead.
3. The IGR staff got together with the staffs of other people on Government Operations (principally Roth and Glenn) to incorporate their ideas into the bill.
4. The staff took the initiative in trying to build coalitions with outside interest groups, although there was less of this than on other bills.
5. When the bill failed to get to the floor in 1976, the staff tried to redraft the bill on its own to meet objections that had surfaced in the Rules Committee. Again, it informed Muskie after the redrafting, not before, and again encountered no objections.
6. When the main cosponsors on Governmental Affairs could not come to an agreement with Senator Percy over the timing of Sunset and regulatory reform in 1977, the staffs were told to "work it out." When they did, most of the bill sailed through the committee without public discussion.
7. To save the bill from certain death before the Rules Committee, Muskie urged Cannon to create a staff working group. This group's delaying tactics in early 1978 was largely responsible for the Senate's failure to act in time to force the issue in the House.
8. To get himself out of the political hole into which the working group's resolution might have put him, Pell asked the GAO and

then the GAO together with the IGR staff to come up with a compromise set of proposals.

9. When Byrd felt a similar sense of uneasiness, he asked yet another group of staff people to give the bill one more massaging.

Through all of these steps, the staffs were actively shaping the bill, taking account of their senators' interests, reporting back to their senators on the agreements they had reached, and arguing the political case for their decisions to their bosses. The senators seemed little in evidence through this whole process. But they clearly were not absent. If you were to ask "who was in charge?" the answer in this case seemed to be the senators, with qualifications. Only a few senators seemed to follow or care about the details of this bill, but they all seemed to know exactly how it might affect them politically. On issues of political importance to the members, the staffs may have become wedded to their own points of view, but they were pulled back more than once by their bosses. What the senators did not seem to know or care about, however, were the different substantive options the staff was considering when the differences in substance had no political impact. (Muskie and Cannon seemed to have followed the issues down to this level, but not the other senators.)

While the senators did seem to be well enough in charge of their staffs to control the political effects of the staff's work, the process this bill went through did not even remotely resemble a civics textbook picture of legislative deliberation. There was a lot of deliberation, to be sure, but it all seemed to be going on between staffs. The senators talked to (or received memos from) their staffs, but they did not seem to talk much to each other. (On a few instances, we even saw a staff member advising a senator to talk to his colleague.) Moreover, while senators may have known more or less what the staffs negotiated in their own names, it seems clear that only Muskie, From, and Davidson—and not even the other cosponsors or many of their staffs—knew why each major item was in the bill in the form it had taken.

Chapter 5

Detailed Negotiations:
The Phantom Conference
on the GI Bill

THE PREVIOUS two chapters have focused on staff aides who happened to work for activist liberal senators. There was a reason for this. Senators have more committee assignments than House members, and liberals have tended in the past to be more interested than conservatives in promoting new legislative ideas. As a result, senators have tended to rely on staffs more than House members, and liberals more than conservatives. But this is changing. New-style conservatives, raised in the age of media politics, are every bit as active as their liberal colleagues in the pursuit of their legislative ends and use their staffs accordingly. (One such aide is Paul Craig Roberts, mentioned in chapter 8 on the House Budget Committee.) And similarly, even the most traditional-style conservative members of the House are choosing increasingly to rely heavily on their staffs.

The negotiations over the 1977 GI Education Bill provide an excellent example of how a liberal activist senator and two traditionally conservative House members used their staffs in one end-of-session "conference." The example also serves an additional

75

purpose: while the chapter on Sunset gave an overview of staff operations on one bill over a three-year period, this one pays attention to the details of staff bargaining in an intense, one-week period. It is, therefore, a better vehicle than Sunset for seeing the negotiation process at work.

In 1977, the House and Senate had passed very different bills extending and increasing educational benefits for veterans. The House acted first, passing a straightforward bill on September 12 that increased veterans' benefits by 6.6 percent. The bill passed under a suspension of the rules by a vote of 397 to 0. The Senate bill, containing a number of significantly different provisions, was adopted on October 14 by a vote of 91 to 0. The Senate vote came about three weeks before the first session of the Ninety-fifth Congress was expected to adjourn. The timing was par for the course for a veteran's bill. For several years in a row the two veterans' committees seemed to have a propensity for bringing major bills to the floor toward the end of a session—a time of the year when the crush of business makes it impossible for most members to focus on the issues, demand regular procedures, or consider taking any action that might endanger cost-of-living increases for veterans.

We used the word "conference" earlier to describe what happened after Senate passage. Actually, it should be thought of as a "phantom conference." Conferees never were appointed and the leading members met only once over an informal breakfast. In 1977, as in previous years, the leaders of the two veterans' committees used the calendar as their excuse for letting the staff do the work of a conference committee. Key staff people simply sat down for three days in late October and early November and resolved the differences between the two bills. These differences went well beyond monetary questions to ones of policy that the committee members saw as issues of principle. As a result, the staff level compromise was no simple split-the-difference affair. To find some common ground between the interests of the key members of the House and Senate, the staffs had to come up with imaginative new formulations significantly changing existing law. These formulations, some of which had never been discussed previously in either chamber, were ratified by key committee members and adopted unanimously, with virtually no debate, by the House on November 3 and by the Senate on November 4.

The Issues

To understand the role the staff played in the phantom conference, it is necessary first to give a brief outline of the differences between the House and Senate bills. The House bill (H.R. 8701) was simply a 6.6 percent cost-of-living increase in the level of GI benefits, together with some provisions correcting administrative difficulties caused by an earlier congressional crackdown on fly-by-night vocational schools living off veterans' benefits. The Senate (in S. 457) generally accepted the main items in the House bill, but added three new and controversial items dealing with high tuition schools (the "accelerated payments" provision), the length of the eligibility period ("delimiting"), and women World War II civilian pilots.

Accelerated Payments. The law in force at the time this bill was being considered gave all veterans forty-five months of equal-sized benefits. Veterans with dependents received more than those with no dependents, but payments did not vary with the cost of the school the veteran attended. The principle of equal benefits for all students was one to which Representative Olin E. Teague (D-Tex.) had been firmly committed since he produced the 1947 GI bill for World War II veterans. As a result, the House bill deliberately did not address the concerns of those who wanted more money for people from states with higher than average public tuition costs. (Teague, formerly chairman of the House Veterans' Affairs Committee, had given up the chair in favor of Science and Technology in 1973, but retained the chairmanship of the subcommittee on Education and Training until he retired at the end of 1978. William Jennings Bryan Dorn of South Carolina chaired the full committee in 1973 and 1974 and Teague's fellow Texan, Ray Roberts, became full committee chairman in 1975. Roberts, Dorn, Teague, and the committee's ranking Republican, John Hammerschmidt of Arkansas, agreed on virtually every issue before the committee.)

The Senate committee took the first step away from Teague's "equal benefits" principle in 1977 with a provision saying that the needy students attending high-cost schools could use up to their last nine months of benefits ahead of time—that is, "accelerate" them. (Most veterans use only thirty-six months of benefits during a four-year program.)

Delimiting. Existing law stated that veterans must complete their program of study within ten years of their discharge from service. Since forty-five months of benefits equals five school years, the delimiting period gave veterans a maximum of five years to start if they wanted to use all of their benefits. The Senate committee bill had originally extended the delimiting period indefinitely for veterans who were prevented from initiating or completing their studies because of physical or mental disabilities or impairments. But the committee, in its only record vote on the bill, deleted the provision by a 5 to 4 margin with the chairman, Alan Cranston (D–Calif.), in the minority. (The full Senate had passed a similar provision in the Ninety-fourth Congress, but the House rejected it in conference.) On the floor, the Senate adopted an amendment sponsored by Cranston and John Durkin, (D–N.H.), that followed the original committee bill by extending the delimiting period indefinitely for disabled veterans who had failed to complete their education within ten years and then, in addition, extended the delimiting period by two years for all veterans who were enrolled in full-time programs at the end of their ten years, granting half of the normal benefit level in the eleventh year and one-third in the twelfth year. Curiously, this floor amendment won the support of Strom Thurmond (R-N.C.), who had offered the motion in committee that had led the committee to drop its less liberal extension. As in 1976, the House bill contained no similar provision.

WASPs. The third controversial section in the Senate bill would have extended all veterans' benefits to women who had been civilians under military command in World War II as Women's Air Force Service Pilots (WASPs). It was added on the floor in an amendment sponsored by Senator Barry Goldwater (R–Ariz.). The Veterans' Administration, in a letter to Representative Roberts, dated June 28, 1977, said that despite the risks WASPs ran and the distinction with which most performed, it opposed "singling out WASP participants for veterans' status" because doing so "would clearly discriminate against those countless other civilians who likewise contributed greatly in times of grave national need."[1] Cranston took essentially the same position in opposing Goldwater on the Senate floor.[2] Roberts appeared to be leaning toward recognizing the WASPs in his hearings on the subject,[3] but a staff aide said the "Roberts' position always has been opposed to recognition for that service."

The delimiting, acceleration, and WASPs issues were the three most politically sensitive of the thirty-five or so differences between the House and Senate bills. In each case, the Senate had liberalized benefits in a manner that ran counter to some deeply held feelings, particularly among the traditional World War II dominated veterans' organizations. Two of the three issues (delimiting and acceleration) pitted the newer Vietnam-era political organizations against the older ones, while the third was treated as a symbolic women's rights issue in which the Veteran's Administration position was labeled sexist. Additionally, the question of accelerating benefits for veterans attending high tuition schools divided members regionally, with people from states where college tuitions were highest (primarily in the Northeast) pushing for the program and people from the low tuition Sunbelt states opposed.

Deciding Against a Conference

When the Senate passed its version of the bill on October 19, it fully expected to finish the first session of the Ninety-fifth Congress by Saturday, November 5. (In fact, Congress did not adjourn until December 15, but sessions after November 5 were largely *pro forma*— one Senate session lasted 4–3/4 seconds—to allow some House-Senate conferences to finish their work.) As of the date of Senate passage, therefore, members thought they had two weeks to finish their work. Normally that should be enough time to appoint conferees and get the issues settled, but Cranston had become Senate majority whip as well as chairman of the Veterans' Committee in 1977. He felt he could not, as whip, ignore floor business to attend a conference. If conferees were appointed, he was faced with two unpalatable choices: accept the danger that others with more time to attend the meetings might exert more influence than he would, or postpone the conference until the new year, when positions might have hardened in a way that would have complicated the process of reaching a compromise favorable to his position.

Cranston's sense of what was politically right for late October 1977 coincided with the way Roberts and Teague traditionally like to do business. "I can't remember but one formal conference being held since 1973, when I came here," said Mack G. Fleming, chief counsel for the House Veterans' Affairs Committee, in an interview. As Teague told the *Dallas Morning News* when asked about this bill, "it's just quicker and easier without a whole lot of people."[4] Thus, there was sufficient reason to believe there would be no objection to the two committees doing without a conference committee, as they had in the past.

This time, however, there was some protest from the House. Under House rules, a chairman must call a meeting of a committee if a majority of its members requests one in writing. On October 25, four members of the committee began circulating a letter calling for a November 4 special session of the committee to consider requesting a conference with the Senate. (The four were Lester J. Wolff, D–N.Y., who ranked behind Teague on the Education and Training subcommittee; Margaret M. Heckler, the subcommittee's ranking minority member; Robert J. Cornell, D–Wis.; and Mark Hannaford, D–Calif.) In part, the letter read:

> We are well aware that it has been the traditional practice of the Committee to seek an informal meeting with the Senate primarily at the staff level, to resolve disagreements between the two Houses. We believe, however, that the issues involved in the two versions of H.R. 8701 are too important and too complex to be left to informal staff discussion. We therefore respectfully request that you convene a special meeting of the full Committee on Veterans' Affairs so that the Committee may vote on the question of requesting a conference with the Senate on H.R. 8701.
>
> We well remember the unhappy experience this Committee and the House had last year when S.969 came to the House in the last hours of the 94th Congress. Because of the shortness of time, the House was faced with the options of accepting the Senate language or allowing the bill to die. Public Law 94–502 was the result. It is indeed ironic that H.R. 8701 is intended in part to correct many of the weaknesses of that hastily enacted legislation. We believe that an open conference with the Senate on H.R. 8701, in which members of the Committee of both chambers can work out the substantial differences in the bill, is preferable to either an informal staff discussion or to waiting until time pressures once again require one chamber to accept the language of the other *in toto.*

Fourteen of the committee's twenty-eight members, one short of a majority, eventually signed this letter or one substantially identical to it. (One of the fourteen eventually withdrew his name.) Thus, the people who wrote the letter were not able to force the appointment of conferees. Nevertheless, their action had an important effect on the outcome. House rules require the Speaker to appoint conferees whenever the House disagrees to Senate amendments to a House bill. A single point of order raised by any member would be enough to prevent the House from disobeying its own rules. Since any one of the signers of the letter could have objected to a House vote on a compromise bill, the threat helped assure that the staffs would consult with all interested parties before they settled on anything.

The Members' Breakfast

Two days after Representative Wolff and his colleagues began circulating their letter, Cranston, Roberts, and Teague held the only direct meeting between members of the House and Senate on the bill. It took place over breakfast on the morning of Thursday, October 27 with four staff aides present: Jonathan R. Steinberg, chief counsel for the Senate committee; Jack Wickes, an associate counsel; Mack Fleming, the House committee's chief counsel; and Francis W. Stover, deputy chief counsel. Cranston, Roberts, and Teague decided quickly that most of the thirty or so differences between the House and Senate could be resolved easily by the staff. Their discussion then focused on delimiting and acceleration, with Steinberg giving a technical explanation of the Senate amendments and Roberts and Teague saying why they thought the amendments were bad policy. At one point, Roberts responded to the concern of representatives from high tuition states by asking why the people of Texas, who already had paid for good state public education, should cough up more federal tax dollars to help states whose public education systems were not as good. Roberts said he thought benefits were adequate for most states. Where they were not, he said, the states and schools themselves should accept their part of the commitment. While Roberts was not fishing for a compromise when he made this argument, his remarks were used by Steinberg and Fleming later as the basis for the agreement they finally reached.

The WASPs apparently were not discussed at the breakfast. According to Fleming, "we did not view it as an issue because it was added on the Senate floor over Cranston's opposition. If the Senate

conferees had wanted to knock it out, we would have been willing."
Cranston seems not to have raised the issue at that time, suggesting
to some that he did not consider upholding the Senate position on
this point to be important for him.

The meeting broke up with the members instructing the staff to
work out a compromise. After three long days of negotiations, the
staff did exactly that.

The Staff

The first staff meeting was held at 2:00 P.M. on the same day as the
breakfast. Representing the two committees' majorities were the
four staff members who had attended the breakfast (Steinberg,
Wickes, Fleming, and Stover) and Edward P. Scott from the Senate
committee staff. Two people represented the Senate Republicans.
One was Garner E. Shriver, a former member of Congress from
Kansas (1971–1976) who, after his narrow defeat at the hands of Representative Dan Glickman (D–Kan.) remarkably decided to become
minority counsel to this committee. The associate minority counsel,
Gary Crawford, helped look after noncommittee member Goldwater's interest in the WASPs. The two important Republican aides on
the House side were John Holden, the committee's minority counsel,
and Peter S. Sroka, an aide for Representative Margaret Heckler
(R–Mass.), the second most senior Republican on the committee and
the leading House advocate at these meetings of the Senate's positions on acceleration, delimiting, and the WASPs. Also present, at
Steinberg's suggestion, was Guy H. McMichael, the general counsel
for the Veterans' Administration. McMichael, as chief counsel of the
Senate committee in 1976, was responsible for drafting many of the
end-of-session provisions, the technical problems of which this bill
was trying to correct.

The staff people present were in many respects typical of the
differences between the newer and the more traditional staffs, with
the House staff being the more traditional of the two. If we were
trying to classify staffs in a meaningful way, at least two different
methods of classifications would seem useful. Political scientist David

Detailed Negotiations

Price, we noted in an earlier chapter, classified staffs by the way they saw their roles. Entrepreneurial staffs were ones who saw their jobs in terms of getting new ideas on the legislative agenda while professional staffs were ones that defined their activity in more limited terms. Later in this book (chapters 5 through 7) we suggest another way of categorizing committee staffs: by the types of people or institutions to whom the staffs owe their loyalty. The basic distinction here is between staffs whose loyalty is primarily to one person (chairman, ranking minority member, and so forth) and those who see themselves working for committees as ongoing institutions. The typical staff of the first type will work on a member's personal staff and then stay with that member on a succession of committee staffs. The classic examples of institutionalized aides are the ones on the nonpartisan staffs of the Appropriations or Joint Tax Committees. These people are hired by committee staff directors for their subject area expertise, without concern for political party, and tend to stay with the committees through changes of chairmen. In between are a wide range of partisan committee staffs who see themselves in varying degrees as employees of specific people or as people likely to stay with the committee through changes in personnel.

Entrepreneurial staffs almost always see their jobs and their loyalties in terms of specific members. In fact, it is precisely because the loyalties are so clear-cut that members are willing to give them such broad hunting licenses. If a chairman leaves, these staffs may transfer their loyalties to a new boss (as Jim Davidson did) but rarely try to make careers on Capitol Hill.

While entrepreneurial staff loyalties may almost always be personal, the reverse is not as true. Not all committee staffs with loyalties to specific members are entrepreneurial. Whether a staff is primarily entrepreneurial or more passive will depend on the member's view of his or her own legislative role. Members who are looking to create and publicize new issues will need entrepreneurial staffs while those who are not, won't.

The House and Senate staffs working on the veteran's bill reflect two different, but not polar opposite, staff styles. The Senate staff clearly has more authority to develop and act on new initiatives—to be more entrepreneurial, if you will. But both staffs are essentially delegates of their chairmen. (In the House, the chairman, Roberts, and former chairman, Teague, acted together as one.) As a result, once the aides had developed the trust of their bosses, they could negotiate on behalf of their "principals" in a way that nonpartisan staffs normally would not consider doing.

Jon Steinberg is almost a classic example of the activist entrepreneur. Born in 1939, Steinberg is a well-known, but not widely loved, figure among people who have dealt with Senator Cranston. The only nonveteran among the key staff people, Steinberg went from Cornell University (B.A., 1960), the University of Pennsylvania Law School (L.L.B., 1963), and a clerkship with Appeals Court Judge Warren Burger (1963–1964), to five years as an attorney for the Peace Corps, the last one as deputy general counsel. After President Nixon took office, Steinberg left the Peace Corps to work for Alan Cranston, then in his first year as Senator from California. Until 1977, Steinberg worked on a succession of Cranston-chaired subcommittees on the Committee on Labor and Public Welfare: Veterans' Affairs, 1969–1970 (the Senate formed a separate Veterans' Affairs Committee in 1971); Railroad Retirement, 1971–1972; and Human Resources, 1972–1977. He became general counsel of the Veterans' Affairs Committee in 1977, when Cranston succeeded Vance Hartke (D–Ind.) as chairman. (Hartke chaired the committee from the time it was formed until his 1976 election defeat.)

Steinberg's congressional career, in other words, has been completely intertwined with Cranston's. They were freshmen together, and Steinberg has always been Cranston's principal staffer on his most important committee assignments. The loyalty of staff to member, and the trust of the member in his staff, is complete. It was not always so. Steinberg had to earn Cranston's trust, and he still cherishes the copy of the *Congressional Record* autographed by Cranston containing their first successful joint effort on the floor. The identification between the two has been so close that one major national magazine was moved to describe it this way:

Jonathan Steinberg, chief counsel of the Senate Veterans' Affairs Committee, is widely regarded as a surrogate Senator. If one watches him whispering and passing notes to Chairman Alan Cranston during committee hearings, it becomes clear why lobbyists for veterans' organizations refer to the Californian as Senator Cranberg. Steinberg's whispered words are often repeated by Cranston as if he were a ventriloquist's dummy.[5]

Detailed Negotiations

Steinberg, needless to say, is not happy with characterizations such as these. In fact, he was so suspicious of the press, based on other critical stories about him,* that he initially refused to be interviewed

*Excerpts from two such stories follow:

"The Senate's High-flying, Powerful Aides"
by Charles Bartlett, *Washington Star*, 26 May 1975:

Some of what is awry in government surfaced the other morning in a meeting between Sen. Alan Cranston, D-Cal, and the advisory council of the Action agency. . . .

On all details regarding Action, Cranston deferred throughout the meeting to a young Pennsylvania lawyer named Jonathan Steinberg. Bushy-haired and bright-eyed, Steinberg has appeared bent on dominating Action like a czar since Cranston gave him control of the subcommittee in 1971.

Steinberg has written legislation which binds Action to his personal concepts of voluntarism. He has prejudices of his own because he was once an employee of the Peace Corps, and where he lacks them, he has friends who can supply them. He obtained enactment of a law, at the age of 32, which denies the agency most of the flexibility it needs to discover better ways of stirring volunteer enthusiasm. It is a bookkeeper's law, much like Steinberg's detailed intrusion on the operations of the Agency.

Subsequently the young aide has waged a running battle against [Action Director Michael] Balzano. When Action officials have come to discuss new programs with Steinberg, he has arrogantly declined to discuss anything except the importance of getting rid of Balzano. His threat in recent months has been that Balzano must leave or the agency's programs will be fragmented. He even drafted a bill to accomplish this result.

This is crude harassment of a program with many vulnerable aspects and a great potential to assist in the country's moral regeneration. If Steinberg were battling on issues of substance, some intrusions would be justified. But his objective in such gestures as blocking for months the confirmation of top Action officials seems largely to be a destructive demonstration of clout.

More significantly, the Steinberg-Balzano affair is a civics lesson in how the government is run and how the laws are written these days. It illustrates how over-stretched senators are turning big bags of power over to callow young lawyers. They pass the laws these young appointees write because they are too busy to look closely at the issues themselves. But they at least owe it to the country to take closer looks at the people to whom they delegate this awesome authority.

Bartlett's column inspired a critical letter from a former associate of Steinberg's ("Bartlett's Column on ACTION Decried," by Eric C. Silberstein, *The Washington Star*, 11 June 1975), a reply to Silberstein by Georgetown University political scientist Jeane Kirkpatrick ("New Bureaucracy Blooms on Hill," *The Washington Star*, 1 July 1975), and a letter supporting Kirkpatrick by a former Senate staffer ("Are Lawmakers Losing Control," by Richard W. Murphy, *The Washington Star*, 9 July 1975). Bartlett's column was his second criticizing Steinberg. His "Voluntarism Vendettas in ACTION" appeared in the *Chicago Sun-Times* of 7 April 1975.

The other reporter to take Steinberg on in print was Inderjit Badhwar in "Balzano Weathers 'Vicious Attacks'," *Federal Times*, 25 June 1975, pp. 1, 6:

Mike Balzano, director of ACTION, the federal volunteer agency, has been the victim of a "vicious, unfounded attack" and continuous "harrassment" aimed at discrediting him, according to sources close to the Ford administration.

These tactics, according to these sources, are part of a two-year "personal on the record about his role on the GI bill, saying he did not see what good it could do for him or his boss. He relented, however, after consulting with Cranston, who was a journalist in the late 1930s. In an interview, Steinberg said, "I feel we have a very unusual and effective relationship. He gives me a lot of latitude because we think alike. If I went to him with a lot of little questions he might ask me why I'm doing that."

Steinberg's present Senate staff colleagues are not as close to Cranston as he is, but they are sufficiently different from the House staff to be worth mentioning. Ed Scott, who was born in 1937, became the committee's general counsel in 1977. He served in the Air Force from 1964 to 1967 and then worked for the Peace Corps from 1968 to 1973, where he met Steinberg. Michael W. Burns, the committee's program director, served in the Navy from 1965 to 1969, including service in Vietnam. The executive director of the Paralyzed Veterans of America from 1969 to 1972, Barnes worked for the Labor and Public Welfare Committee from 1972 to 1973 and from 1975 to 1976 and the Veterans' Committee in the intervening years.

The personal backgrounds of Steinberg, Scott, and Burns reflect the basic differences in approach between the House and Senate committees. Steinberg's personal service to his chairman is not all that different from his predecessor McMichael's, who was press secretary to Hartke's 1970 campaign and then was chief counsel of the committee under Hartke, leaving for a political appointment in the Veterans' Administration in 1977. Steinberg's and Scott's Peace Corps connection and Burns' association with an organization that was concerned particularly with the problems of severely disabled Vietnam veterans all differ markedly from the organizational and military backgrounds of those on the House staff.

Mack Fleming was clearly the most important staff person from the House in the 1977 meetings, but he might not have been had they

vendetta" that has been waged against Balzano by a key aide to Sen. Alan Cranston, D–Calif., who has oversight responsibility over the volunteer agency.

The aide is Jon Steinberg, a former Peace Corpsman who reportedly "hates Balzano's guts" because the ACTION director has tried to lead the agency in a direction different from what it followed during the Great Society days when Steinberg was in the agency. . . .

During this entire period, Balzano had not been able to arrange a single meeting with Steinberg's Senator—Alan Cranston. . . .

For nearly two years now, sources in ACTION report, Steinberg has tried to "paralyze" the agency. "Thousands of man-hours have been spent on just answering Steinberg's mail and the mail he has generated."

taken place one year earlier. Oliver E. Meadows came to work for the committee in 1953, became staff director in 1955 when Teague became chairman, and remained staff director under Dorn and Roberts until 1976, when he retired and became National Commander of Disabled American Veterans. "As long as he was here, there was no question that whoever chaired the committee, Meadows would be the staff director," Fleming said. "We have had three chairmen in the 1970s and there have been no staff changes except as people left." Meadows was succeeded as staff director by A.M. (Monk) Willis Jr., a politically experienced sixty-one-year-old World War II veteran from Roberts' (and, before Roberts, Sam Rayburn's) congressional district. Willis seems not to have been involved directly in the negotiations over this bill.

The forty-six-year-old Fleming served in the Army from 1956 to 1958 and went to work for Congress in 1960, when he began a five-year stint as Dorn's administrative assistant. He was director of congressional affairs and assistant counsel for the Veterans' Administration from 1965 to 1968, went back to Dorn's staff in 1969, practiced law from 1970 to 1974, was brought back by Dorn to be the committee's chief counsel in 1974, and was kept in that position by Roberts. His principal assistant in the negotiations, Frank Stover, is a World War II veteran who became the committee's deputy chief counsel in 1976. Before that, he was a registered lobbyist for the National Legislative Service of the Veterans of Foreign Wars.

Thus, the House staff (like the Senate's) was largely hired at first because of political connections to individual members. But the different political interests of the members led to a very different staff. It was an older staff with extensive experience in the Veterans' Administration—World War II veterans' organization network Teague and Roberts had been supporting for years. (Sroka, who worked for Heckler, was cast from an entirely different mold: the thirty-five-year-old native of New Bedford, Massachusetts was a part-time Antioch Law School student with a background in journalism.) These people, plus a few others whose roles were less central, were the ones who negotiated the controversial issues in the 1977 GI bill.

The Staff Meets

The first meeting of the staffs began at about 2:30 on the afternoon of Thursday, October 27 (the day of the breakfast) and continued for seven and a half hours. The administrative provisions were discussed until about 8:00 P.M., leaving only about two hours for the controversial issues. The first such issue to come up was the proposed extension of the ten-year delimiting period. According to Fleming:

> I started out by saying I didn't think Teague or Roberts would accept an extension of the delimiting period. That was the firm position of the members on our committee. Right away, the Durkin amendment was not the issue. We know their committee did not want it, so my comment was: this is not in the House bill, so what do you offer? I said we would see no problem with physical and mental impairment [i.e., extending in cases where impairment caused a person to fail to finish within ten years.]

Steinberg responded to this by pulling out a typed sheet with an elaborate offer that: (1) retained the Senate committee provision extending the delimiting period indefinitely for people with physical or mental impairments; (2) retained the provision added on the Senate floor extending the delimited period for an eleventh and twelfth year for all veterans enrolled in a program at the end of their tenth year; (3) dropped the Senate bill's benefit payments for the eleventh and twelfth year; and (4) increased the maximum student loan for all veterans from $1,500 to $2,500 per year, including the eleventh and twelfth year for students made eligible by this provision. Thus, Steinberg's proposal retained almost all of the important features of the Senate bill. In exchange for dropping direct veterans benefits for students in their eleventh and twelfth year for reasons other than physical or mental impairment, Steinberg was asking for a sweeping liberalization of the veterans' loan program—something not previously discussed in the Senate or House in connection with this bill. Fleming thought for a minute and then said he would take the proposal to Roberts. With that, the first day's meeting adjourned at about 10:00 P.M. (Roberts, apparently backing off from his staunch 1976 opposition to extension, told Fleming that he preferred not to reach a decision about the loan idea until he saw what came out of the discussion of accelerated benefits.)

The staff group met again the next morning at 10:00, with accelerated payments the main order of business. Steinberg offered to tie the problem of high tuition states to the liberalized loan provisions: let students eligible for loans accelerate their borrowing if they attend a school whose tuition exceeds $700 per term. Fleming, knowing that the Senate bill had called for a grant and well aware of what had happened to other loan bills in the past, asked Steinberg whether he would be willing to say the Senate would not be back in two years asking for loan cancellations. Steinberg said he could not give any such assurances without talking to Senator Cranston. "At this point," one participant said, "there was a little rumble and chuckle because the Senator was already there."

It is not clear who proposed what next. According to Steinberg, the Senate staff had met the previous Monday and decided that some form of loan cancellation was the least they could bring back to their senators. Fleming said he knew from the Thursday breakfast that he had to get the states involved. Moreover, by Friday Fleming and Steinberg both knew what the other one needed without having it spelled out in block letters. As a result, the interchange developed a momentum of its own, to such an extent that all of the participants claimed to be unable to remember the exact order of the proposals and counterproposals. Apparently, Steinberg at one point suggested a one-third loan cancellation. Fleming asked what about the states' responsibility for the tuition level in their own state schools. Then, either Fleming or Steinberg—the accounts conflict—suggested a one-third federal loan cancellation only if a state also paid one-third. Whichever one put the proposal forward (it does not really matter), the other agreed to take it to his member for approval.

Thus, in a single, intense negotiating session, the staff agreed to a "compromise" that in fact was very different from the House bill, Senate bill, or anything in existing veterans' law. The idea of a state matching grant for cancelling a federal loan was a completely new departure no member had thought about, let alone debated in public. Roberts' concern for states meeting their responsibilities gave the staff its inspiration for this hybrid grant. No one pretends the House chairman had anything like this in mind over breakfast, but he and Cranston both bought the proposal the staff had worked out.

Next, the staff turned to the WASPs. Initially, Teague, Roberts, and Cranston had opposed legislating veterans' status for WASPs for two different, but related, reasons: first, because well over a hundred thousand people who had served in World War II in some twenty-five civilian organizations (such as the Merchant Marine or Civil Air Patrol) could be expected to claim that they were entitled to whatever benefits the WASPs might receive; second, Teague and Roberts felt the secretary of defense had the authority under existing law to classify service in the WASPs or any similar organization as equivalent to military service for veterans' purposes. The Veterans' Administration (VA) and Office of Management and Budget (OMB) also opposed the WASP provision on budgetary grounds. Until the staff meetings, the Department of Defense had taken no position on the merits of recognizing the WASPs, but it had rejected the view that they could be recognized by administrative fiat.[6]

Before the meeting, Sroka and other staff people who worked for members pushing for the WASPs had been working with Antonia Chayes, the assistant secretary of defense for Reserve Affairs, Manpower and Installations. (Chayes, like Heckler, is from Massachusetts.) Because of her efforts, Deputy Defense Secretary Charles Duncan wrote a letter to Goldwater and Heckler saying the department felt the service of the WASPs during World War II was equivalent to active military service and it supported the legislation formally recognizing that equivalency.

Gary Crawford, Thurmond's aide, had been given a copy of the letter by Goldwater's office. When he read it out, it clearly surprised the VA's McMichael, who telephoned OMB's acting director James McIntyre to reaffirm OMB's continued opposition. Thus, the administration position was split at the last minute by some well-planned, lower-level lobbying of the Defense Department. This split made it somewhat more difficult politically for Cranston to drop the provision in conference than it otherwise might have been.

When it became Sroka's turn to speak about the WASPs, he made even clearer to Steinberg and Fleming just what the political price of opposition might be. He said that the WASP provision was easily the most important provision in the bill from Heckler's point of view. Steinberg interrupted to say that if Heckler was going to raise a point of order against the bill, he would appreciate knowing ahead of time.

Fleming followed, saying that the Senate's amendment on the WASPs could not be accepted by the House because it was not germane to educational benefits. (The WASPs stood to gain hospitalization and pension benefits but were long past the time when educational benefits would apply.) Sroka then indicated that his threat that Heckler might raise a point of order was intentional and said that if Teague or Roberts were to claim the issue were not germane, Heckler would respond by calling it germane to the sociopolitical agenda of the time. He proceeded to read from a comptroller general opinion of 1943 rejecting an Air Force request to commission the women without special legislation that contained language considered sexist by current attitudes. At this point, as it became clear that WASP supporters would use this language to embarrass their opponents, Steinberg reportedly became visibly uncomfortable.

When the meeting broke up at about 5:00, Sroka was convinced that the WASP issue had not been resolved, but Steinberg and Fleming said that it was. Steinberg said that he privately gave Fleming some language on Friday that would give the secretary of defense the unambiguous authority to recognize the WASPs and other similar groups. Fleming said he took this proposal to Teague and Roberts, and they agreed right away because it fit with the position they had taken previously. On the Senate floor, Cranston mentioned the compromise to Goldwater, who also approved it. Then there was an apparent breakdown of communication. Because Sroka thought there was no agreement, the Congressional Women's Caucus decided to make a public display of their concern, which they did in a succession of one-minute speeches on Tuesday, November 1. When Sroka went to see Fleming after the women's floor speeches, Fleming told him about the proposal to which he and Steinberg had agreed.

Wrapping It Up

The last meeting of the staff was a drafting session that settled a number of detailed issues. It lasted from mid-afternoon on Wednesday, November 2 until 4:00 A.M. on Thursday, November 3. According to Fleming, "when we finished at 4:00 A.M., I went back home and went to bed. I got back to my office by 7:30. At about 8 or 8:30 we were putting together our explanatory statement that was hand delivered to all of the members of the committee."

By 2:00 P.M., the compromise came up on the House floor. The explanatory statement was inserted in the *Congressional Record,*[7] but it was clear from the ensuing debate that no one, including Roberts and Teague, had read the bill or was able to answer misleading questions relating to its contents. (Steinberg said, "I am positive that no member saw the bill. Certainly, no senator saw it.")

The staff compromise was accepted, but not without some nervous moments for Roberts and Teague. Earlier that day, Teague had asked Speaker Thomas P. (Tip) O'Neill (D–Mass.) to move the bill from his "unanimous consent" to his "suspension" calendar, which would have allowed two-thirds of the House to suspend the rules. By refusing this request, O'Neill magnified the power of any person with a substantial stake in the bill whose interests might not have been protected. Heckler and Edgar[8] spoke vigorously against the lack of a conference, but Teague and Roberts knew they would not withhold their consent. However, they were worried about some people not on their committee, at least one of whom gave the impression until the last minute that he might object.[9] He did not, and the bill went through unanimously. There was much less trouble the next day in the Senate. Two senators did question the lack of a conference briefly, but the whole bill sailed through unanimously with little real debate and almost without public explanation of its provisions.[10]

A comparison of the two debates does make clear one difference between the House and Senate. A majority in both chambers was willing to accept the staff's compromise as the work of a conference. But in the House, the members who argued against letting staff do the work of legislators knew they were appealing to the prevailing ethos in their chamber. When Heckler and Edgar served notice that this would not be tolerated in the future, they had every reason to think they were getting a sympathetic hearing. In contrast, the two complaints raised in the Senate were shut down quickly with an impatient demand to get on with the business at hand.

Conclusion

Yet, while Heckler and Edgar could appeal to their colleagues' sense of pride, one has to wonder whether the House is not becoming more like the Senate. Phantom conferences are exceptional, of course. So are House staff negotiating committees of the sort that reworked the Senate Sunset Bill four different times and so are House committee staffs that have the Senate Small Business Committee's overriding spirit of entrepreneurialism. But House members do seem to be delegating more than they used to, hiring more entrepreneurial activists and letting staff-to-staff conversations begin to replace direct communications between the members. Thus, while the past three chapters may not be enough to show how the "typical" staff in the House or Senate works on a "representative" bill, they do show some phenomena that are strikingly common in the Senate and may be becoming more so in the House.

PART 3

More Information, But Better Informed?

Chapter 6

Overseeing and Overlooking: The Energy and Power Subcommittee

HAS congressional staff growth helped Congress deliberate about complex legislative issues? Congress has repeatedly justified staff growth by saying that members need to know more if they are to make complex policy choices without relying entirely on predigested information from the executive branch or interest groups. "Knowledge is power," members have repeated in countless speeches justifying this or that increase in the size of their staffs. Always left unspoken, with good reason, are the minor premises: that more staff means more knowledge and therefore better informed policy decisions.

The justifications for large staffs gloss over an ambiguity that is central to our understanding of the way they work. More staff clearly does mean more information pouring into one place or another in the legislative branch. But does the information improve deliberations within and help increase the relative power of the legislative branch as a whole, or do the interests of the staffs and their bosses conflict with these broader institutional goals? In other words, knowledge may be power—but whose knowledge and whose power? Of course, the interests of chairmen and of the institution as a whole are not directly opposed. If they were, members would scarcely be willing to delegate committees any power at all. But neither are their interests identical, and this lack of identity creates the ambiguity we intend to explore here. Do knowledgeable committee staffs use their expertise to shape the way their chairmen view the options open to them and thus influence the decisions themselves? To what extent do chairmen do this to their colleagues? Even if chairmen and their committee and subcommittee staffs do distort information, or use it to serve their own ends, is it not still possible that Congress is better informed with the staff increases of recent decades than it would be without them? If so, is the current pattern the only alternative? Must members put up with the uncertainties of giving subcommittee chairmen control over the information flow if Congress is to have any chance of keeping up with the executive branch in today's complex world? Or are there ways to serve the needs of chairmen while better serving institutional needs, by utilizing different staffing patterns or alternative structures from the ones that have grown up so haphazardly since 1947?

Not surprisingly, our view of these questions becomes different as we move from committee to committee. The basic analytic distinction between staffs remains the one between chairmen's staffs and those staffs, generally nonpartisan, that see themselves as employees of their committees as collegial entities. Of course, the two types may cover many variations: even the most nonpartisan staff spends more time with the chairman than anyone else, while chairmen's staffs may vary as widely as the staffs of the House Veterans and Senate Small Business Committees. Yet, while there may be no "pure" types, most committee staffs do shade toward one or the other tendency and the shadings seem clearly related to the way they seek and disseminate information for Congress.

In the chapters that follow, we look first at two subcommittees whose staffs view themselves as employees of their chairmen, the House Commerce Subcommittee on Energy and Power and the House Commerce Subcommittee on Oversight and Investigation. Much about the two subcommittees is similar. As two subcommittees in a highly decentralized committee, they share a common environment. The two chairmen at the time of this study were close personal friends with similar policy views. The similarities become even greater when we examine only a restricted portion of each subcommittee's work, energy oversight, to allow an even more direct comparison.*

Yet despite all the similarities, the two subcommittees and their staffs went about their business very differently. In a sense, they represented opposite tendencies, or problems, relating to the role of chairmen's staffs: one staff director consistently overgeneralized from the information uncovered by his staff's investigations, using it almost as propaganda; the other, reluctant to upset too many political apple carts over issues he considered unimportant, hesitated more than once before doing anything with the facts at his disposal. In both cases, the staff directors apparently went beyond the wishes of their chairmen in some of the specific examples examined, but both chairmen approved basically of the way their staffs worked. Thus, the situations uncovered in these two chapters seem likely to relate to problems that potentially could affect any chairman's staff and therefore tell us something about this mode of staffing in general.

In chapter 8 we observe two collegial staffs in which the independent role of the staff is minimal, the nonpartisan staff of the Joint Committee on Taxation and the core staff of the House Budget Committee. We discover that the use of collegial staff may be a partial answer to the informational problems caused by relying on staffs beholden solely to their chairman, but that the work done by nonpartisan collegial staffs raises its own problems. These, in turn, seem to relate to the members' desire to get two kinds of information from them: objective summaries of arguments made by others and independent policy analysis based on the staff members' own expertise. Because of its centrality to understanding of nonpartisanship, therefore, the utility of policy analysis becomes the theme of the final chapter of this section, Chapter 9—a detailed review of the staff analyses used in Congress's debate over natural gas deregulation to see how the analyses helped inform (or misinform) deliberation.

---

*Oversight was chosen rather than legislation because of the stark way in which oversight presents the conflict between a chairman's desire to control what is happening and the claim made by other committee members—sometimes supported by some of the chairman's own staff—that they should have complete and immediate access to whatever the staff learns.

The Energy and Power Subcommittee

The House Committee on Interstate and Foreign Commerce did not have an Energy and Power subcommittee until January 1975. Energy was not a major concern of the United States Congress before the Arab Oil embargo of 1973, and Torbert MacDonald (D–Mass.), chairman of the subcommittee on Communication and Power from 1967 through 1974, had no difficulty handling his subcommittee's two disparate subjects. His negative approach to his jurisdiction helped: he limited his subcommittee generally to subjects within the purview of the Federal Power and Federal Communications Commissions. But the ailing chairman understood that this approach would not suffice in a postembargo world. He readily agreed in 1975 to have his subcommittee's jurisdiction divided, keeping the less demanding communications field for himself. (MacDonald died of bone cancer on May 21, 1976.)

MacDonald's decision came in the middle of a major upheaval on the committee. The Commerce Committee was one of the few to suffer serious jurisdictional losses in the committee reforms of 1974. (It lost all of its jurisdiction over transportation, except railroad regulation—of particular interest to the chairman.) Many on the subcommittee blamed the losses on the pleasant, but not very dynamic, chairman, Harley Staggers of West Virginia. The Democratic Steering and Policy Committee contributed to Stagger's difficulties by putting twelve freshmen (most of them liberal and reform-minded) on the committee. (The committee had only seventeen returning Democrats.) Most of the new members combined with at least some of the senior ones in January 1975 to take the Oversight and Investigations Subcommittee away from Staggers and give it to John Moss of California. Michigan's John Dingell, who publicly supported Moss's challenge, was given the Energy and Power Subcommittee. (Moss was third in committee seniority behind Staggers and MacDonald. Dingell was fourth.)

Staggers, temporarily embittered, refused to call a meeting of the committee to set a budget. Finally, in early March, the committee Democrats essentially took the budget away from Staggers—leaving the full committee staff with its clerical and administrative aides, parceling out the few substantive full committee aides to the subcommittees and leaving most of the rest of the committee's budget (except for the minimal amount given the minority) in the hands of the subcommittee chairmen. The subcommittees, in other words, were set up as a series of almost separate committees, each with its own sizable and completely separate staff. The members came together only to mark up legislation. When they did so, they had to be served by staff aides who were responsive essentially to the subcommittee chairmen.

Dingell and Moss were both appointed to the Commerce Committee in 1957. There, following the customs of congressional seniority, they sat next to each other in full committee meetings for twenty-two years, until Moss retired. In other words, they spent more time with each other than most politicians spend with their families. The two were close politically as well as personally. For most of their years together on the committee, they were the leading activist liberals on a committee dominated by moderates and conservatives. Moreover, their approach to energy oversight appeared to be similar. Dingell utilized a Small Business subcommittee in 1973–1974 to hold hearings on alleged anticompetitive practices and withholding in the industry. These were the precise themes on which Moss said he would concentrate as he prepared to challenge Staggers. From the perspective of early 1975, in other words, an observer would have had every reason to expect the Moss and Dingell subcommittees to remain as close substantively as the two men were personally. It did not work out that way.

Staffing the Subcommittee

When Dingell became chairman of the Energy and Power Subcommittee in 1975, a new rule just adopted by House Democrats forced him to give up the chairs of a Small Business Subcommittee on Regulatory Activities and a Merchant Marine Subcommittee on Fisheries, Wildlife Conservation and the Environment. He had chaired the Small Business Subcommittee since 1965 and used it in 1973 and 1974 as a forum for examining energy matters. Dingell's major legislative reputation was developed, however, on the Merchant Marine Committee, where he broadened the role of the traditionally conservationist subcommittee he took over in 1966 and made it into a major forum for developing the environmentalist legislation of the late 1960s and early 1970s. These two subcommittees became Dingell's starting point for building up the staff of Energy and Power. True to normal congressional practice, Dingell began staffing the subcommittee with people who had worked with him, even though they had no background in energy. They were hired for their loyalty, not for their expertise.

Frank M. Potter, Jr., Energy and Power's staff director, was the first person Dingell hired for the subcommittee. (Dingell also was able from the start to rely on a few holdovers from the full committee staff, such as Charles Curtis, who stayed on the full committee payroll.*) Potter had been Dingell's principal staff assistant on his Merchant Marine Subcommittee since 1971. His background before that was largely as an environmental activist. Born in 1932, Potter was graduated from the University of Chicago Law School in 1957. After four years of private law practice, he worked as an attorney in the Interior Department from 1961 to 1965. In 1966 and 1967, he was a special counsel for the Scenic Hudson Preservation Conference, the highly publicized ad hoc preservationist organization that was dedicated to fighting Consolidated Edison's plans to build a pumped storage hydroelectric power plant on Storm King Mountain, across the river from Potter's native Westchester County.[2]

Potter got to know Representative Richard Ottinger during the Storm King fight and came to work for him as a legislative assistant in 1968. He left later that year, with Ottinger's blessing, to form the Environmental Clearinghouse, an information resource for Congress and a forerunner of the present Environmental Study Conference. The Environmental Study Conference has become a major staff-sharing operation, with some twenty people writing weekly reports that analyze legislative and administrative developments of interest to members concerned with environmental issues. When Potter started the operation, however, it was pretty much a hand-to-mouth operation and a good example of how one small staff-sharing organization can play an important coordinating role in Congress. Potter's success in that job brought him to the attention of Dingell, whose Merchant Marine Subcommittee was responsible for the National

---

*Curtis' service with Dingell, in true "network" fashion, apparently worked to his advantage in his later job as chairman of the Federal Energy Regulatory Commission.[1]

Environmental Policy Act (NEPA) in the House. Dingell hired Potter for the subcommittee in 1971, where Potter helped develop the Marine Mammal Act and the Endangered Species Act.*

Potter's energy interests were consistent with his environmentalist background. Convinced that fossil fuel supplies were running out, Potter believed that Congress should be encouraging conservation—through higher prices if need be—and the development of exotic fuel sources. With his eye on long-range issues, Potter tended to downgrade the interest of some staffers in such mundane questions as price-fixing or regulatory foul-ups. Hired because he had earned Dingell's trust with his handling of environmental legislation, Potter brought with him a perspective that was different from the one Dingell had pursued in his Small Business energy oversight hearings.

The first person Potter turned to for help after he became staff director was Peter Hunt, an old acquaintance from his environmentalist network. One year younger than Potter, Hunt earned his Masters in business administration from Columbia University in 1961 and set up a consulting firm that ultimately did some work on biological and economic issues for the opponents of Storm King. He did not meet Potter during the Storm King battle, but he did meet Representative Ottinger, who later urged him to come to Washington to meet Potter and William Kitzmiller, another aide of his. (Kitzmiller replaced Curtis in 1977 as the full committee staff person assigned to Dingell's subcommittee.) Hunt was asked to testify and work on several bills, including NEPA and the Environmental Education Act, during the time Potter headed the Environmental Clearinghouse. Still, Hunt said he had no real thought of working for Congress until Dingell asked him on April 1, 1975 and he agreed to do so.

Next, Potter decided to hire an economist. He wanted a senior person familiar with energy economics who did not work for the industry. After asking around in the networks, Potter finally gave up on the thought of getting someone senior. Instead, he hired Walter W. (Chip) Schroeder, a young man conversant with economic modeling.†

---

*Dingell was less of an "environmentalist" by the mid-1970s, favoring labor on issues that seemed to pit jobs against tighter environmental regulation. He did not rely on Potter for these battles, since they fell outside the subcommittee's jurisdiction. He used a personal staff aide on such issues as his 1977 effort to relax the Clean Air Act's auto emission standards.
†We shall learn a great deal more about Schroeder's work in the chapter on natural gas policy analyses.

The staff grew quickly after the initial appointments, and many of those hired after the first three had at least some experience with energy policy. Peter Stockton and William Demarest moved laterally from Dingell's Small Business Committee, where they were responsible for Dingell's investigations of oil company withholding in 1973 and 1974. Stockton continued doing investigative work for Energy and Power, but Demarest worked more on legislative issues, gradually became more conciliatory toward the industry (as did many of the staff aides who worked primarily on legislation), and left the staff in early 1979 amidst charges of "conflict of interest" to start a lucrative private legal career with the Washington office of Foreman, Dyess, Perwett, Rosenberg and Henderson—a Houston-based firm with many energy industry clients.* Michael Barrett joined Dingell

*The following news account of one of Demarest's last actions on the staff is reprinted here in its entirety for the insight it gives into the importance of staff on issues of legislative detail. It is published with permission from *Newsday*, March 23, 1979, pp. 3 and 11.

"Washington's Fine Gray Line" by Bob Wyrick

Washington—two weeks before resigning from the congressional payroll, a young staffer named William F. Demarest Jr. went before a federal regulatory agency and volunteered testimony that helped persuade the agency to enact a ruling that will give the natural gas industry an estimated $1 billion a year in additional profits.

That action, which would have been considered unusual under any circumstances, has touched off a wave of criticism by consumer advocates and some of his former colleagues, because at the time he gave the testimony to the commission Demarest already had made plans to join a Houston-based law firm which handles important oil and gas clients.

Demarest himself said in a recent interview that he didn't do anything improper, and in fact had acted with the approval of his committee chairman.

But his appearance before the commission, and the position he took, has touched off both resentment and astonishment among many of his former colleagues, and also raised questions about the "revolving door" pattern in which government employees move easily, and often profitably, into the pay of industries they have regulated or shaped legislation for while in government.

The question is one of propriety, not legality. The 1978 Ethics in Government Act sharply limits the activities of former government officials once they return to the business world. But it does not go into effect until July 1.

Among those upset by Demarest's surprise appearance Jan. 19 before the Federal Energy Regulatory Commission was his immediate boss, Frank M. Potter, Jr., staff director for the House subcommittee on energy and power. "It's a bad smell, I agree," Potter said in an interview. "I wasn't in town when he did this. If I had been, I would have suggested that he didn't."

Later, Potter added: "A lot of people were . . . (angry). It looked bad . . . It would have made me very nervous."

Demarest acknowledged that his position and that of Dingell often were identical with the arguments the major gas interests were making at the same hearing. But he said he had no conversations with the gas interests about the presentations and felt there was not conflict.

after quitting John Moss's staff over an issue we shall examine in the next chapter. James Phillips, a former journalist for *Congressional Quarterly,* the *Washington Post,* and *National Journal,* was hired as an investigator. Phineas Indritz came from the Government Operations Subcommittee on Conservation and Natural Resources, where he had worked for more than a decade under two chairmen, Robert Jones of Alabama and Henry Reuss of Wisconsin. His assistant on the Reuss subcommittee, David Finnegan, joined Dingell in 1976, after working for two years on a Science and Technology Subcommittee on fossil fuel research chaired by West Virginia's Ken Hechler. David Schooler was hired straight from Harvard Law School in 1976 and earned his spurs by working closely with Finnegan on several important projects. In 1977, the subcommittee added William Braun (a young attorney who went from the Federal Power Commission to Moss to Dingell) and Michael Ward (another who had worked on Dingell's Small Business Subcommittee.)

By congressional standards, Potter had assembled a senior staff with a fair amount of legislative experience. Counting clerical help, the staff was up to thirteen by the end of 1975 and twenty-one by 1978, about half of whom were lawyers. The budget request for 1978 was $764,460. To those twenty-one on the payroll should be added three who were detailed to the subcommittee from the full committee, plus one who is generally there on loan from the General Ac-

---

"There was no impropriety," he said. "The firm I now work for was not directly involved in the proceedings."

But one staff source on the commission who asked not to be identified said, "Never mind if they had a specific client. Every regulation applies to every producer, whether they chose to file comments before the commission or not. The way I see it, he had done such a fine job of writing the bill for the producers and now he's getting his reward and he's telling us what the bill means when it will help the people he's going to work for."

The new gas act, among other things, allows higher price ceilings for newly discovered gas to encourage exploration. One of the complex issues before the regulatory commission was to decide whether these higher ceilings should be permitted to apply to newly discovered gas in older fields where contracts already existed between producers and pipelines at lower rates.

One of the things the commission did, and a position argued for by Demarest and the industry, was to permit prices on this type of gas to rise under certain conditions. Companies are permitted to pass along these higher prices to consumers.

Demarest said his critics apparently harbor grudges against him for various reasons. "You can't be smart and aggressive on the Hill for 5 1/2 years without making some enemies," he said. "Just spell my name right and put in my phone number. It's great for business. All you need is a thick skin."

Copyright 1979, Newsday, Inc. Reprinted by permission.

counting Office, one on loan from the Department of Energy, and one rotating graduate student fellow from the American Society of Mechanical Engineers. The subcommittee majority's staff thus had become big enough to match many full committee staffs of only a few years ago. The Republicans on the subcommittee had only three aides and contended, understandably, that they were too swamped to follow oversight.

If any subcommittee is justified in having a large staff, this one surely is. The subcommittee had major, omnibus energy bills thrust at it in each of its first four years. In addition, it had to deal with the usual run of authorization bills and specific pieces of energy legislation. Despite the heavy legislative workload, the subcommittee had been far more conscious of oversight than most legislative subcommittees. It held only a few formal hearings limited to oversight issues; it got into a larger number of oversight questions in its legislative hearings, particularly the authorization hearings; and it dealt with even more in an informal way, through letters and telephone calls initiated and followed up by the staff.[3]

Although the staff initiated and did the work on virtually all of the subcommittee's oversight, it did not and could not afford to operate as if it were independent. Their success ultimately rested on their ability to get Dingell to demonstrate his personal interest in a subject and in the bureaucracy's fear over his control over its budget. Whenever people in the Energy Department had reason to suspect that the chairman was not committed personally to a staff member's pet project, the staff member's effectiveness was virtually nil. When Dingell backed the staff up—as he did usually, but not invariably—the department might stall, but at least made a show of being responsive. And, when Dingell's continued interest was shown by his repeatedly coming back to a subject—not only in letters, but also by taking his own time away from other things to raise questions in a hearing, private meeting, or telephone call—then the department knew that the cost of not going along may be high indeed. The secret to the staff's oversight power, in other words, had to do with the continued personal commitment of the chairman. The chairman relied on the staff to get him started on something, and then used his own judgment to decide which of the many things the staff started he would pursue. In Dingell's case, he might or might not be briefed on something before the staff started questioning a witness in a hearing. If he had not been briefed, he listened. If he listened and thought the subject peripheral, he might stay relatively silent. If he thought the subject important, he would followup the questions on his own. When he did that, the department was on notice. When he did that with the same subject repeatedly, the department acted. On a number of important issues in the Ninety-fifth Congress—most notably, the department's pursuit of old compliance cases—departmental action, for which the press had been giving the department most of the credit, had come about largely because of the specific prodding of Dingell's staff, backed up by the chairman's repeated personal intervention. But it took a great deal of staff infighting to reach this point, as we shall see.

Oversight and Legislation

There was a basic distinction on Dingell's staff between "overseers" and "legislators." The distinction was not over what they did—most did both—but over the importance they attached to each activity. Some, such as Potter and Hunt, looked primarily toward the future, with their eye fixed on the major issues Congress should address by legislation. Others, such as Stockton and Phillips, primarily liked to ferret out maladministration. A few in the middle, such as Finnegan, Schooler and Barrett, had a taste and competence for both.

The differences between the oversight-first and legislation-first staffers on the subcommittee are common on Capitol Hill. *The Washington Monthly* in December 1977 published an article by Gregory Rushford, an investigator who said he was fired by Senator Thomas Eagleton because he had turned up information that could have caused Eagleton political difficulties with important members of the House and Senate Appropriations committees. Rushford concluded that the tension between legislation and investigation is inescapable and said that from Eagleton's political perspective, the senator probably was right to fire him:

> The art of politics is not compatible with the art of investigation. In the legislative process, the best players are moderates, people with principles but not rigid ideology, who know how to horsetrade, compromise and temper disagreements. . . . But to be effective, an investigator has

to follow the path wherever it leads—to Democrat or Republican, friend or foe.[4]

John Dingell's record showed him to be more concerned with oversight than Senator Eagleton. But Dingell was first and foremost a legislator. The interests of his staff director reflected and even magnified this.

The legislative pressures under which investigators work can be illustrated with two stories involving Dingell's subcommittee: a 1976 investigation into a pamphlet about natural gas published by the Federal Energy Administration (FEA) and a 1978 inquiry into the possibility of bringing geopressurized natural gas to market much more cheaply than administration or industry spokesmen were saying could be done. In each case Dingell put off the investigation because it might have endangered a high priority piece of legislation.

The FEA's public affairs office published "The Natural Gas Story," shortly before the House narrowly defeated a gas price deregulation bill in February 1976. By May, subcommittee investigators Stockton, Phillips, and Barrett had learned that the FEA had submitted the proderegulation pamphlet to the American Gas Association (AGA) for comments before it was published, and then tried to cover up the AGA review when these investigators learned about it. The staff's findings were summarized by Dingell in a closing statement he made at a September 17 subcommittee hearing devoted to the pamphlet. According to Dingell:

> (1) The American Gas Association, an industry trade group committed to higher gas prices, was involved in the clearance of the FEA's publication, *The Natural Gas Story.* It made material changes that sharpened the pamphlet's deregulation pitch.
> (2) Top FEA officials engaged in a deliberate scheme to withhold information about the clearance procedure from the subcommittee.
> (3) This material was withheld in the face of a specific Congressional request for it.
> (4) The files were withheld because FEA recognized their disclosure would be embarrassing and would adversely affect the Administration's efforts to deregulate the price of natural gas:
> —Before the files were finally delivered, two senior officials removed pertinent information from the files.[5]

Overseeing and Overlooking

If we leave the story with this statement, it would look like a straightforward example of a subcommittee catching an agency doing something it shouldn't and then, appropriately, slapping its wrists in public. But the subcommittee's role was more complicated. The staff knew most of the story in May and, according to the staff, was ready for a hearing in June. The hearing was held in September to minimize the embarrassment for FEA at a time when its life was at stake. Representatives Floyd Fithian (D–Ind.) and Pat Schroeder (D–Col.) wanted the agency to go out of existence, and their position commanded a substantial number of votes. When the FEA's original authorization expired on June 30, 1976, it was forced to limp along with a temporary extension until reauthorization finally was passed in August. Only then were the oversight staff people permitted to "complete" their work on "The Natural Gas Story."

A similar situation seems to have occurred toward mid–1978. At that time, Dingell was spending most of his time trying to pass an omnibus energy bill that would phase in natural gas deregulation after an eight-year period of controls during which new gas prices would be allowed to rise from about $1.75 per thousand cubic feet in 1978 to about $3.75 in 1985. (The controlled price for new gas discoveries before the bill was passed was approximately $1.45 per thousand cubic feet.) The bill Dingell was working on also said that "high cost" gas would be deregulated within one year instead of seven to give gas companies the incentive to develop new technologies for retrieving gas, known to be plentiful, from unconventional sources. Specifically included within this category was gas derived from geopressurized resources.

The compromise made it almost certain that geopressurized gas would be brought to market only in a deregulated environment at prices higher than those for conventional natural gas. The compromise was reasonable, from the point of view of a person who supports controls, if and only if unconventional gas cost more than conventional gas to produce. However, a first draft of an Energy Research and Development Administration (ERDA) study that was suppressed by the White House during the debate over the president's energy plan asserted that vast amounts of geopressurized gas could be produced for about only $2 per thousand cubic feet. (Even the version of the study that finally did get out to the public spoke of prices of only $3 to $3.50).[6]

During the fall of 1977, Bryan Hodgson, a member of *National*

Geographic's senior editorial staff, came to see Peter Stockton. (Subsequent meetings included Peter Hunt, who had been following geopressurized gas issues for Dingell.) Hodgson had been spending months on a story about natural gas that finally was published in November 1978.[7] The article laid out several still controversial theories held by hydrologists and geologists which, if borne out, would support the original ERDA suggestion that the nation could be awash in geopressurized gas at prices that would at least be competitive with the price of gas from conventional sources. While Hodgson did not venture to predict a specific cost for producing this gas, he did strongly suggest that the cost should not be unduly high and even had a photograph of a well capped by Chevron U.S.A. that was producing enough gas to repay the $5 million cost for deep drilling in only twenty-nine days of production. While Hodgson's article recognized the uncertainties involved, it raised a number of serious doubts that the intellectual credibility of the arguments made on behalf of the Carter administration's and Dingell's compromise position in the 1977–1978 natural gas deregulation debate.

Hodgson's information was a political hot potato. If Congress really wanted to deliberate about the natural gas policy it was about to vote up or down, it clearly was the sort of information it should have. However, Congress was not at the start of a session working with a new bill. The bill it was considering was the product of eighteen months of negotiations that had produced a carefully crafted, politically structured compromise. For a long time during 1978, it appeared that no policy would be able to command majority support as three major factions—those wanting deregulation, those wanting continued regulation at current prices and those like Dingell and the President who were willing to compromise—continually jockeyed to get language that could pass. The difficulty of the task is shown by the final tally: on the final day of the 1978 session, the House affirmed the administration's position on the key procedural roll call by only one vote.

In this charged atmosphere, Hunt asked Potter and Dingell about scheduling informational hearings for August or September of 1978 based on Hodgson's article. The idea was shelved. "It would be like rolling a bomb under the gas act," Hunt reportedly was told. Liberal Democratic subcommittee members who opposed the bill were not happy but, like Fithian and Schroeder in 1976, they had no staff or forum to hold hearings on their own.

Overseeing and Overlooking

When Dingell was asked in an interview about the decisions to postpone hearings on "The Natural Gas Story" and on geopressurized gas, he said:

> In each instance the legislation was the paramount responsibility of the subcommittee and the oversight was a secondary responsibility. I have not gone out of my way to create problems for legislation that I was supposed to move forward, and I don't regard that as making particularly bad sense. Getting this gas legislation through has been almost as difficult a task as I have ever had to face in the Congress. . . . I'm not going to go out of my way to create controversy that will surround a piece of legislation that I have to handle. That would be just plain poor sense. . . .
>
> You've got to remember that the price you're going to pay for geopressurized gas is highly speculative. The pricing pattern we arrived at was a highly political set of judgments.

These views about the primacy of legislation to oversight are shared, not surprisingly, by Potter. Potter even took them a step further in several conversations in which he made clear his view of the relative status of staff aides that perform one task or the other: The highest status goes to lawyers or people with quasi-academic interests who spend substantial portions of their time on legislation. Investigators, he said, tend to get to wrapped up in "nickle and dime stuff."

Potter's opinion about his staff colored his judgment about the substantive worth of the material they brought him. His judgments roughly followed the same lines as Dingell's and he had his boss's complete trust and confidence. However, as is typical of many superior-subordinate situations, Potter went much further than his boss in his impatience with oversight. In one instance, for example, Potter turned away a case brought to him by his investigators that interested Dingell a year later, when he read about it in a newspaper. Two aspects of the relationship between the active member who is interested in oversight and his staff will become more clear after a review of this example: the member's reliance on his staff to sift information for him, and the ability of lower-level staff people to use channels, such as other subcommittees or the press, to bypass the staff director.

The Whistleblower and the Staff

The case involved Ralph Rohweder, a man in his sixties who knowingly jeopardized his career to "blow the whistle" on some of his colleagues at the FEA. Rohweder worked from 1974 to 1978, on a "temporary" basis in the aviation fuels section of the FEA. In 1974 he was responsible for allocating controlled amounts of aviation fuel produced in the United States to domestic airlines. At that time, he shared an office with William T. Zale and others. Zale's job was to allocate these fuels, which were cheaper than fuel sold in the world market, to foreign airlines. During 1974, U.S. carriers reduced their consumption of aviation fuel by some 900 million gallons (about 10 percent) while carrying more passengers than they had in 1973. Over the same time, foreign carriers increased their fuel consumption by about 500 million gallons, or about 25 percent of their total U.S. consumption. As should be evident from the gross figures, Zale's allocations were more generous than his coworker's. For understandable reasons, domestic carriers such as Pan American Airways began pressuring Rohweder in the spring of 1974 to give them the same kind of treatment the foreign carriers were getting. Convinced, along with many of his coworkers, that the applications from foreign carriers should be given tougher scrutiny, Rohweder began asking his superiors to review the situation. About the only result of this at first was to get Rohweder fired in June. After some pressure from above, he was rehired on a temporary basis in August to act as deputy general manager of the aviation fuels section. (Virtually everyone in FEA was hired at first on a temporary emergency basis. Zale and most of the others in the section except Rohweder were converted to civil service status in 1974.) While he was in his new position, Rohweder pursued the question of Zale's allocations and concluded not only that had Zale failed to do his job properly but that, more seriously, he and perhaps his superiors might be getting paid off. Each time he aired his suspicions to a superior and the superior did nothing, Rohweder became convinced that this person also must either be covering up or in collusion with Zale.

When Rohweder's immediate superior, Aviation Fuels Manager E. Lloyd Powers failed to act, Rohweder went to Powers' boss, George Hall, the FEA's general fuels manager. Hall ordered an investigation that ended up finding Zale's allocations excessive and then, remarkably, recommended that Zale be transferred from foreign to domestic carriers—doing the exact same job for different companies. Rohweder then wrote a January 1975 memo to Hall's superior, John Vernon. Rohweder's memo to Vernon specifically repeated his charges of Zale's "dishonesty" and offered as evidence an offer UTA French Air Lines had made to Zale of a free tour of the South Seas. That January memo resulted in a full fledged FEA investigation that ended up both condemning Zale and failing to support Rohweder. A confidential FEA investigative report to an internal personnel "suitability panel" specifically:

1. Upheld Rohweder's allegations that Zale had allocated fuel excessively without documenting the reasons for his decisions;
2. Rejected the charges of dishonesty, saying that there was no evidence to support the charge; and
3. Turned up new information, not known to Rohweder, that Zale had failed on his application for employment to mention a federal income tax conviction and a previous job from which he allegedly had been fired.

The suitability panel essentially accepted the investigative team's findings in June 1975. By December, a letter to Zale had been drafted as the first step toward firing him. The letter said he was to be dismissed because of:

1. Incidents prior to his employment reflecting on his honesty;
2. Intentional and repeated misrepresentations on employment and security questionnaires;
3. A lack of judgment, indicated by a failure to document reasons for increasing fuel allocations, thereby giving the appearance of favoring special interests; and
4. A lack of judgment in off duty conduct.

So far, there is nothing remarkable about this case. Rohweder made his charges, there appears to have been a thorough internal investigation partially sustaining his allegations, and the agency took the first step toward remedying the situation. The career civil servants working on security did their job. Now the complexities start.

The draft letter to Zale was dated December 19, 1975 and written to be sent over the signature of George Hall. For some unknown reason, however, the letter was never sent to Zale. On December 23rd personnel gave the file to the FEA's general counsel's office, where it languished—along with most other items sent in that direction. After a year of inaction, the general counsel's office decided that the case was too stale to pursue. An internal memorandum dated February 3, 1977 indicates that people in FEA felt that because of the lack of timeliness—caused entirely by the way FEA handled the case —it would be difficult to sustain the charges on appeal.

The net effect of all this on Zale was that he got to keep his GS–14 career civil service job, paying in excess of $30,000 per year. He had his career status and it was simply too much effort, or perhaps too embarrassing, for political appointees at FEA to do anything about it.

And what about Rohweder? He was the only person in his section who had *not* been converted to career status at the time of his January 1975 memo. The subsequent investigation supported many of his charges, but not the most serious ones. (Neither were they refuted, however: that is not the job of an investigative team.) Rohweder was perceived as a "knight on a white charger," a do-gooder who, like other whistleblowers in the civil service, was seen as the problem instead of the exposer of problems. Rohweder was not fired, but he was shunted off to a corner to do "make work," where he was kept on temporary indefinite status.

January 11, 1977 was the third anniversary of Rohweder's "temporary" assignment at the FEA. He still had no *right* to a career position, but after the third anniversary, the FEA could convert him without competitive procedures if it wanted to. That, in turn gave Rohweder the right to ask his immediate superiors to convert him and then, if they refused, to move the issue up the bureaucratic ladder. (Rohweder filed a formal grievance on May 11th.)

After more than two and a half years of internal battling, Rohweder also decided at this stage to take his case outside the FEA. Shortly after his third anniversary on the job, Rohweder was introduced to Jim Phillips of the Energy and Power Subcommittee staff. After hearing Rohweder's story, Phillips set up a thirty-minute meeting with Frank Potter. The staff director was less than interested in Rohweder's case. As with many other oversight issues with more obvious policy implications, Potter did not like to do investigations that might tarnish the reputations of the political people with whom he had to work on a daily basis. He is far from unique in this respect. Some staff people delight in being nasty to some of the people with whom they have to deal, but most find it both in their interest and more pleasant if they have a cordial relationship with at least some of the people who are regularly under their jurisdiction. For a number of staffers, this means being cordial to environmentalists and public interest lobbyists while playing the tough guy with private industry. For others, it is the other way around. Potter's background is as an environmentalist. However, he (like Dingell) went out of his way to maintain close relationships with the top political appointees at FEA in the Ford administration, particularly the administrator, Frank Zarb, and his deputy, John Hill. (Dingell remained close to Zarb after he left the FEA and in late 1978 Dingell's subcommittee gave him a consulting contract.)[8] Potter never rejected Rohweder's case on the merits, but he saw no advantage in pursuing the matter and did not.

Phillips did not let the case die there, however. His personal situation on the subcommittee staff would have made it fruitless to try to go over Potter's head to Dingell. Instead, Phillips talked about the case with Frank Silbey, an investigative trouble shooter on John Moss's personal staff. Silbey got the FEA to send him a full file of documents relating to the case. Without these files, no one working for Congress could have done anything for Rohweder. Once Silbey had the files, Phillips was able to get Dingell to request them from FEA. Others on Capitol Hill soon got their own copies. The issue lay dormant for months, as Rohweder's formal grievance worked its way up the FEA. Then, in January 1977, Grievance Examiner Isadore Risen recommended in a report that the Department of Energy (which by then had absorbed FEA) grant Rohweder his career status. Risen found that the decision not to convert Rohweder was legal but unfair. On January 24, Risen's recommendation was rejected by David J. Bardin, the administrator of the Economic Regulatory Administration in the new department. Bardin's memo, which was signed for him by his deputy Hazel Rollins, justified his decision by noting that the aviation fuels section's work was being phased out. It did not discuss the merits of the case.

That brought the issue to a third and more public phase. Rohweder's case had been discussed briefly in a Jack Anderson column of February 1, 1977,[9] but never went further in the press or in Congress after the meeting with Potter. The story was different in

1978. About a month after Bardin's decision, Martin Dyckman wrote a long story about Rohweder that began on the front page of the *St. Petersburg Times* and was obviously based on information from one of the files floating around Congress.[10] If Phillips did not leak the story, it must have come from one of the other staff aides who learned about the case directly or indirectly from him. One month later, Anderson took up the case again in a column dramatically headlined, "Hero in Scandal Faces Dismissal." Anderson wrote:

> A four-year-old scandal, involving an estimated $63 million worth of bootleg aviation fuel, has been gathering dust in the Energy Department. Meanwhile, the official who blew the whistle faces dismissal, and the associate who was implicated in the scandal has been promoted.[11]

Anderson's column caught Dingell's eye. Potter was in Alaska on committee business at the time, so Dingell called Stockton at home and told him to find out what was going on at the Department of Energy. When I asked Dingell later whether he minded learning about the case from the newspaper when his staff director had known about it a year earlier, Dingell said something revealing about the dependence of an overworked member on his staff:

> Frank serves as a very useful filter. There is an endless amount of work or trouble that I could take on if I had vastly more time.

As long as he needs a filter of some sort, Dingell indicated, he has to accept the fact that he will miss some things he would rather see. The filter is useful as long as it *generally* tells him what he wants to know. More than that cannot be asked, as long as the filter does not systematically miss a whole category of issues the member would like to know about.

Stockton and Barrett took over the case after the Anderson column and from there, given Dingell's personal interest, things began to happen. (Phillips had left the staff in August 1977 to work for a Senate Judiciary subcommittee chaired by Howard Metzenbaum of Ohio.) After a little more than a month of investigation, the staff was ready to take action. On May 11th, Potter called O'Leary to tell him he "had a problem." On the next day, O'Leary's administrative assistant called Barrett to say that no immediate steps to fire Rohweder were being taken and that "the underlying personnel problem" was being referred to the DOE's inspector general. On May 19th, O'Leary sent a letter to Rohweder rejecting Bardin's decision and accepting the recommendations of the hearing examiner. The subcommittee did not yet know about this letter, however, so it continued to work. Furthermore, the letter had enough loopholes to allow DOE to convert Rohweder or not, depending on how the bureaucrats decided to play the civil service rules. Therefore, the issue was far from closed.

On the same day, May 19th, Stockton and Barrett drafted a letter about the case for Dingell to send O'Leary. The draft concluded that the department's actions were:

> Nothing short of shocking—promotions for misfeasors, firing for the one who reports the misfeasor. This is Agency conduct which neither I nor the Subcommittee will tolerate. . . .
>
> If you disagree with what seems to be clear evidence in support of Mr. Rohweder's being promptly given a permanent position and suitable responsibilities within the Department, the Subcommittee will be pleased to receive your testimony justifying such actions, and to conduct a more complete investigation.

These sentences never reached Dingell. Potter, in his words, "blue-pencilled" them. The draft Dingell saw toned down the language and deleted the threat of a hearing. Still, the version Dingell did send on May 22nd was strong enough to prompt O'Leary to reply on May 25th that "an attempt" would be made to convert him to career status.

O'Leary's letter settled nothing, but Dingell's had given the staff the backing it needed to pursue the case. The subcommittee staff leaked the story to the *Federal Times*,[12] *St. Petersburg Times*,[13] the Scripps-Howard chain,[14] and the *Washington Star*.[15] The resulting articles served to remind people in DOE that their failure to convert Rohweder would be publicized. For the next month and a half, Stockton called DOE every few days to keep the pressure on. Finally, on August 28th, Rohweder was given the papers converting him to career status. He was also assigned to a new and more satisfying job writing oil pricing regulations.

Rohweder credits his success entirely to congressional staff. "I owe it all to Jim Phillips, who was the earliest to care about the case and continued to care after he went to work for Metzenbaum; to Frank Silbey, who demanded the documents that proved my case; and to

Pete Stockton, who was absolutely tireless once he got the documents, calling over here every three days for months." Rohweder's success was essentially a personal one; he was vindicated for having acted out of public spiritedness. But, had he failed—as he surely would have done if Phillips had not gone around Potter to Silbey—the failure would have been much more than personal. It would have been a signal to everyone in the agency that they should ignore the errors of their coworkers if they cared anything about their own necks.

Georgiagate

The Rohweder case involved a disagreement between a cautious staff director (Potter) and eager subordinate (Phillips) in which Dingell learned of the case after the subordinate went "outside channels." There was a second and politically more sensitive case at roughly the same time in which Potter again apparently sidetracked a Phillips investigation. Once again, Dingell learned about the issue months later from the press and once again he seemed to support Phillips' initial judgment by promising a full-scale investigation. But this time, the investigation never took place. No one of the staff stepped in and carried the case forward, as Stockton did with Rohweder, and Dingell never returned to it to get the staff to move. It is impossible to know whether Dingell's failure to come back to the issue was deliberate because of its political sensitivity, or inadvertant. There is more than enough evidence from the busy chairman's other behavior to support the more innocent explanation. Many times during complicated, legislative negotiations staff members have had to remind Dingell about other subjects to get him to sign a letter. The workload of Dingell's staff is simply more than Dingell or any other single human being can keep in the front of his mind in all of its details. But whether inadvertant or not, Dingell's failure to return to the subject had the effect of confirming Potter's decision to bury the investigation. And whatever may be the explanation for Dingell's inaction, Potter's decision clearly appears to have been based on his own political instincts.

The investigation in question grew out of the implementation of some FEA oil allocation regulations in Georgia. The events under investigation began toward the end of Jimmy Carter's term as governor and indirectly involved two Carter family members and two people who later were appointed to the Carter administration in Washington.

Under FEA regulations after the 1973 Arab oil embargo, a "state set-aside" program was established under which a state was permitted to require oil refiners to reserve a portion of the refined product entering the state in a special pool for emergency allocations to hospitals and similar institutions. The gas, which was often sold for less than the normal wholesale cost, was not supposed to go to retail gas outlets.

In Georgia, the full pool of gasoline that refiners set aside under the program never was needed for the kinds of emergencies contemplated in the regulations. Instead of curtailing the program, however, the state allocated hundreds of thousands of gallons of gasoline from the "emergency" pool to people who sold the gas to retail gas stations, including Billy Carter's station in Plains, Georgia. To make the following account of this convoluted case easier to follow, here are some of the names that came up in the subsequent investigation:

- Kenneth L. Dupuy, the acting regional administrator of FEA for the Atlanta Region until mid-1975. Dupuy was the federal official responsible for overseeing the Georgia State Energy Office's implementation of its oil allocation plan.
- William E. Corey, president of U.S. Transport, Inc. in Conyers, Georgia. U.S. Transport was an Atlanta area chain of gas stations and truck stops that received twenty-one emergency allocations during 1974 and 1975, more than anyone else in Georgia.
- Lynn Gamble, Dupuy's secretary. Gamble testified in a sworn affidavit that she and Dupuy had sexual relations frequently during the first half of 1975 in an apartment rented by Corey. Gamble also testified that on other occasions she and Dupuy were guests of other oil company executives and said that she once noticed a laundry tag at the Corey apartment with the name "Lew Spruell" on it.
- Lewis Spruell, director of the Georgia State Energy Office until April 1976. (He held the office during the administrations of both Governor Carter and Governor Busbee.)
- Omi A. Walden, Spruell's successor, appointed by Governor

George Busbee. She was appointed by President Carter in 1978 to serve as the assistant secretary of Energy for Conservation and Solar Applications.

- James McIntyre, who succeeded Bert Lance as President Carter's director of the Office of Mangement and Budget and headed the Georgia Office of Planning and Budget under Carter.
- Billy Carter, whose retail gas station received monthly emergency allocations signed first by Spruell and then by Walden. Some of the forms also had McIntyre's signatures. There is no evidence of kickbacks or payoffs relating to Billy Carter but, like most of the questionable allocations, Carter did not justify his requests as required under federal regulations.
- "Chip" Carter, the President's son, who was an intern in Spruell's office at the time of the allocations to Billy. There is no reason to think Chip Carter knew about the allocations, but his name frightened people dealing with the case once it appeared in the files. (It appeared before Billy Carter's.)

With this skeleton cast of characters in place, we may begin outlining the chronological development of the case. The excessively permissive energy allocations by the Georgia State Energy Office began in 1974 under Spruell (Carter was governor until the end of 1974) and continued at least through the end of 1976 under Walden. Dupuy and Gamble began using Corey's apartment on December 23, 1974. One week earlier, on the 16th, Dupuy had asked the FEA's national office to change the regulations to increase the amount of oil for the state's set-aside programs. (The request was turned down on January 3, 1975.) Thus, Spruell, Corey, and Dupuy were involved in what was at least a questionable and interwoven set of relationships by the end of 1974, at the latest.

Dupuy was investigated by the FEA's Office of Security and Safety during the first half of 1975. The investigators developed what the Energy and Power Subcommittee staff described in a memo to Dingell as an "airtight case of gross misuse of [airline] travel privileges, misuses of GSA vehicles, unauthorized expenditures and unauthorized absences from duty" that were essentially unrelated to the allocation program. The investigators put together formal charges, but these were buried. Dupuy reportedly had letters in his file from Senators Strom Thurmond and Jesse Helms and Governor George

Wallace recommending him for the job of deputy administrator of FEA. These political connections may well have cooled any desire top FEA political appointees had to fire him. Whatever the reasons, Dupuy got off with a transfer from Atlanta to Washington, followed in July 1975 by a reprimand from FEA Administrator Frank Zarb. (Dupuy has denied all of the charges against him and told one interviewer that he was "the best federal employee the government has ever had from 1776 to the present.")[16]

At about the same time as the internal investigation of Dupuy's alleged abuses of his federal privileges, the FEA security office received another allegation linking Dupuy to Corey's apartment. This information was not followed up at the time.

The set-aside case was investigated by FEA security officers in December 1975 in response to a complaint by the Standard Oil Company. An internal FEA memorandum to the file shows that investigators knew the essential outlines of the apparent irregularities in the Georgia state office by December 17th. The FEA did not prosecute the case, but it did send a letter on June 10, 1976 to Governor Busbee describing the possible violations.

Dingell's staff became aware of the first Dupuy investigation shortly after the letter about the set-aside program was sent to Busbee. In a June 21st letter to Zarb, Dingell said he had learned of a FEA investigation of compliance activities in the Atlanta region that might relate to the subcommittee's continuing probe of the FEA's compliance efforts. Specifically, Dingell asked for "all FEA files regarding the Dupuy investigation." Zarb sent the files on July 7th. In his accompanying letter, however, Zarb said that the investigation of Dupuy resulted from a "house-keeping" audit of Dupuy's activities and not an alleged violation of compliance standards. The statement was essentially accurate, but there were allegations in Dupuy's file about the Corey apartment that clearly related to compliance. Phillips followed up these allegations in a trip to Atlanta during which he learned about and interviewed Gamble, substantiating the charges about Dupuy's use of Corey's apartment.

Phillips summarized the result of his trip in a memo to Potter dated July 20, 1976—one week after Carter received his party's presidential nomination. On the 20th or 21st, Dingell, Zarb, Potter, and Phillips met in Dingell's office. (Zarb brought along the FEA's two deputy general counsels, Douglas Robinson and Eric J. Fygi, both of whom were asked by Dingell not to sit in on the meeting.) Dingell went over the points in Phillips' memo with Zarb—specifically stressing Dupuy's tie with Corey and Corey's gains under the allocations program—and demanded that Dupuy be prosecuted. Zarb said he would put Robinson in charge of another FEA investigation of Dupuy. He also said that the allegations about Dupuy and Corey related to another case the FEA was investigating.

On July 21st, Phillips called Special Investigator James W. Grimes of the FEA's Compliance Division in Atlanta to learn more about this other case. Grimes said that Zarb must have meant the state set-aside investigation and then refused to say anything more about it. Phillips asked to see the files for that case. Grimes said he was still working on it and would need sixty more days. Potter agreed to let him have the two additional months. Grimes then interviewed Gamble on the 26th, obtaining the sworn affidavit mentioned earlier.

Robinson visited Atlanta on July 28th and told Grimes and others working on the investigation to put the state set-aside case on the back burner and concentrate instead on the house-keeping charges against Dupuy. In subsequent statements, Robinson has said that he split the two cases because he and Zarb thought Dingell's concern clearly made the Dupuy case a higher priority, particularly since Spruell had resigned his position with the state office.

Michael Butler, the FEA's general counsel and Robinson's direct superior, did not learn of this decision until October, when he called it "disturbing". He based his unease partly on the fact that Robinson left the FEA after he finished with the Dupuy case to work for Jimmy Carter's presidential election. There are enough ambiguities surrounding Butler's October memorandum to make any observer suspicious of taking it at face value. For example, Robinson's assignment in many ways undercut Butler's authority. Zarb had told Robinson to report directly to him on the Dupuy case because the first investigation was done by people under Butler and Fygi's jurisdiction. Robinson also claims that Butler was out to embarrass the Carter campaign. (Butler told CBS News in December 1977 that he did speak to President Ford's number-two White House lawyer, Edward Schmults, shortly after writing his memo.[17] Schmults, according to Butler, said the administration would sit on the information for fear that divulging it would look like a "dirty-trick" and backfire politically.) But whether Butler's actions were politically inspired or not, his memo raised an important question. Moreover, a Justice Department official in December partly confirmed Butler's impression by saying that the Dupuy and Spruell cases involved a "common nexus" and should have been investigated together. Robinson, on his behalf, says that he did not stop the one investigation by speeding up the other.

While all this was going on within FEA, congressional investigators still were unable to learn anything about the substance of the case. When Phillips was in Atlanta with Stockton on another compliance case on September 22nd, he asked Grimes again for the set-aside files, pointing out that sixty days had elapsed. Grimes set up a conference call between Phillips, Potter, and Butler and asked for sixty more days. Again, Potter agreed, thus putting off any congressional investigation until after the election.

Dingell still had not gotten the files on March 18, 1977, the day Frank Silbey received them along with eighteen other sets of FEA files about whose existence he had learned from Phillips. (These included the files about Rohweder and a number of compliance cases to be mentioned later.) As soon as Phillips heard Silbey had the set-aside files, he called Grimes and asked for a briefing. Grimes refused unless he saw something in writing. The staff drafted a letter making this request in Dingell's name, which Dingell signed on the same day. FEA sent the file to Dingell on March 24th. Potter let Phillips look at the files for about an hour and then he put them in a locked safe to which only he and his office manager had the combination. That is the last anyone on the subcommittee staff ever looked at the issue for more than eight months. Then CBS reporter Charles Thompson revived the subject. In a December 1977 interview with Thompson, Dingell expressed outrage at the administration's performance and said he would hold a hearing on the subject. The hearing never took place, but Dingell did demand that the DOE's inspector general investigate any possible connection between the way Robinson handled the set-aside investigation and his decision to join the Carter campaign. (The inspector general had jurisdiction because Robinson, after much controversy in the early part of 1977, landed a job in charge of writing the Carter administration energy regulations.)

The inspector general concluded in January 1978 that Robinson's decision to pursue the Dupuy case separately from the investigation of Carter's appointee Spruell, combined with Robinson's subsequent decision to work for the Carter campaign, created a "potential appearance of a conflict of interest." Robinson's reply in an interview with this author was that a "potential appearance" is so subjective that he could not answer one way or another. He flatly denied that there was an actual conflict, claiming that he had no communication with the Carter campaign in June or July of 1976, after sending in his resume in the Spring. He said that he went to Zarb and offered his resignation within an hour or two of getting an offer from Carter in early August, but stayed at FEA until August 28th at Zarb's request to finish the Dupuy case.

David Bardin, the head of DOE's Economic Regulatory Administration and Robinson's boss in 1978, called a press conference on February 3rd on the supposedly secret inspector general's report shortly after it was finished. In the press conference, Bardin mischaracterized the report, saying that it had completely exonerated Robinson and that the only "potential conflict" the inspector general could have meant would have been the impropriety of one Ford administration appointee (Robinson) investigating another (Dupuy). Bardin's misleading statements were exposed in an article based on a leaked copy of the inspector general's report.[18] That article then was used by Dingell's staff a month later in two days of DOE Authorization bill hearings in which the staff raised questions about Bardin's press conference. For some inexplicable reason, the press conference came up not when Bardin himself was testifying, but later. David Finnegan, the staff person who questioned Bardin, devoted his time to other issues, although he had the subject on his list of possible topics to pursue. David Schooler and William Kitzmiller later asked about Bardin's press conference when they questioned the inspector general and the director of Public Affairs.[19] Asked about this strangely indirect way of getting at the issue, Dingell—who was *not* present during most of the questioning because the hearings conflicted with natural gas conference negotiations—said that he often trusts his staff to develop questions for hearings and place them in order of priority without clearing them in advance with him. Dingell said that Finnegan must have thought the questions he asked were more important, and Dingell supported his judgment.

While Bardin's handling of the inspector general's report was discussed in a public forum, neither Dingell nor his staff ever returned publicly to the substance of the set-aside case. Despite Thompson's revival of the issue for television, Potter's decision to lock up the file in March, 1977 effectively put an end to the subcommittee's investigation of the Georgia program. There was some renewed interest in the Senate when President Carter nominated Omi Walden for her

DOE job, but the Carter administration in Washington said that it had "cleared" her and that statement was accepted without further investigation. If, for some unforeseeable reason, the set-aside case ever does get investigated properly, we can be sure of one thing: it will not be because of any pressure from Dingell's subcommittee.*

Phillips was upset with the subcommittee's handling of the Dupuy and state set-aside investigation on three different counts. First, he questioned the decision to let the FEA reinvestigate Dupuy internally instead of pursuing the case in a public hearing. "If we had held a hearing right away, everything would have come out." (That, of course, may have been precisely what worried some people.) Potter's response on this point was that "the decision to bring Zarb in and have him handle the problem internally, as opposed to having a big hearing, was our decision and I think we got Dupuy out of there a lot faster than we would have if we had turned it into a confrontation." Dupuy resigned from the FEA under pressure in August, but never was prosecuted.

Phillips second complaint was that Potter was too willing to give the FEA whatever extensions it wanted, until the Moss subcommittee got the files. Potter said in an interview that he could not remember precisely why he agreed, but that "sometimes things just fall between the cracks, or you make a conscious decision that it is not worth escalating to the next stage."

Phillips third and most serious complaint, was that Potter locked up the files on the day he received them, thus ending the subcommittee's investigation. Phillips said Potter specifically was concerned about seeing Chip Carter identified as an employee of the Georgia State Energy Office's allocation division. The FEA's regional administrator in Atlanta had a similar reaction, FEA internal documents reveal. When he first saw Chip Carter's name mentioned in connection with the case in November 1976, he ordered his investigators to stop all work on the case. The memorandum revealing this was in the file the subcommittee received on March 18, 1977.

Potter admitted he was concerned that someone in the press might try to make something out of Carter's fairly trivial job in the state energy office, but denied that he ever stopped the subcommittee's investigation of the state set-aside case. "As far as stopping the investigation, not only did we not lock it up but that question was never

*The Justice Department finally declined to prosecute Dupuy on October 1, 1979.

even raised," Potter said. "It's hard for me to recall but my strong recollection is that it was one of those things that was perking along and then it stopped and I did not have a good enough filing system to tell me, 'hey, whatever happened to the Georgia state set-aside case' to fire up whomever it was to get him started. There was never a decision made that we were going to stop working on the case." However, when Potter was asked specifically if the file was put in a locked file in his own office, he acknowledged that "it was always in my locked cabinet. It never got out because that is the way we handled files like that." Nevertheless, he said his decision to keep the files secure was not a decision to suspend the staff's investigation.

Potter's response was puzzling for two reasons. First, others on the subcommittee staff have said in interviews that they often keep sensitive files at their own desk—sometimes openly on top of the desk— while they work on them. Second, Potter would have one believe that he locked the papers up for safe-keeping and expected Phillips to keep working on the case, but that Phillips for mysterious reasons let the case slide. Some other staffer might have behaved this way, but not Phillips. Barry Direnfeld—general counsel for the Metzenbaum subcommittee that employed Phillips after Phillips left Dingell—, said that "if anything, he (Phillips) needs to be held back. Once he gets on something, he is willing to work on it twenty-four hours a day. He is the most persistent advocate of an idea I have seen. I never have had to ask him what happened to something he has been working on. It has always been the opposite." Direnfeld's opinions are consistent with those of just about everybody who ever has worked with Phillips.* If anything, the complaint about him is that he is too zealous. For him to have let this case "slip through the cracks" would be like a rabbit refusing to mate—not impossible, but somehow not in the nature of the beast.

Some Oversight Successes

The cases examined so far in this chapter all were ones in which there was a significant gap between the staff's gaining some information

---

*I worked with Phillips for a time at *National Journal.* We were never close, but I share this view of his character.

and the information getting through to the chairman, other members of the subcommittee, the House, or the public. We should not leave the Dingell subcommittee, however, with that as our only impression of it. There were any number of times during the Ninety-fourth and Ninety-fifth Congresses that Dingell's staff uncovered something, Dingell acted on it promptly, and the agency changed its behavior as a result. For example, David Schooler learned in late 1976 that the FEA under Frank Zarb had failed to meet mandated conservation program deadlines. Dingell brought the matter to the attention of John O'Leary, Zarb's successor, in early 1977 and O'Leary got the agency to act. Phillips learned of similar problems with the coal conversion program in the spring of 1977, and Dingell followed the issue through in the coal conversion section of the National Energy Act of 1978.

Probably the subcommittee's single most sustained oversight effort has been with the FEA's and DOE's inadequate compliance enforcement program. Phillips and Stockton learned in the summer of 1976 that the FEA still had not finished compliance investigations it could well have forwarded to the Justice Department in late 1974 or early 1975. Phillips was convinced the problem stemmed from the failures of the two people with the most direct responsibility for compliance cases: Deputy General Counsel Robinson and Gorman Smith, the assistant FEA administrator for Regulatory Programs. Potter, suspicious that his non-lawyer-investigators were again looking at "nickel and dime stuff" told Mike Barrett to go with them on a field investigation and report back. Barrett told Potter there was nothing in what Phillips and Stockton were finding. (He subsequently has acknowledged that this assessment was wrong.) Phillips and Stockton nevertheless drafted a memorandum in November alleging there was "rampant white collar crime" in the energy industry. Potter did not take the memo to Dingell for further action—he thought the subject was not worth the subcommittee's time. But the memo was leaked to the press, and the resulting stories laid the basis for all of the oversight that followed.[20]

Robinson—by this time a member of President-elect Carter's transition team—was mentioned in the first draft of the white collar crime memo, but his name was removed at Potter's insistence. Phillips apparently spoke about Robinson to reporters anyway. He hoped to forestall Robinson's probable appointment to a high position dealing with energy policy in the Carter administration. Robinson felt that Phillips was trying to destroy his career and demanded a face-to-face confrontation with Phillips before Dingell. The two of them spent four hours arguing in Dingell's house "ruining a perfectly good Sunday" Dingell said. Dingell was impressed by some of Phillips' points, but not entirely convinced. He asked Schooler and Finnegan (both lawyers) to look over the material and recommend whether he ought to support or oppose Robinson's getting an apointment in the new administration. (Potter, who was the only other person at the confrontation, supported Robinson vigorously.) Finnegan and Schooler waffled somewhat by drafting a letter for Dingell that called Robinson an honest, trustworthy, and capable lawyer, about whom one may nevertheless "legitimately question the wisdom of appointing . . . to a position in FEA." Dingell signed the letter but Robinson eventually wound up with an appointment anyway. The letter more or less resolved that personnel issue from the subcommittee's point of view, although the after-effects were felt for months within the office staff and resulted in Potter eventually managing to cut off Phillips' direct access to Dingell.

Finnegan was able to get the subcommittee back to the basic compliance issues in the "white collar crime" memorandum by divorcing his treatment of it from assessments of personal responsibility and by using his direct access to Dingell to overcome Potter's latent resistance toward oversight. Finnegan's detailed memorandum of February 28, 1977 became the basis of a hearing on FEA's compliance program conducted by Dingell on April 6th.[21] The hearings prompted FEA Administrator O'Leary to create a Task Force on Compliance and Enforcement chaired by the Security and Exchange Commission's respected director of enforcement, Stanley Sporkin. The "Sporkin Report"[22] of July 13, 1977 recommended sweeping changes, many of which, in a September 28 Dingell subcommittee hearing, O'Leary promised to adopt.[23] One result was a new DOE Office of Special Counsel whose intensified audits of the major refiners have brought significant results.[24] Other compliance cases have not been handled as well by DOE, but an investigation by Stockton and Barrett that covered the second half of 1978 again brought subcommittee pressure to bear on the department.[25] In fact, whenever the department reaped headlines from its successful settlement or prosecution of an important compliance case during 1978 and 1979, subcommittee pressure and staff investigation almost invariably were there behind the scenes.*

Summary

This chapter is not, and has not pretended to be, an assessment of the Dingell subcommittee's complete oversight record for the Ninety-fourth and Ninety-fifth Congresses. The subcommittee staff did a lot of creditable oversight, only some of which has been mentioned. While most of the work was done by calls and questions raised in DOE authorization hearings and other legislative hearings, or by letters and telephone calls, the work done by Finnegan, Stockton, Barrett, Schooler, Phillips, and others would stand up well when stacked up against oversight done by most legislative and many investigative subcommittees. The subcommittee's legislative responsibilities seem to have helped the staff's oversight by providing it with a detailed knowledge of the way the FEA's and DOE's administrative structure and statutory authority were supposed to work. This knowledge gave the staff a head start, but the size of the staff and the interests of the chairman seem to have been even more important ingredients without which nothing could have happened. The staff's size meant that the subcommittee could perform its essential and burdensome legislative duties without using up all of its staff resources. If we recall our earlier chapter (chapter 3) on entrepreneurial staffs, however, we realize that the chairman's interests were decisive: somehow, the staff got the idea during these four years that Dingell would be willing to let at least a few people on the staff use their time looking into the way the administration worked rather than dreaming up new legislative worlds to conquer.

It seems doubtful that this situation will continue, however. When faced with an unexpected budget cut that hit all of the subcommittees on the Commerce Committee, Dingell decided at the end of March 1980 to fire Peter Stockton. The decision is bound to effect the

*On the other hand, department officials said privately that they have lost several big cases that were brought to trial without adequate evidence because of pressure from Dingell.

work of the remaining staff. Stockton has a reputation among journalists for being one of the two or three top investigators on Capitol Hill. The official line is that he had become a luxury, since he was the only person on the staff who worked only on investigations. But there seemed to have been more to it. Stockton's tenacious devotion to oversight rubbed a number of people the wrong way. One of them was Frank Potter, who specifically lumped Stockton together with Phillips as nickel and dime hit artists. It is unclear whether Dingell's decision to fire Stockton resulted from his own view, quoted earlier, that legislation is more important than oversight, or from his willingness, evidenced on many occasions*, to let his staff set his priorities for him. In either case, the decision is an excellent example of the job conditions under which staff members work and the way loyalty operates on Capitol Hill: staff members are supposed to show unwavering loyalty to their boss, but only an unusual member will return that loyalty in kind. Stockton did get a few weeks notice, so maybe he should be happy for small favors. When Stockton's 1973 energy investigations for Dingell's Small Business Subcommittee upset full committee chairman Joe Evins (D–Tenn.), Dingell reacted at the time by giving Stockton only five days to pack up and leave.

Had this chapter been a broad essay on the relationship between oversight and legislation, these themes would have been presented at much greater length. Instead, we have spent most of our time on four specific examples that tell us about the role of staff: the "Natural Gas Story", geopressurized gas, Ralph Rohweder, and the Georgia state set-aside program. In each case we found some reason to question making too easy a connection between increased staff size and a better-informed Congress. Large staffs may be essential for Congress's effort to keep track of the bureaucracy, but any number of things can affect whether Congress learns what is known to the staff. Some of the ones we have described include: the chairman's desire not to harm an important bill's chances with an oversight hearing; a desire on the part of the staff and/or chairman not to embarrass their party's presidential candidate (and later, president); a desire not to embarrass friends in the agency being overseen; and a desire on the

---

*For one typical example, see his statement quoted earlier about letting the staff determine the priorities for staff questions to witnesses in Department of Energy authorization hearings.

part of staff not to offend the people in the various Washington issue networks who hold the keys to their future careers.*

Thus, there may be gaps between what is known by a staff and its chairman or between the chairman and the rest of Congress. What is learned at any one stage will be carried on further only if the information passes through the political and other "filters" along the way—or if someone privy to the information passes it on quietly to another subcommittee or to the press.†

---

*We referred early in the chapter to one staff member's potential conflict of interest before joining a law firm. The staff's delicate approach to the set-aside case and to Robinson's role on compliance *might* have been related to similar considerations, although we cannot be sure: Robinson and former committee staff aide Charles Curtis worked together on President-elect Carter's energy/environment transition team and the people who worked for the subcommittee had the normal Washington ambitions for administration appointments.

†It was fairly easy for this to happen in energy, where large numbers of subcommittees have similar jurisdictions. It would be much harder if congressional reformers had their way and eliminated or minimized jurisdictional overlaps. In fact, the importance of maintaining alternative avenues for bottlenecked information may well be the strongest argument for accepting the organizational inefficiencies produced by unclear lines of jurisdiction. On March 25, 1980, the House of Representatives rejected a proposal that would have created a single energy committee. Instead, it adopted a resolution that should reduce conflicts over energy jurisdiction somewhat, but by no means entirely. The resolution also increased the jurisdiction of the Commerce Committee over energy. Dingell is in line to be named chairman of the full committee in 1981, after Staggers' expected retirement.

Chapter 7

Partisanship and Prejudgment: An Investigative Subcommittee

THE EXAMPLES from the Dingell subcommittee discussed in chapter 6 show that there are often many steps between a subcommittee staff member's learning something and anybody else's getting to share it, particularly when the sharing has political or legislative implications. John Moss's Oversight and Investigations Subcommittee gives us a chance to look at almost the opposite problem: the use of staff to discover a few facts which then are artificially made to appear as if they form a pervasive pattern. Whereas Dingell and his staff occasionally held things up for legislative or political reasons, Moss often charged ahead for the sake of creating a climate that would influence legislative events. Like Dingell, Moss's tendencies were abetted and even exaggerated by the gate-keeping actions of a principal member of the subcommittee staff. Unlike Dingell, the key staff person did not stay for the full four years studied. When he left in mid-1977, the staff's behavior changed, even though everything else about the subcommittee, including its chairman, remained the same.

Harley Staggers chaired the Oversight and Investigations Subcommittee as well as the full committee from 1967 through 1974, but he lost the subcommittee in the dramatic multiballot contest of January 1975 mentioned in chapter 6.[1] Since Moss retired at the end of the Ninety-fifth Congress, the four years covered by the case studies in this book span the full period of his chairmanship. To be fair to Moss, however, we should state at the outset that the bulk of this chapter deals with Moss's first two and a half years as chairman, until the departure of the subcommittee's chief counsel.

Moss always described himself as an intensely partisan liberal Democrat but, despite his self-perceptions, he never was a "party-first" person. Deeply admired by people active in consumer groups and other "public interest" lobbies, Moss's best known legislative achievements were the Freedom of Information and securities law reform acts. Considered a little difficult to control by some of his colleagues, Moss was never particularly close to the House Democratic leadership. Depending upon whose version one accepts, he was either bypassed or removed himself from consideration in favor of John McFall when McFall was named assistant whip by his state delegation in 1969.

As with the switch from Bible to Nelson on the Senate Small Business Committee (see chapter 3), Moss's assumption of the subcommittee chairmanship led to an enormous increase in subcommittee activity: from 17 days of hearings in the Ninety-first Congress (1969–1970), 16 in the Ninety-second (1971–1972), and 23 in the Ninety-third (1973–1974) under Staggers to 71 days in the Ninety-fourth (1975–1976) and 122 in the Ninety-fifth (1977–1978) under Moss. Some of this increase resulted from giving the subcommittee to someone other than the chairman of the full committee, whoever that chairman might be. Separating the tasks reduces the time conflicts and inevitably increases the amount of work possible. In addition, Staggers' style led him to favor settling as many conflicts as he could quietly, without public hearings.

But the differences between Moss and Staggers were greater than could be explained in these terms. Moss liked to stir things up. Staggers, in contrast, felt comfortable describing Congress by saying that "we react." His reactive style meant that the subcommittee generally waited for an issue to hit the front pages before it was investigated.

Moss talked about oversight in an interview in which he mentioned his debt to former speaker Sam Rayburn:

Rayburn had the feeling that oversight was far more important than legislation. He felt that to know what was happening in the departments and agencies, to let them know that you were alert to the way they were operating, could do more than passing a bunch of new laws. I have preached oversight ever since I have been here. I think it's invaluable, the most important legislative tool we have. We don't do enough of it and it isn't adequately understood either by the members or by the public. But I'll tell you, once an agency has gone through a tight oversight, it's understood by the agency.

Moss's commitment to oversight earned the admiration of his colleagues and the label, bestowed on him first by Ralph Nader and then picked up by the press, as "the man who perfected oversight."[2] Yet, despite his statement about the relative importance of legislation and oversight, the topics Moss chose for energy oversight in the Ninety-fourth Congress were selected because he was trying to influence his colleagues' opinions about legislation pending before Dingell's subcommittee and others.

Moss's view of the relationship between legislation and oversight was made clear by the first statement he made in 1975 about his intended agenda as subcommittee chairman. In a January 27 "Dear Colleague" letter soliciting support for his challenge to Staggers, Moss listed possible investigative topics for the Ninety-fourth Congress (1975–1976), about half of which he ended up pursuing. The energy topics included "natural gas reserves and withholding," "the effect of vertical integration," "Federal Energy Administration conflicts of interest," and "FEA's implementation of petroleum price controls." All of these topics were the subjects of pending bills. Four more were listed under health, and another half dozen were scattered over the rest of the full committee's jurisdiction.

Michael R. Lemov, the first person Moss hired for the oversight staff, expanded on the "Dear Colleague" letter in a February 3 memo. Lemov proposed dropping the six topics scattered across the full committee's jurisdiction and focusing the subcommittee's work on three subjects: energy, health, and the performance of the independent regulatory agencies. His justification for choosing the last two were explicitly political in part. Health care costs and the performance of the health insurance industry, Lemov wrote, would make good topics because "the Ford Administration is vulnerable in this area because of its decision not to support national health insurance at this time." Similarly, Lemov said in an interview, the importance of regulatory reform as a prospective campaign issue for 1976 influenced his decision to emphasize it in the memo. The suggestions relating to health care and regulatory procedures were accepted.

Lemov's memo also influenced the subcommittee's direction in the energy field, but not as strongly. Noting that the topics in Moss's letter related primarily to current legislative issues Dingell's subcommittee would be likely to address, Lemov said that what the Congress really needs "is a definitive study, collecting and summarizing the work already done by other committees and agencies, filling in some major gaps and ultimately pointing toward long term legislative solutions." Although Lemov followed Moss in listing "reserves" and "vertical integration" as primary areas for study, his proposed second-level investigations (revenues and profits of the major oil and gas companies, horizontal integration and international operations) had a longer-range focus than Moss's emphasis on FEA's implementation of the law. Neither these second-level studies nor anything else broadly "definitive" ever was done during Lemov's tenure with the subcommittee, however.

There were several reasons for this, but one seems to stand out as most important. Moss and Lemov let the issues of natural gas reserves and price deregulation dominate their energy investigations. Moss's interest in preserving low natural gas prices went back to his 1948–1952 career in the California State Assembly. He believed that the fundamental cause of the natural gas shortages of the 1970s had little to do with geology or with the level of profit incentives inherent in the wellhead gas prices set by the Federal Power Commission (FPC, now FERC, the Federal Energy Regulatory Commission).[3] Shortages have occurred, according to Moss, because gas companies are withholding supplies in anticipation of higher prices under deregulation. Let the FPC just require gas companies to pump what they have found and there will be no shortage and hence no need for deregulation, he concluded. This conclusion influenced most of the subcommittee's energy investigations.

Moss's personal interest in the effect of natural gas prices on the consumer had two effects on the staff. First, on the positive side, the subcommittee staff was given the incentive to discover and reveal some important information that Congress might otherwise have missed. The second effect was negative. The staff under Lemov's direction had a tendency to conduct its investigations and, more important, report its findings in a way that smacked of partisanship and prejudgment. Later, we shall see that the responsibility for this must be shared by the chairman and chief counsel. Right now, however, it is important to emphasize that this negative conclusion is based only on the way the subcommittee conducted energy investigations until the time Lemov left to enter private law practice (September 30, 1977). We are not analyzing here the work done by the subcommittee in the fields of health policy or regulatory reform nor are we looking at the many different oversight investigations Moss conducted on other subcommittees.

Staffing the Subcommittee

Any time a member assumes a new chairmanship, he has to make some basic staffing choices. Does he want to keep some of the old staff from the previous chairman or does he want to start with a fresh slate? Moss, unlike Dingell, was taking over an ongoing subcommittee. Furthermore, the nature of the transition was such that Staggers did not have new jobs to give his old employees. Nevertheless, Moss's pledge to make a fresh start suggested a need for new faces.

What Moss ended up doing was keeping most of Staggers' clerical staff and three of his ten professionals. He then hired twelve new professionals of his own, thus increasing the size of the professional staff by 50 percent. These numbers went up again in subsequent years. From fifteen professional and four clerical staff in 1975, Moss went to fifteen professional, and six clerical in 1976, twenty-one professional and eight clerical in 1977, and twenty-two professional and nine clerical in 1978. As with the Dingell subcommittee, these were supplemented generously by people on loan from the full committee staff and the General Accounting Office.

Moss put his own stamp on the subcommittee not only by hiring a larger staff but also by looking for a qualitatively different kind of professional from the ones hired by Staggers. As David Price has noted:

> A comparison with Stagger's staff roster reveals striking differences in patterns of recruitment, although under neither regime has Investigations been a repository for political appointees. Four of the ten profes-

sional aides working for the Investigations subcommittee in 1974 had FBI backgrounds, and three had occupied legal positions in one or more of the regulatory commissions. By 1977, only one FBI man remained, and few aides could claim experience in the agencies or commissions. "Oversight" and the kind of background relevant to it were conceived somewhat differently. Moss's staff came from three main sources: congressional offices, "public interest" organizations, and the universities. The result was a staff more conspicuously reformist in inclination than their predecessors, more broadly focused on policy questions, more sensitive to the political requisites of having a policy impact, and more inclined to carry on their investigations in a public forum.[4]

The first person hired, the forty-year-old Lemov, was a Harvard law graduate from a congressional office—Moss's Consumer Subcommittee. Elliot Segal, hired to run health investigations, had been an assistant dean at Yale Medical School. John Galloway, an energy investigator subsequently put in charge of energy oversight, is a political scientist who taught at Hunter College and wrote for *Consumer Reports* before Ralph Nader and Joan Claybrook recommended him to Lemov. Richard Falknor, the first person put in charge of the regulatory reform task force, came from another congressional staff. Lowell Dodge, his successor, was director of Ralph Nader's Center for Auto Safety from 1969–1974. (He left the subcommittee in 1978 to go to the Consumer Product Safety Commission.)

The staff's organization was somewhat confusing at first. Although the work was more or less divided into three units—health, energy, and regulatory reform—the staff was not divided formally into three separate task forces until the last half year or so of Lemov's tenure. For the first two years, Segal and Dodge were informally in charge of three to four staff professionals each. Segal had direct access to Moss, and Lemov did not interfere with Segal's work. The energy picture was more obscure. Galloway emerged as a staff leader only over time. During the early years, Lemov tried to keep control over all of the energy material by having the staff energy specialists report through him and by having his own central core of six or so generalists doing "quick hits" on energy subjects as he thought politically expedient. Needless to say, the situation made for a great deal of tension. Turnover is a good indicator. While the Dingell subcommittee lost only two or three professionals in its first four years, by early 1978, before he announced his retirement, Moss had lost nine of the fifteen hired in 1975. Remarkably, only two professionals left after Moss made his announcement.

Procedural Partisanship

During most of Moss's chairmanship, the Republicans had to work with only one staff professional, Bernard J. Wunder, and even he was on the full committee's payroll. (A second minority professional was added in late 1977.) Moss defended the ratio in an interview by saying that the staff worked for the whole subcommittee. But the fact is that the staff worked for Moss first, a few interested junior Democrats next, and the Republicans not at all.

The numbers only begin to tell the story of the handicaps under which Wunder had to function. An attorney in Augusta, Georgia from 1973 to 1975, Wunder had worked on ranking minority member James Collins' personal staff from 1969 to 1970, from the time he finished service in the Air Force until he started law school. Wunder was not expert in any of the subcommittee's subject areas when he was hired, although that scarcely matters when one has to cover so broad a field by oneself. Even the most technically competent member of a staff is bound, like a member, not to have specialized knowledge about most of what this subcommittee does.

For the most part, the people who worked for Moss were generalists like Wunder. However, they had a much easier time of it than he did. Given a narrow enough subject, enough time to work on it, and a chairman like Moss who would back up his staff whenever they asked for documents, a patient and intelligent investigator can, in time, learn enough to put together a meaningful hearing. Understaffed and forced to react to investigations started by others, the minority can never get fully in command of all the subjects it should. At best, it picks the ones it considers most important.

The conditions under which Lemov forced Wunder to work were far from the best, however. From the time Wunder arrived in April 1975, until Lemov's departure in September 1977, Wunder said that he was almost never told the topics to come up for a hearing until seven days before the hearing was scheduled—the *minimum* advance notice required by the rules. He would not learn what the hearing was expected to produce until one or two days before it was held, when Moss's staff would give the members' staff a very sketchy outline of what they planned to do. As for looking at the evidence on his own to prepare questions for his members, Wunder said:

138

Their interpretation of the rules is that they don't have to give it to me as a matter of right. If I was afforded it, it was a matter of privilege. I couldn't say, "let me see all your stuff." What I saw depended on which staff was doing an investigation. In the health area, they gave me fairly good information, much more so than in the other areas, especially energy.

This attitude carried over to the handling of reports, Wunder said. For example, Moss would not circulate a draft report until about three days to a week before it was to be approved. After approval, the minority would get almost no time to write a reply. "The rules say a minimum of three days. We usually had only three," Wunder said. Then, even if he would submit his report at the close of time, he would find that somehow the chairman managed to extend the time for himself to file "additional views" responding to the minority report. (The practice of filing a surrebuttal is rare in Congress but was normal on this subcommittee during the Lemov period.) To get around this, Wunder once sent his minority report on a particularly sensitive subject to the Government Printing Office in a sealed envelope.

The practices described by Wunder do happen on other committees, but they are not normal. Minority staff people often work at a disadvantage, but this was an extreme case. When Wunder tried to persuade other minority staff directors to push for changes in the House's rules to guarantee some procedural rights, they would not support him. What Wunder wanted to guarantee in writing was much less than what most minority staff directors had achieved informally. They feared that if they codified his requests, other chairmen might use them to worsen the minority's position on other committees.

When asked about Wunder's complaints, Lemov claimed he had a good reason for giving the minority fewer procedural rights than they have on other committees. In an interview, he said:

We were not just investigating some ma and pa stores. We were investigating some of the biggest corporations in the United States. When we did give advance notice of our information very early in the game, we sometimes found that information getting to the companies we were investigating. . . .

After all, documents do disappear. [One person under investigation] told the FPC that he had no documents to give them. We sent our staff investigator there and he found a file several inches thick.

If we'd have tipped our hands too far in advance, that file might not have been there.

There are two kinds of responses to this. First, Wunder claimed he never leaked anything either to a person being investigated or, unlike others on the staff, to the media. He said that could be seen from the very investigation Lemov cited. He did have advance information about that one, because the subcommittee met to vote a subpoena. But no one was "tipped off" and the files were there.

Second, other investigative subcommittees working on equally sensitive subjects follow fairer procedures. For example, Wunder's complaints were mentioned to Stuart Statler, then the minority counsel for the Senate Governmental Affairs Permanent Subcommittee on Investigations. Statler said that "it's nothing like that here. All investigative memos are supposed to come to me and almost everything is done in the name of the chairman (Henry Jackson or Acting Chairman Sam Nunn) and the ranking minority member (Charles Percy)." When asked about Statler's statement in an interview, Lemov countered:

> Did they take on the oil industry? Nobody else has taken on Mobil, Gulf, and Texaco the way we have. Energy is so sensitive. . . .
> We didn't fool with little boys. You don't get results by being Mr. Nice Guy. You have to be tough and embarrass people. There are lots of ways people can delay you when you want information. It's worse to have a dud hearing than to have nothing because they go away laughing and it is hard to get things from them in the future.

There can be no question that the subcommittee made a point of embarrassing people in its hearings. But to stick to Lemov's main procedural reason for not giving the minority more access to information before a hearing: Did the Senate subcommittee take on the oil industry? Yes. And, in hearings that started August 1, 1978, it took on the criminal underworld as well.

Interestingly, John Moss did not defend Lemov on the point, "Lemov has been berated on that," he said. "I'm not going to go into personnel matters, but there were some very rough spots with Lemov that would have required corrective action if he hadn't made his own determination that he was willing to go into private law practice." Apparently, the chief counsel went beyond the chairman's wishes. After Lemov left, Wunder said he began getting much better access to information the committee staff had discovered. Energy Task Force Director Galloway said the improved access was "for both ethical and tactical reasons. If we level with them and our information is good and right, there is a good chance they will go along with us. For example, Collins went beyond us on the cellulose insulation industry investigation. There is no reason for this to be partisan if you have a good case."

Substantive Partisanship and Prejudgment

The problem of procedural partisanship is not the same as the related and more serious one of prejudgment. When a staff member knows that his boss has prejudged an issue, it clearly affects the way he does his research or investigation. Moss was convinced that his two most frequent congressional opponents, big business and the executive branch, were almost always in the wrong. And, as was the case with Potter, Lemov carried his boss's attitudes to an extreme.

One key difference between Moss and Lemov came on questions of substantive partisanship. Lemov said he felt distinctly uncomfortable trying to perform oversight during a Democratic administration. "That was one reason I didn't want to stay on as chief counsel. You make a lot of enemies." He did not say so, but Lemov reportedly had been trying for an appointment to the Federal Trade Commission and that might have contributed to his discomfort. Moss, in contrast, never has minded making enemies in his own party. He recalled:

In October, 1966 I had filed a report on the Agency for International Development's stewardship in Vietnam that had President Johnson terribly disturbed. Some of the Democratic party leaders were also disturbed because I filed it just a few weeks before the November elections in '66. But I pulled no punches and I didn't hold up the timing of it.

And during the twelve years it took to write the Freedom of Information Act, spanning the Eisenhower, Kennedy, and Johnson administrations, there wasn't an agency that came before the committee that was not taken to task very sharply when they were found guilty of any withholdings.

This attitude continued into the Carter administration. During 1978, long before other Democrats were willing to take on the president in public, Moss criticized corrupt patronage in government agencies,[5] demanded the resignation of two top officials in the Civil Service Commission,[6] called President Carter's proposed civil service reforms a set of "pseudo-solutions,"[7] charged the White House Office of Telecommunications Policy with violating the law in 1977 by awarding a noncompetitive contract for a wiretap study,[8] and blasted as "confused and disoriented" a three-volume, 1,300-page report on the accounting profession released by the Securities and Exchange Commission.[9] Perhaps even more revealing was the rhetorical extreme he went to in a 1978 interview in which he said that "the overall thrust of the Carter administration is toward a degree of secrecy greater than I have seen in any administration since I have been in Washington." That included the Johnson and Nixon administrations, to name just two. The feeling was reciprocal. Jack Anderson's nationally syndicated column of August 8, 1978 quoted a Hamilton Jordan White House memorandum that said "Moss is an A—." (Expletive deleted in the column.) When Anderson asked Jordan about the memo, Jordan denied only the particular word, saying "It's more likely that I called him a jerk."[10] Finally, what prompted Jordan's reaction was a Moss-led subcommittee effort in August 1978 to cite Health, Education, and Welfare Secretary Joseph A. Califano for contempt of Congress after Califano refused to turn subpoenaed data about drug processing over to the subcommittee.[11]

So whatever else may be said of Moss, the way he handled issues was not based on which political party would benefit. The problem of prejudgment in Moss's case was more subtle than that. Moss acted as if he were a prosecuting attorney out to catch villains. There was nothing in the consumer-advocate background of most of his aides to counter this tendency. This goes a long way toward explaining the kind of working hypotheses investigators set out to prove or disprove as they gathered their facts. They generally went looking for issues where there were identifiable "bad guys"—from withholders of oil and natural gas to participants in an international uranium cartel. The implication, not accepted by all on the staff, was that wrongdoing was at the heart of the energy crisis.

The prosecutorial mentality affected more than just the kinds of issues the subcommittee looked at. It also colored the way it reported its findings to Congress as a whole. Given the search for wrongdoing, one might expect the reports to follow a legal format. They did but, especially during Lemov's tenure, the tone was not that of a judicial opinion rendering a verdict based on the facts before the "court." Rather, the reports read like prosecutorial arguments to a court, ignoring some facts while extracting as much as possible from those on the prosecutor's side of the case. One minor example and two major ones illustrate the point. All relate to natural gas.

Staff Pamphlet on the Natural Gas Shortage

The minor example is a report issued just as the House was preparing for its floor debate on natural gas price deregulation of February 1976. That debate took place in the middle of a winter when gas shortages had produced severe curtailments and even, in some portions of the Midwest, factory closings. To help prevent what Moss thought was a headlong rush toward price deregulation, which ultimately failed by only four votes after passing the Senate, the subcommittee staff issued a twenty-six-page staff report, "Questions and Answers About the Nature and Causes of the Natural Gas Shortage." Lemov had a subcommittee press person prepare the report, over the objections of some energy aides. By issuing it as a staff product with the specific disclaimer that it had "not been approved or disapproved by members of the subcommittee," Moss and his staff were able to put out the rhetorical broadside without a subcommittee vote and, probably more important, without including minority views. The overall argument of the pamphlet was as follows:

1. The natural gas shortage is not caused by price regulation (which producers claim decreases supplies) but by aggressive producer advertising that has stimulated demand. (The relevance of this distinction is lost on this author, since the advertising works only because of gas's price advantage.)
2. There is evidence of extensive withholding of natural gas by producers in anticipation of deregulation. (The pamphlet did not estimate how extensive this alleged withholding might be. We shall return to the withholding issue below.)

3. Deregulation would not increase supplies significantly.
4. Deregulation would be expensive.

The arguments for and against saying deregulation would increase supplies will be analyzed in chapter 9. Suffice it to say here that the Moss staff report presented a complex and debatable issue as if there were no question about its conclusion.

But the treatment of the cost of deregulation is even more revealing of the report's true character. Three estimates were cited:

- A 1974 Federal Energy Administration conclusion that deregulation would cost consumers $23 billion in 1985 while producing almost no additional supplies;
- A December 1975 study by the Congressional Research Service's Lawrence Kumins claiming the first-year cost of deregulation would be $20.3 to $22.4 billion;
- A General Accounting Office estimate that the cumulative cost of deregulation for the ten years ending in 1985 would be $75 billion, with gross producer revenues increasing from $9 billion in 1975 to $31 billion in 1985.

The numbers in these estimates no longer mean anything, if they ever did, because of the dramatic changes in the price of both gas and home heating oil since then. What is important for our purpose, however, is what the press aide and Lemov did with the evidence available at the time. To put it bluntly, they distorted all three of the studies cited while ignoring others less favorable to their political conclusion:

- The GAO study actually said that that cost of deregulation would be relatively modest per household and that it would produce significant additional supplies.
- The Federal Energy Administration's 1974 study was based on assumptions that had no relevance to the 1976 debate. As the staff was preparing its report, however, it had available to it a January 1976 FEA study of the bills then before Congress. That study put the cost of deregulation at about $5.5 billion for its first year. It was not cited in the staff report.
- Kumins' study for the Congressional Research Service was highly controversial, a fact the pamphlet did not bother to men-

tion. Moreover, the pamphlet used a number that Kumins himself found misleading.

Thus, the staff report distorted information from each of the sources it used. It also ignored any of the competing econometric estimates of deregulation's cost, all of which were lower. The point here is not to argue which numbers were more accurate, but to say something about the rhetorical purpose of the report. Intellectual honesty would seem to have required the staff to at least have acknowledged the existence of competing estimates, even if it then went about refuting them. By failing to do this, and by not allowing for a minority report, the staff was taking advantage of the ignorance of noncommittee members to lead them to a prejudged conclusion. Despite the question-and-answer format, the report was not meant to educate the members but to fool them. It was a piece of propaganda, pure and simple. If the report had been issued as a press release, members might have seen it for what it was, but giving it the subcommittee's imprimatur increased its importance manifold.

Natural Gas Withholding

The two other examples of prejudgment are more involved, more ambiguous and more important. One involves a sin of commission: the way the subcommittee presented its findings about withholding. The other is a sin of omission: the failure to report the results of an investigation into the American Gas Association's natural gas reserve data after Moss's highly publicized charges about the AGA failed to pan out.

Taken together, the subjects of natural gas supplies, reserves and withholding took up seventeen of the twenty-seven days of hearings the subcommittee devoted to energy in the Ninety-fourth Congress (1975–1976). Two more days were spent on other natural gas topics, five on Federal Energy Administration enforcement and three on all other energy subjects. The subcommittee spent forty-four days in the Ninety-fourth Congress on other subjects—principally health and regulatory reform. The ratio changed dramatically in the Ninety-fifth Congress, as Lemov's importance went down and Galloway's went up. In the entire Ninety-fifth Congress, the subcommittee spent exactly two days of hearings on gas reserves in January, 1977 and eight more between February and May 1977 on allegedly adverse personnel actions at the FPC that Moss claimed were taken in retaliation for FPC staff cooperation with the subcommittee on withholding. Both of these hearings were continuations of 1976 investigations of actions taken by the Republican appointees to the FPC. Once the hearings were finished, Moss did nothing more on natural gas. During the rest of the Ninety-fifth Congress, the subcommittee devoted ten days to uranium, ten to other energy subjects, thirty-six days to health, twenty to consumer issues, seven to regulatory commissions, ten to athletics, six to securities, and three to other subjects.

The subcommittee held hearings or issued reports on six different individual cases of natural gas withholding during John Moss's tenure as chairman, all under Lemov's general supervision during the Ninety-fourth or early Ninety-fifth Congress. The last two of the six cases were more solidly investigated than the other four, but only one, Galloway's, proved anything that suggested withholding—and even that was questioned by the secretary of the interior. Yet, the six cases were treated by Lemov and Moss as if they formed part of a pervasive pattern of intentional withholding that was the unseen conspiratorial cause of the nation's natural gas shortage. We gain a better appreciation of the tenor of these investigations by looking briefly at the majority-minority debate in the six cases. The point of this exercise is not to claim that the minority was right and Moss was wrong in the individual cases, but to indicate the kind of technical information needed to decide one way or the other and the impossibility of generalizing from the individual cases to the gas industry as a whole.

Cities Service. On July 18, 1975, the subcommittee published a "Preliminary Staff Report Concerning Delays in Natural Gas Production by the Cities Service Oil Company."[12] No final report was ever issued, although Moss referred later to the preliminary report as if it were final. The subcommittee staff claimed that Cities Service deliberately put off repair work on a drilling rig in the Gulf of Mexico in 1974, that the delay resulted in substantial disruptions of natural gas delivery to the Northeast during the 1974–1975 winter shortages, and that the shortages were created to stimulate Congress to deregulate the price of natural gas. The minority replied that the rigs and material the majority said were available for repairs in the spring of 1974 were not right for the job. The minority also claimed that the work was performed expeditiously and that there was "not a scintilla of evidence that the decision concerning when to perform the workover was made for the purpose of intensifying pressure on Congress for deregulation."[13]

Garden City and Bastian Bay, La. In October and November 1975, the subcommittee issued reports that gas production and delivery in two major Gulf Coast Fields, Garden City[14] and Bastian Bay,[15] Louisiana, were declining at a precipitous rate. The subcommittee claimed that the companies holding leases from the federal government for developing these fields had deliberately drilled only a limited number of wells in each field, thus preserving gas for a future when prices might be higher. The minority said that the assertion that gas could be recovered more quickly from Garden City was made without reference to the risks or economics involved. For Bastian Bay, the minority said the field was approximately 73 percent depleted and that additional drilling meant a considerable risk of a blowout.

Grand Isle. In February 1976, the subcommittee charged the Mobil Oil Corporation with deliberately withholding gas during the winter of 1975–1976 from Grand Isle Field No. 95 in the Gulf of Mexico by delaying its application for acceptance of an FPC certificate until too late in the year for it to begin drilling before the dangerous winter seas.[16] The minority said Mobil developed the field quickly, applied for an FPC certificate within six days after signing a pipeline contract, and consistently urged the FPC to act expeditiously to allow deliveries before the winter. The delay was caused, the minority said, because the contract contained some clauses favorable to Mobil which the FPC had allowed in past contracts but which the FPC decided to review before granting Mobil this certificate. In the minority's view, the delay was clearly because of the FPC and not Mobil: "It is grotesque to cite this case as support for an effort to extend the demonstrably cumbersome and counterproductive FPC regulatory proceedings."[17]

Gulf's Warranty Contract. A February 1977 subcommittee report[18] charged the Gulf Oil Corporation with failing to deliver a promised 625,000 mcf (thousand cubic feet) of natural gas per day to the Texas Eastern Transmission Corporation. The first of the majority's six recommendations in the report called on the FPC to enforce the amount of gas FPC certificates "require." The second said that if the FPC fails to enforce delivery obligations, Congress should compel enforcement by statute. The minority agreed that Gulf had failed to meet its contractual obligations but claimed that the shortfall was the result of "an honest mistake" Gulf had been trying to rectify. More important, given the majority's policy suggestions, the minority noted that the contract in question was one of only four warranty contracts. The remaining 9,000 or so contracts do not guarantee delivery and therefore cannot be used to reach any general conclusions about FPC enforcement.

"Behind The Pipe" Reserves. Also in February 1977, the subcommittee held hearings on "behind the pipe" gas reserves in fields in federal offshore lands leased by the Texaco Corporation. No subcommittee report was issued on the subject but the issue raised in the hearing again had to do with the rate of recovery from a well. The standard way of draining a reservoir is to drill to the lowest geological layer that holds expected reserves and then work up. Reserves are called "behind the pipe" if they could be developed by drilling additional wells into higher strata. If such wells are drilled they increase the *rate* of recovery from a reservoir and increase the *cost* of exploitation, but *do not effect the total amount* of gas retrieved. John Galloway said in the hearing that the question raised by the investigation was whether gas companies or the government should determine the rate of development on field lands. Moss, going beyond Galloway, said, "I have every reason to believe Texaco's problems . . . are closely representative of other producers similarly situated."[19]

Moss's hearings had been held February 22 and 23 to highlight an Interior Department finding, released February 17, that Texaco's "Tiger Shoal" field did offer a good opportunity for accelerated development. On the basis of this finding, the department said it would review five other fields to see whether the situation was representative, as Moss claimed. Interior Secretary Cecil Andrus released the results of that investigation on April 27 of the next year. According to Andrus, three of the five fields offered no opportunities for increased production, one presented an opportunity for some increase but at high cost and substantial risk, and the fifth would allow for increased production, but only on economically imprudent terms. Furthermore, Andrus stressed, no evidence of what properly could be called "withholding" was found in any of the six fields, including Texaco's.[20] Moss never went back to correct his statement of the previous year and no subcommittee report was issued.

Overgeneralizations

The six cases the Moss subcommittee used to make its case for withholding share some common features. All required a considerable amount of staff investigation. All help point out the gaps and uncertainties between finding natural gas and getting it to market. All help demonstrate that there may be more gas in the world's known wells than finds its way to pipelines. Some of the cases may even involve withholding. But, despite four years of massive staff effort on an item of high personal priority for the chairman, Moss failed to present a single case in which *intentional* withholding was demonstrated clearly. The majority-minority differences summarized previously only began to scratch the surface. When one gets into the technical insides of the subject, one finds in each case that the specific technical facts needed to make a case—such as what kinds of pipe of what diameter were available where—were all open to dispute.

It would be difficult to understand Moss's willingness to devote a high proportion of his staff resources to this subject (he made much firmer cases on others), if it were not for his interest in influencing his colleagues' opinions on pending legislation that would have deregulated natural gas prices. Having his own oversight subcommittee with its own staff thus gave Moss a forum for pursuing a specific line of investigation designed to buttress his own point of view on legislation not before his subcommittee. Free from having either to pass mandatory authorization bills or respond to administration priorities across the spectrum of energy policy, Moss was able to devote a great deal of staff time to one aspect of one legislative issue.

Before his staff even started its work, Moss had no doubt that there was significant withholding and that withholding was an important factor in the natural gas shortage. Moss's "Dear Colleague" letter of January 27, 1975 specifically stated his desire to investigate natural gas "withholding" and not the broader, more impartial subject of "shortages." Asked about the prejudgment the word "withholding" implied, Moss said that even before becoming chairman, "I knew there was withholding. I know of fields right out in my congressional district where gas has been found and wells have been drilled and there is no production."

The question raised by Moss's subcommittee, however, is not whether there are individual examples of nonproducing wells, but whether there is a pattern of intentional withholding affecting the basic supply and demand picture of the industry. Moss, convinced that there was such a pattern, did what he could to prove it.

The methods used in the Garden City and Bastian Bay cases were extreme, but they provide informative examples that show what such a prejudgment can do to oversight. The subcommittee staff reviewed data from more than forty Gulf Coast fields to identify those that looked statistically as if they were likely candidates for a finding of underproduction. From those fields, two were singled out to make a case for what Moss then described as a "pervasive problem."[21]

Some of the investigators and former investigators who worked on withholding for the Moss subcommittee were disturbed by this tendency to take their findings and overgeneralize them. Yet, these unhappy staff aides tended to let their blame fall short of the chairman. One, speaking of the Gulf warranty contract case, called it a "well-done, carefully constructed study that they tried to make cover the whole industry." The Garden City and Bastian Bay studies, however, were described by this same aide as:

> . . . something else. The guy who did them was straight out of law school and learned the industry on the spot. There was a general feeling that those reports were sort of cooked to prove the points made at the hearing. There was a dedication to keep a lid on gas prices, whatever it was necessary to do.

Another staff person who worked on withholding for Moss said that most of the overgeneralizing took place at the staff level:

> You would write something and it would get changed. Other sections would get crossed out. By the time it was finished it would be one sided, like a legal brief. Mostly this happened in the editing, and the editing was done exclusively by Lemov.

Wunder, the minority counsel, said this kind of editing led him to write his minority reports as if they were legal briefs for the other side. For every statement in a majority report saying a particular example shows the need for tough regulatory policy, one can find a statement in the corresponding minority report offering the example as a convincing argument for deregulation.

Lemov accepted the responsibility for editing the reports but claimed his job was to tone down the language, not make it more extreme. This is disputed by several on the staff. Furthermore, Lemov admitted that he often edited with an eye toward the press's tendency to pick up broad and oversimplified statements. He did this, he said, because "the press is vital if you want to make oversight work." At least some on the staff were unhappy with the results, but sorting out the roles played by Lemov and Moss is no easy task. We shall return to this after laying out the facts of the reserve data investigation.

Reserve Data

Any one who ever has worked for or with Congress is familiar with the kind of distortion we saw in the withholding cases. Whether done consciously or unconsciously, members (in fact, people in general) often leap to unwarranted conclusions based on overgeneralizations and misinterpretations, and then communicate these conclusions to the staffs who are charged with discovering the "facts." In this fairly common situation, the results of the staff's research are made public. What is open to question are not the facts, but the hypotheses that lead staff to spend time seeking the facts in the first place and the interpretive framework within which they are presented. A less common and even more questionable situation occurs when a chairman publicly presents his hypotheses, complete with damaging allegations, before the research has been done, and then fails to make the staff's research public when it does not support the chairman's public statements.

That was the way Moss handled his subcommittee staff's investigation of the American Gas Association's (AGA) data about natural gas reserves. At a June 9, 1975 hearing, Moss released an internal Federal Trade Commission (FTC) memorandum, written by the staff of the FTC's Bureau of Competition, that urged the commission to file suit against eleven major oil and gas corporations and the American Gas

Association for *"concertedly* maintaining a deficient natural gas reporting system." The exact legal meaning of the word "concertedly"
is open to dispute but, at the least, it implies that the companies and
the AGA knowingly acted to gain mutual benefit from the way they
reported reserves. (The word "reserves" refers to known, tapped and
economically recoverable oil or natural gas. It is much narrower than
"resources.") Moss wholeheartedly joined the Bureau of Competition's allegation at the hearing by using the phrase "concerted
effort," and by saying that the staff memorandum was "alarming."
He even suggested a motive for the alleged illegal activity by noting
that "it is in the interest of the gas producing industry to underestimate reserves," because reserves are an important component in
determining the Federal Power Commission's regulated wellhead
gas prices.[22]

After his brief opening statement, Moss turned the hearing over
to Lemov for almost the entire morning. Letting staff develop the
case in an investigative hearing does have some merit, because it
facilitates the presentation of a complex body of evidence. Other
investigative subcommittees have followed the practice, but it can
have partisan side effects when it is abused.

In this instance, Lemov spent the morning taking testimony from
three Bureau of Competition staff members who wanted the FTC to
bring suit against the gas companies. Neither Lemov nor Moss
pointed out that morning that the FTC's Bureau of Economics disagreed with the Bureau of Competition's conclusions. Representative
Collins, the ranking minority member, tried to get Bureau of Economics people on the stand at the same time as the people from the
Bureau of Competition. Moss refused, putting off their rebuttal for
more than two weeks. Collins compounded the political impact of
Moss's decision when he finally was given all of five minutes, near the
end of the morning session. (Moss defended the allocation of time
with his fiction that the staff worked for everyone.) Instead of bringing the internal FTC disagreement out in the open, Collins spent his
precious minutes, as he did on other occasions, questioning the academic credentials of the people from the competition bureau.

This served Moss's ends perfectly. Since Moss apparently
wanted to create skepticism about the gas industry among his colleagues (or, as he might put it, to make them aware of the factual
basis for his skepticism), he had to present his findings in a way
that would attract their attention. Committee reports are useful

for some purposes, but members cannot get the attention of busy colleagues with a fifty-page printed document. Something brief is needed. To be most effective, that something should be given to the members at a time of day when they are not distracted by other business. Ideally, it should also be presented in a fashion that suggests that the information is of concern to the general public and not just to specialists.

The vehicle that best meets all these requirements is a front-page story in the *Washington Post.* Unlike newspapers from the home district, which come to a member's office, the *Post* comes with breakfast, at home. On the morning after the hearing, the front page of the *Post* carried a story headlined "FTC Suit on Gas Data Urged" which failed, through no fault of the reporter's, to mention that the opposite was also urged elsewhere in the FTC.[23]

The *Post* continued to give the story good play well into the summer. When the subcommittee voted on June 16 to subpoena the records of seven oil companies that had failed to cooperate with the FTC, the story was given the right-hand lead position on the first business page.[24] A week later, when Moss still had not set a firm date for a hearing to take testimony from the Bureau of Economics, Collins finally released that bureau's staff memorandum. That resulted in a *Post* story on an inside business page on the disagreement within the FTC.[25] Two days later, Moss's "grilling" of the economics bureau position was back on the first business page.[26] On July 15, the *Post* headlined a statement made to the subcommittee then Federal Power Commission Chairman John Nassikas acknowledging that there were "gross deficiencies" in the AGA's reporting program. Only in the eighth paragraph did the story get to Nassikas' statement that despite the deficiencies in the reporting system, he thought the data were "reasonably" accurate.[27] Then, in the public relations *pièce de resistance* of the series, the *Post* on July 23 published a picture on its first business page of two subcommittee staff aides receiving an armored truck load of subpoenaed oil company documents for the reserve data study.[28] Despite Moss's claim that he never sought publicity for himself or his subcommittee's work, it should be noted that photographers were there only because the subcommittee staff had tipped them off. As Lemov told David Price: "Kirk Smith [a subcommittee aide] spends maybe half his time making sure the press is informed. After all, this is a fast league up here; there's a lot going on. You have to make sure people know what you're doing."[29] The resulting coverage was a predictable result of this kind of spoon feeding from the staff.

The July 23 *Post* photograph was the last anyone ever heard of the allegedly concerted actions for more than two years, until Collins forced the issue at the end of 1977. What happened in the interim smells suspiciously like a subcommittee cover-up of material that proved not to substantiate the serious charges Moss had aired.

The subcommittee had received about three-quarters of a million pieces of paper—about forty-odd file cabinets full—from the major gas companies. Michael Barrett, a Staggers holdover with Federal Trade Commission and Securities and Exchange Commission experience, was put in charge of the investigation. He was helped by six auditors from the General Accounting Office. By the fall, Barrett became convinced that the documents did not prove concerted action and that there were not, as Lemov was charging, three sets of books kept by the companies. Lemov, not satisfied with this conclusion, told Barrett to keep working on the material. Ultimately, Barrett went to Moss and resigned, specifically tying the action to his dissatisfaction over the reserve data investigation. Barrett had no other job at the time he resigned, but got one fairly soon with Dingell's subcommittee.*

John Galloway was asked to head the investigation after Barrett left, but he also failed to turn up any direct evidence of concerted action or deliberate underreporting. However, the subpoenaed material did allow the subcommittee for the first time to make a direct field-by-field comparison of AGA and U.S. Geological Survey (USGS) reserve estimates for Gulf Coast fields. Neither the USGS nor AGA could make such a comparison on its own because each considered the information that went into its estimates to be proprietary.

The comparison showed the USGS reporting some 37 percent more in gas reserves than the AGA. While Galloway did not speculate on the cause of this discrepancy, Moss did. In the hearing at

---

*Moss, in an interview, denied that Barrett resigned over the AGA investigation, although the resignation was described to me by several on the staff. Moss claimed that anyone who said Barrett left because of the reserve data case was "lying." Moss insisted that Barrett left the subcommittee with an offer from Energy and Power in hand and that he has come back to work for the Moss subcommittee on specific assignments, such as the investigation of the National Collegiate Athletic Association. It was obvious from the interview, however, that Moss had confused Barrett with another staff member, Mark Raabe, who left and later came back to work with the subcommittee on the NCAA investigation.

which Galloway's findings were released, held two weeks before a floor vote on deregulation, Moss said that "very serious questions would be raised if this Congress deregulated natural gas on the basis of the industry's own self-serving data."[30] Within weeks, the February 1976 staff question-and-answer pamphlet, mentioned earlier in this chapter, referred to the understatement of reserves by the AGA as "a form of withholding."[31]

The next step came May 4, 1976 when Galloway wrote a memo to Lemov saying the "staff with the assistance of GAO personnel *has completed*" comparing AGA's reserve ledgers with the records of the individual companies. He concluded that the "comparison appears to support the AGA" on first glance. A closer analysis, however, shows that the data bases used by the companies differ from each other's and from the AGA's. This made the comparison "a mostly pointless exercise." He recommended that the subcommittee leave things with the apparent 37 percent discrepancy between the AGA and USGS, since the USGS data "constitute the only non-biased, non-industry reserve data available for comparison."

Galloway's memo claimed the comparison of oil company to AGA data on individual field was "pointless" because it did not prove anything. However, the very failure to prove something did undermine any basis for a charge of collusion. Since Moss had raised this specter in a public hearing, and repeated it several times, one might think he would have a responsibility to clear the people whose personal reputations were questioned. He never did. In fact, for months after the Galloway memo, Moss said the investigation was still going on and results would be coming out soon.[32]

The issue was brought to a head publicly in late 1977, when Collins learned of Galloway's May 1976 memorandum to Lemov. On November 2, 1977, Collins wrote to Moss asking that he be given the results of the staff's comparison of the oil company and the AGA data. He also asked Moss to have Galloway brief Collins and Wunder on those results. Moss, in a November 10 response, said that Collins, but not Collins's staff, could look at the data subpoenaed by the subcommittee. Moss was silent about Collins' request to see the staff's analysis of the data. Collins was allowed to look at the files on November 17 and that is when he first saw Galloway's memorandum. In a letter written to full committee chairman Harley Staggers that day, Collins said that "since this document contains no proprietary information, I hereby request that it be made public." Collins said he wanted the memorandum public because it would help show "that there has been a cover-up of conclusions which should have been reached and made public." Moss, not Staggers, answered Collins in a November 21 letter that took him to task for bringing the dispute to this full committee chairman and said that "the majority under our system is charged with the full responsibility for what happens."

Obviously at an impasse in the Commerce Committee, Collins brought the issue up on the House floor on December 6.[33] His position was buttressed by a *Wall Street Journal* lead editorial the next day strongly supporting him.[34] Moss gave in on December 15, when he inserted Galloway's May 1976 memorandum in the *Congressional Record*.[35] But he did not do this until Galloway and three other staff aides wrote another memo, dated December 12, 1977, about the memo of the year before. The second memo said that nothing significant had been covered up by the failure to release the first because the earlier one neither supported nor undermined the AGA's data. The second memo again stressed the 37 percent disparity between the AGA and USGS figures.

Galloway's 1977 memo obscured many of the same points that had been muddied by earlier subcommittee statements on the subject. The individual company data may say nothing about the validity of the AGA's data but it does suggest a lack of evidence to support the charges of collusive company behavior. Galloway appears to have been careful not to say things he could not comfortably support—his memo was silent on the charge of collusion—but he felt no compulsion to report the whole truth publicly until Moss asked him to, when doing so would have contradicted what Moss had said in open hearing. Galloway's reticence on this point seems perfectly proper: the responsibility is and should be the elected member's. But it dramatically points out the conflict between the notions of "professionalism," to which a scholar or pure investigator might adhere and that of the lawyer-advocate congressional staff aide.

One final point should be made about Galloway's memo. By referring back to the 37 percent difference between USGS and AGA, Galloway reiterated a consistent subcommittee suggestion that the gap in some way undermined the credibility of the AGA's figures. However, the subcommittee never went back after January 1976 to either the AGA or the USGS to learn the cause of the 37 percent disparity. If it had, it might have learned that the difference resulted from things that had nothing to do with deregulation, collusion, or any of the other causes suggested by Moss.

This author, on August 3, 1978, interviewed Gary W. Horton, one of the USGS experts who testified before Moss in January 1976. According to Horton, most of the difference between the AGA and USGS stemmed from nothing more sinister than a difference in definition. Both started from identical data collected by independent contractors. The USGS included in its figures reserve data from wells that had been tapped but were not yet in production. The AGA, in contrast, would not add a well to its reserve inventory until it could do a flow test, which assumes at least some previous production. The difference in technique would not normally have produced a 37 percent difference in estimates but, according to Horton, the data used by the subcommittee happened to include substantial Pleistocene (Ice Age) belt deposits just discovered and counted by the USGS, but not yet in production and therefore not yet included in the AGA's figures.

The point here is not to get in a dispute over the USGS or AGA definition. If Moss had limited himself to looking at the technical questions relating to reserve data, there would be no question about what he had done—just as there would have been no objection to a careful analysis of the rate of gas recovery from known wells. But in the reserve data case, as in the withholding investigation, Moss went well beyond the technical issues to allege that the industry was engaged in a self-serving and perhaps illegal conspiracy. He put the staff to work to find the conspiracy, and when they could not find one in the withholding cases, he had them write the reports as if they had. Similarly, when his staff's reserve data investigation flatly disproved Moss's worst allegations, the conclusion was buried until Collins forced it out.

The Role of the Staff

We earlier deferred examining the extent to which the staff exercised independent influence over the chairman's approach to energy oversight. On one level, the answer is obvious to anyone who ob-

served Moss directly. John Moss, more than most people with comparable workloads, was in charge of what went on in his name. Yet, on
a different level, the issue is more complex. Moss's wishes, or his
presumed wishes, did guide the staff. But when one person is in
charge of a subcommittee staff of thirty that generates enough detailed information to sustain a public hearing one of every two days
Congress is in session, the problems of management start mounting.
Moss acknowledged this in an interview:

> It's impossible for me to read everything that comes into the commit-
> tee. But I'm no different from any other official in Washington. None
> of them can do everything. But you can very quickly change your staff.

Thus, Moss said his ability to control his staff rested at least implicitly
on his ability to fire them at will. However, the power to fire can
come into play only if the chairman learns what the staff is doing.
That is no small task on any subcommittee, but subcommittees that
do investigations pose more difficulties than others. The potential
problems may range from the way staff treats potential witnesses at
the start of an investigation to the generalizations in the written
report at the end. In Moss's case, the problems discussed in these
pages occured toward the end of the process, when reports were
written. On other subcommittees (such as Dingell's) they came earlier, when it was time to decide which investigations should be followed through.

Moss's major point of control over his staff came as he prepared for
a hearing and during the hearing itself. According to Galloway, about
half of the hypotheses the staff investigated came from Moss and
about half from the staff. Moss then let the staff develop the evidence
until they thought they were ready to brief him. According to Galloway:

> Oversight gives the staff tremendous power. There is no way I can
> imagine a staff person investigating a subject for three or four months
> and not persuading a member to hold a hearing at that stage, if you have
> done your homework. Ultimately, you'll be found out, though, when the
> person being investigated comes in to answer.

Galloway described what it meant to him as an aide to work in a
situation where the control comes only after he has put his reputation
on the line.

> The real control is in the hearing. I got up in one hearing with TV cameras there and accused Texaco of withholding. That's one hell of a control on staff. When you take a controversial issue and stick your neck out, you have to have done your homework.
>
> Before one hearing, when I was planning to make some pretty heavy allegations, I went in with my testimony to Moss. [Moss has his chief investigator on a subject present his findings in testimony.] He smiled and said, "do you think you know what you're saying?" I said I did. He said, "we'll see." I would rather he made some kind of response, but he didn't. He just sat there and said we'd see.

Once Moss was briefed, he was in control. The problem according to several staff members who worked on energy, was that they found it difficult to get to Moss without Lemov. (The same complaints did not apply to the health task force or to energy after Lemov left.) These people say they think that disagreements within the staff over how to interpret the evidence never got to Moss. In particular, they felt they had a hard time presenting the case for a narrow interpretation of the withholding evidence. They also wondered whether Moss knew the staff had already finished looking at the AGA reserve data material when he repeatedly said the investigation was still under way.

In these two major instances, Moss claims he was aware of the staff's differing opinions, even if the staff did not always know it. The withholding issue was brought to him directly at least once. Lemov wanted to bring the cases together in a single wrap-up report on withholding. Galloway thought they had done enough. There was no wrap-up so, in that instance, Galloway prevailed. The individual reports, however did make charges that went beyond the individual cases.

Galloway and Lemov also differed over whether to publish a report critical of AGA's reserve data. Lemov said in an interview after he left the staff that he did not think the evidence showed intentional conspiracy, but he did want to hit the companies for their sloppy recordkeeping and lack of uniform standards. As we have seen, Galloway's May 4 memo did not even support a charge of sloppiness, although it talked about a lack of uninformity. In any case, there was no report until Moss's December 1977 *Congressional Record* insert.

While Moss appears to have been aware of some of the key internal staff disagreements on major issues, the staff nevertheless did not feel

free to go around Lemov to dispute his judgment. That was the issue
Barrett raised by his resignation. Lemov concedes some of the substance of the complaint, but denies it affected anything major.

> I don't recall any situation where an issue of significance was not
> brought to his attention. I think we ran a tight ship and issues didn't get
> lost. They were all brought to his attention.
>
> I would say this much. I was a tough chief counsel, and with thirty
> staff members coming to me with problems ranging from insignifi-
> cant to very important, ranging from the White House all the way
> down to some little bureau in an obscure agency, there had to be
> some decision on what was primary and what was not. And I had to
> make that decision. That was my responsibility. Considering the im-
> mense number of agencies we were involved with, there had to be
> someone who said "listen, put this one off for a few weeks." I cer-
> tainly wasn't going to have this lineup outside of Moss's office of doz-
> ens of people who wanted to see him. It was my job to make sure
> that he got the issues in order of priority and I took the responsibil-
> ity for seeing that the priorities were reasonable, that he heard
> about the important things first.
>
> Anybody could grab the phone and call him, and did. But the thing
> is that when a staff member undertook to go to the chairman, outside
> of the normal order of priorities, outside of our regular group meetings
> with him, then they had to be responsible for their judgment. *And if
> the chairman and I thought they had wasted his time, that wasn't going
> to help them.* [Emphasis added.]

Lemov described his job here essentially as that of a neutral gate-
keeper who let all major points of disagreement through to the chairman in the right order of priority. The story is similar to ones told by
chiefs of staff everywhere, from the White House to corporate board
rooms. What really goes on is difficult for any outsider to know with
certainty. In this case, several on the energy staff say Lemov's gate-
keeping went beyond setting priorities to controlling which of several disputed interpretations of the facts would go to the chairman
for his signature. When one former energy staff aide making this
charge was asked whether he ever brought his disputes over Lemov's
head to Moss, the aide said he saw Moss only three times while he
was on the staff, twice with Lemov and once, alone, to resign. Another said he never saw Moss alone.

Once again, Lemov's account agrees with these in many specifics
while presenting a different conclusion. Asked how different points
of view among staff normally were resolved, Lemov said:

It varied, depending on the seriousness of the problem. Normally the entire staff met. If it was a gas-withholding issue, the energy group would meet first and normally we would work it out. If we couldn't, we would get the staff together. Then sometimes we would even pull in the executive staff—my deputy and our operations director—and we'd work it out then. And if people still wanted to go to the chairman, they did. It happened, sometimes.

The problem with this structure, from the point of view of the staff below Lemov, is that it did everything to discourage them from bringing their disagreement to the chairman. Should a staff aide decide to buck the system and go to Moss, he had one more problem to face: Lemov, as the earlier quotation indicates, considered it a black mark against an aide if he "wasted" the chairman's time.

Although he lived with it for almost three years, Moss said this is not the atmosphere he wanted, whether or not all the important issues reached him. Moss said he had told all of his staff they should always feel free to come to him without clearing everything through Lemov. When I said that many of his staff nevertheless felt they had to work through him, Moss insisted:

They did not. They only did to the extent that they lacked the backbone to bring things directly to me. But there has never been a time when a staff member had any difficulty getting in that door. All they had to do is walk in the office.

Nobody could be fired there without my concurrence, ever, and no one could be hired without my concurrence, ever. Now, when you bring a staff in and meet with them, and meet with them individually, and I've done that with every one of them, and you tell them what the rules are, if they choose to be spineless there is nothing I can do to put spine in them until I find out what's happening, and then I try again to see that they don't have to get into this carefully structured bureaucracy that likes to emerge in Washington.

You know, running staffs in Washington is not the easiest thing in the world if you want to give them freedom and give them some latitude to exercise judgment or to disagree. I've always had the policy in that they can disagree as vigorously as they want and express it as strongly as they want *until a decision is made.* Then they're supposed to support the policy that's decided upon.

Moss genuinely did want to encourage his staffs to be open with him. The aides agree with him on this. The problem came with knowing when a decision had been made, or when Lemov's expressions about what the chairman wanted (or was presumed to want) in fact represented decisions by the chairman. When I persisted in saying that a different impression was created in the minds of some staff by Lemov, Moss said:

> Lemov was a very aggressive chief counsel. He was an excellent man who would take every piece of power he could, if you would let him. It's like everything else in government or in a corporation. You have to fight for everything you get. If you're not willing to do battle, you'll be walked on.

After Lemov left for law practice, Moss decided not to go back to having a single chief counsel. Having separate task force directors was meant to encourage the flow of dissenting opinion to him.

> I find it coming to me more directly, rather than by rumor, as was more likely under the structure that existed under Lemov. Lemov is a strong personality who had to be dressed down quite sharply in my office on several occasions. I expect to have differences with good staff. You get someone who's completely compliant and is always trying to make you happy, I don't want him.

Let us assume for the moment that Moss was right and that most of what came to Moss directly during the year after Lemov left would have come to him earlier in one way or another. (Moss's detailed statements about the substance of the staff disagreements in an interview for which he could not have prepared makes that assumption highly plausible.) What difference does it make who was chief counsel, or whether there was one?

The influence of the chief counsel may come less in the answers a committee adopts than in the questions it asks. Thus, Lemov's departure coincided with the change in the subcommittee's focus that we noticed earlier. The staff spent literally no time on natural gas after the early months of Lemov's last year. According to Galloway, interviewed in early 1978 during conference negotiaions on natural gas deregulation:

> Here Congress is doing natural gas and I'm doing home insulation. Deregulation has to be settled by a political judgment now. There is nothing I can add to the debate, no new facts. I have two cases of withholding I am not doing anything with, but what does that have to do with the energy bill? Lemov would have said you have to

keep the pot boiling but I like things that have a discernible truth at the end.

Galloway's comment points to another important difference between himself and Lemov. Not only did they investigate different subjects for Moss, but the work was done in a different spirit. Galloway did not contradict his boss's overblown assertions, but tended himself to be more cautious in the conclusions he would draw from his data. Lemov, in contrast, was willing to wring every possible bit of political and public relations juice out of the information at his disposal.

These kinds of differences can affect everything a committee does. As one former staff director said in an interview, "the staff director and chief counsel are educators." When subcommittee staffs have little congressional or investigative background—a far more common situation now than twenty years ago—the director becomes the key person in setting the moral and intellectual tone of a staff operation. A lawyer who thinks it a mark of professionalism to "prove" as much as he can with whatever facts are available will convey that attitude to junior investigators. A more cautious staff leader will similarly teach the junior staff what they have to do to win his approval. The proof, as Lemov repeated several times in interviews, is in the product.

Conclusion

These last two chapters, chapters 6 and 7, have shown that the Dingell and Moss subcommittee staffs were anything but neutral information conduits. The staffs clearly increased the ability of the two chairmen to influence congressional policy, but whether they left Congress as a whole better informed varied idiosyncratically with each issue in a manner no nonspecialist member could be expected to discern.

The problems we discussed in chapters 6 and 7 resulted partly from the sheer size of the two subcommittee staffs and partly from the system of personalized committee staffing that has come to predominate over the past few decades. The size of the staffs was important because the volume of the work they generated for their chairmen forced Dingell and Moss to delegate a great deal of authority to their staff directors, who saw their job as requiring them to sift the staff's work and help set the chairmen's priorities. The chairmen were willing to do this because, under a personalized staffing system, the staff members are expected to owe their primary loyalty to the person who hires them. The member, counting on that loyalty, is willing to delegate responsibility and let the staff person do things in the member's name. The staff person's self-interest *within* Congress requires him to act within bounds set by the claims of loyalty. However, because of the new career patterns that have developed as members look for an element of entrepreneurialism in their aides, the staff member often has his eyes on a career *outside* Congress, in the Washington issue network related to his committee's or subcommittee's jurisdiction. For that reason, the staff person finds it important to develop a reputation for himself that, while not conflicting with his loyalty to his chairman, establishes his reputation as someone to be reckoned with in his own right.

Potter and Lemov both seemed to understand the limits and opportunities of the system within which they worked. One tended to overplay the results of his investigations while the other tended to downplay them. In both cases, however, they were maintaining a regard for what they perceived to be the political interests of their boss while, *at the same time,* establishing their reputations as people in positions to make that determination.

Phillips' situation on the Energy and Power Subcommittee was another matter. What happened to the results of his investigations shows how personalized staffing can not only distort but stifle the flow of information to Congress. At the same time, it points out the dangers to a chairman within a personalized system of delegating authority to the staff. Phillips is a tenacious investigator who would not even consider tailoring an investigation to curry favor either with the agency being investigated or with potential future employers. He came out of the world of journalism where his job was to investigate, discover, and report to the public, without complications. He carried those standards over to his congressional work—as do many staff aides, whether journalists or not, who see themselves primarily as investigators. When a representative or senator delegates authority to a dedicated investigator (and an investigator who is not dedicated is one who is not likely to learn anything), the representative or senator has to be aware that the staff may turn up something that is not in the boss's immediate interest. The boss always has the authority to turn the investigation aside or delay it, but by the time he does this, the investigator has put in a great deal of time and developed a commitment to the subject on which he has been working. In some cases, those results may get leaked to other subcommittees or to the press. In others, the staff member will let himself be muzzled. When that happens, there is a residue of bitterness or cynicism on the staff's part that can be avoided only when the staff member finds a boss with whom he fully agrees, as Phillips apparently does with Metzenbaum.

From the point of view of the representative or senator in whose name the staff member is acting, it makes perfect sense to let the elected member of Congress be the final judge of whether an investigation, even a meritorious one, should be aborted. It makes sense, that is, as long as the member is making the decision and not the staff director, and as long as subcommittee staffs and subcommittee agendas are considered to be the personal property of their chairmen. The institutional question we must consider is whether Congress is well served by the growing dominance of subcommittees and staffs that operate in this personalized manner. There are good arguments to be weighed on both sides of this issue. Before we consider them, however, we shall turn to an examination of two committees that use their staffs in the nonpartisan collective manner envisioned by the authors of the 1946 Legislative Reorganization Act.

Chapter 8

Tensions and Advantages of Nonpartisanship: Staffs of the Joint Taxation and House Budget Committees

WE NOW ENTER a different world. The surroundings look familiar: the same overcrowded offices; the same overstuffed congressional furniture filled with waiting lobbyists; the same harried looks on the staff as they write conference reports over long weekends. Yet, something is different. The staffs seem to know their work is significant without feeling self-important about it. They know the difference between staff and member and honor it. While working for no one person, they keep their several masters happy. We are in the shrinking world of nonpartisan staffs.*

*There is some dispute over which committees have nonpartisan staffs and which do not. Everyone agrees that the staffs of the two appropriations committees and the Joint Committee on Taxation are nonpartisan. The House Armed Services Committee staff is also nonpartisan, but junior members of the committee—particularly but not only the liberal Democrats—have said they have trouble getting access to the staff's time or information when they disagree on policy. One person basically satisfied with the staff acknowledged that they "do carve out fiefdoms of power like all committee staff."

166

Tensions and Advantages of Nonpartisanship

Coming out of the personalized committee staffs we examined in chapters 6 and 7, the transition comes as a real jolt. Our passage might be easier if we at least acknowledge some way stations along the route. There are some committees whose staffs, while partisan, nevertheless see themselves as having long-range professional responsibilities to their committees as committees, and not simply to their chairmen.

To mention just one example, the Bronx-born Richard J. Sullivan was hired as chief counsel of the House Public Works Committee in 1957 by chairman Charles Buckley, who chaired the committee from 1955 to 1965 and who also came from the Bronx. But Sullivan outlasted Buckley, staying on as chief counsel during the chairmanships of George H. Fallon (1965–1971), John A. Blatnik (1971–1975), Robert Jones (1975–1977), and Harold T. Johnson (1977). In the process, he developed a reputation among insiders as an indispensable person to know if you are interested in a pork barrel project. The people serving with Sullivan on the full committee staff's top positions also have long terms of service; most have worked for at least four chairmen. More interesting is the way the majority and minority staff work together. On other committees, the majority accepts the responsibility for doing the administrative work and writing committee reports, while the minority limits itself to writing additional views on points of disagreement. On Public Works (and Senate Armed Services at least through 1978 and a few other committees), the minority staff shares the workload with the majority on all points except those on which the members specifically disagree with each other. (In the Senate, the Environment and Public Works Committee staff does not share its workload in the same way, but Bailey Guard has been the minority staff director under four different ranking minority members with different political perspectives.)

The Senate Foreign Relations staff was nonpartisan through 1978, when chairman John Sparkman retired and ranking minority member Clifford Case was defeated. Republicans asked for and were given their own staff in 1979. The Senate Armed Service Committee's small staff of sixteen professionals was formally designated nonpartisan through 1978, but Republicans had a *de facto* minority staff for some years before that. The chairmen of the Senate Committees on Finance (Russell Long) and Agriculture (Herman Talmadge) both claim that their small staffs are nonpartisan and the staffs on both, particularly Finance, do make themselves available to the minority. Nevertheless, Republicans on both of these committees helped lead the fight for the two major 1970s Senate staffing rules changes on personal committee staff aides and minority staffing, and each now has a minority staff. The House Budget Committee has a mixed partisan-nonpartisan staff and will be discussed later.

Although Sullivan and Guard have long records of service when compared to most other partisan committee staff aides, the nonpartisan staffs of the two appropriations committees probably have the strongest records of career staffing in Congress. It is worth looking at them briefly before we turn to the tax and budget committees.

Like the partly partisan Public Works Committees and the nonpartisan House Armed Service Committee, the two appropriations committees try to hire people in mid-career with specialized executive branch experience. They emphatically are not looking for, and do not attract, young people who are out to make a reputation before they move on. As one Senate Appropriations staff member said:

> People who are looking for some "Hill Experience" are not going to come to Appropriations. They just would not have the latitude or the legislative vehicle to show off their creative work. All you get to show for your work here is a change in a number in a bill that otherwise looks the same year in and year out.

A House Appropriations staff member agreed with this, saying that "there is a tradition of people staying for quite a while and retiring from this staff."

Longevity on a professional staff is usually a clear indication of a staff that is able to serve different committee and subcommittee chairmen and ranking minority members with different political outlooks. On the two appropriations committees, most of the staff members work for subcommittees, where almost all of these two committees' work is done. Continuity of staff service is made easier in the House by the fact the House Appropriations is the only committee on either side to base its nominations for subcommittee chairmanship on subcommittee seniority. Thus, Joseph P. Addabbo's 1979 accession to the Defense Subcommittee chair long held by George H. Mahon may lead to significant changes in defense policy, but it did not mean a change in subcommittee staff. During his years under Mahon on the subcommittee, Addabbo had been well served by subcommittee aide Ralph Preston and there was no reason for him to think that would not continue.

The more remarkable story about institutional continuity has to do with the Senate Appropriations Committee. Until the early 1970s the House and Senate Appropriations staff almost mirrored each other. Then the Senate staff was hit with a rash of retirements at precisely the time when the ethos of professionalism seemed no longer to carry weight with the senators. Twelve of the thirteen new subcommittee "senior clerks" were promoted from within, as befits a "professional" staff, but the newer subcommittee chairmen began trying to place people loyal to them in the entry level professional staff slots. By the second half of the decade, the committee was going along with the other Senate committees that were hiring designated minority staffs and personal committee aides for the junior members.

As if this were not enough to produce a change, Warren Magnuson became chairman of the Appropriations Committee in 1978. Magnuson, we recall from an earlier chapter, was the senator who made entrepreneurial staff activity famous with the latitude he gave Michael Pertchuck and others on the Commerce Committee in the 1960s. Magnuson even imported some of this style to his Appropriations Subcommittees when—to the consternation of his committee colleagues—he put Harley Dirks on the staff. Dirks had worked for Magnuson for a year on the Democratic Senatorial Campaign Committee when Magnuson had him hired for Appropriations in 1966. Perhaps the only person on the staff hired with no previous budgeting experience, Dirks had been active in Washington state politics for years before his home state senator brought him to Congress in 1965 for a political job. He was considered a "Magnuson person" throughout his eleven years on the staffs, until he was fired for the "phantom hearings" we mentioned in chapter 3. (Dirks became legislative director of the American Medical Association after leaving the staff—another uncharacteristic move for an Appropriations staffer.)

When Magnuson became Appropriations chairman, there was every reason to believe he would try to change things. He immediately hired two of his leading aides from the Commerce Committee, Thomas Allison and Edward Merlis. Speculation ran high that there would be more of the same. However, it has not worked out that way. Within a year, the two activists had moved on: Allison to the executive branch and Merlis to the Judiciary Committee. Magnuson neither expanded the central committee staff nor hired political people to replace these two. He thus seemed to confirm a thesis proposed in an interview by the now retired Congressional Research Service senior specialist Walter Kravitz. "My feeling is that staffs, like all organizations, take on lives of their own," Kravitz said. "The kind of a tradition that is established on the staff is very important. Then even the chairman and the members have to face up to it, and even if they don't go along entirely, they will be influenced."

Kravitz had this thesis very much in mind when he built up the nonpartisan core staff of the House Budget Committee that we shall examine later. But the staff he used as his model was that of the Joint Committee on Taxation.

Joint Committee on Taxation

The Joint Committee on Internal Revenue Taxation (as it was called until 1977) was set up in 1926 as an investigative committee, but quickly became a holding operation for the professional non-partisan staff that served as the principal staff for both the House Ways and Means and Senate Finance Committees on tax legislation. Although the staff's role has declined from its 1964–1976 peak under staff director Laurence N. Woodworth, it still serves as an example of the important role nonpartisan staffs may play on highly partisan issues.[1]

Woodworth came to the joint committee staff in 1944, earned his Ph.D. in public administration from New York University in 1960 and became the committee's third chief of staff in 1966 when Colin Stam, the staff director since 1938, died. Stam had been hired originally in 1927 to participate in the investigation of the refunds that had led Congress to set up the joint committee. By 1929, he had begun a ten-year project to codify the tax code, and by 1930, the committee was using the staff on tax legislation. Throughout his twenty-four years in charge of the staff, in both Democratic and Republican controlled Congresses, Stam insisted that his job was merely to provide the Finance and Ways and Means Committees with information and analysis while leaving the decision to the members. But this self-assessment was considered too modest by those who watched the committee closely. E.W. Kenworthy, writing about Stam in 1963, considered the following 1957 remark by Harvard tax expert Stanley S. Surrey, "representative" of the ones informed people made about Stam: "the task of policy formulation and policy guidance to the Congressmen appears to be reserved exclusive to the chief of staff."[2]

170

Tensions and Advantages of Nonpartisanship

Stam's influence had been noted some years earlier by Stephen Bailey and Howard Samuel in their study of the excess profits tax of 1950:

> It has been estimated that Stam exercised more influence on the preparation of tax legislation than any other single person in the federal government. Stam was lukewarm to the idea of an excess profits tax, however, and despite the sentiment expressed by a majority of the members of both houses, he indirectly tried to delay its passage.[3]

Stam was not only influential but apparently used his influence to achieve specific tax policy goals. While it is true that he was not a partisan Democrat or Republican, his actions were often criticized by liberals for favoring the two tax committees' bipartisan conservation majority.[4] By the time Woodworth took over in 1966, neutrality was not what many members had come to expect from the staff.

Woodworth worked hard to change this and he succeeded. By 1972, he had become the first Congressional employee ever to win the Career Civil Service Award of the National Civil Service League. Tributes to him ranged across the political spectrum. Early in his time as chief of staff, liberal Democratic Senator Paul Douglas told David Price, "The staff situation is better now. . . . I like this guy Woodworth. He's very able and fair, whereas Stam was impossible. The liberals just couldn't get to him."[5] By 1974, members of both parties felt comfortable giving Woodworth the sensitive job of auditing President Nixon's 1969–1972 tax returns.[6] Woodworth was admired by Republicans as well as Democrats. When he died at fifty-nine, after less than a year as President Carter's assistant secretary of the Treasury for Tax Policy, the ranking Republican on Ways and Means, Barber Conable, said in an interview that he felt as if he had "lost a brother." Perhaps the most revealing story about him was one the *Wall Street Journal* included in its obituary:

> Sen. Bob Packwood remembers Larry Woodworth this way.
> Last year, as the Senate Finance Committee wrestled with what later became the Tax Reform Act of 1976, Sen. Packwood was wrestling with a more personal problem: He was growing blind. Cataract surgery later restored much of the Oregon Republican's sight. In the meantime, all he could read were brief notes, printed in giant letters by his staff. Reading amendments to the Internal Revenue Code was out of the question.
> Then, early one morning, Larry Woodworth, Congress's staff expert

on taxes, came to Sen. Packwood's office, unbidden, and explained what the committee would be taking up that day—the law as it was, the law's shortcoming and the possible solutions. Mr. Woodworth came again the next day and the next and every day until the committee had finished with the tax bill, ultimately giving hours of his time to a junior, minority member of the 18-man Finance Committee.

"He didn't try to sell me," recalls Sen. Packwood. "He just wanted to make sure I was informed."[7]

The story tells a lot about not only Woodworth as a person and as a nonpartisan but also about the way he saw his job. More than anything else, Woodworth and his staff were teachers. While academicians on more partisan staffs have found themselves performing as legal-style advocates, the lawyers and accountants on this staff performed as researchers and teachers. The staff put in an extraordinary amount of effort before the committees started to work on a major tax bill, preparing voluminous pro/con material that laid out the arguments and political interests on each side of the major issues to be considered. While all staffs do this to some extent, the joint tax committee went beyond normal partisan staff briefings to publish the material in advance of the committee's deliberation. In that way, members on and off the committee at least had access to the issues before the committee closed off any options. While members not on the committee would seldom read the material themselves, Woodworth would spend hours explaining the issues to reporters so that, through the press, the other members and the general public would know the political implications of the technical debate going on in the committee.

This educational posture had important political benefits for the Ways and Means Committee. The House expected the committee, when it was chaired by Wilbur Mills (1958–1974), to be a "responsible" body whose judgments would end up as a carefully compromised reflection of the will of the whole House. The geographically balanced membership came from politically "safe" districts. While the Democratic members through 1974 were nominated by their state or area delegations, the leadership of the committee and the party always looked for people who believed in compromise and whose political security let them withstand interest group pressure. The House's "closed rule" policy for tax bills, whereby the House had to accept or reject committee bills without amendment, was a tribute both to the House's faith in the committee and to its unwillingness to face the chaos that would result from members feeling forced to posture in public floor debate in support of amendments that would benefit special interests in their district.[8] By giving the press a balanced education early, Woodworth helped make the system work. Members of varied political persuasions would be alerted that something of interest was going on before the committee locked itself in and a closed rule made it too late to change.

Woodworth was an educator of a different sort for the members of the committee: less a lecturer and more a counsel helping the members see the implications of the choices before them. "I always felt he was trying to bring out the best in me, rather than explaining himself," Conable told the *Wall Street Journal.*[9] But Woodworth's role in committee went well beyond this. Because he had won the members' trust, they let him take the lead in developing compromises and they utilized him as a filter through which lobbyists had to pass before the members would consider special-interest amendments. In both of these roles, Woodworth's technical skills were what the outsider was likely to notice at first. However, in both roles, the members knew that what they were getting grew as much out of his knowledge of the members' politics as out of his familiarity with the details of the Internal Revenue Code.

Let us start with the staff's role as a filter, which did not change after Woodworth left. If a representative or senator offers an amendment to a tax bill, particularly a minor one, he usually will be asked whether the language has been checked with the joint committee staff. If it has not, the chairman almost always will ask the staff to look at it overnight before the committee takes it up. If the staff agrees that the amendment relieves some people of a burden created unintentionally by the way the code is worded, the committee will probably take the staff's word with little discussion or debate. (Obviously, this sort of judgment involves the staff knowing what the members wanted in the first place, both politically and technically.) If the staff thinks the amendment is designed not to correct a general problem but to help only a few specific people or businesses, it will let the committee know discretely. Finally, if the staff thinks an amendment opens up a can of worms, the amendment probably will be rejected out of hand. One respected Washington tax lawyer described the process this way:

> If I am representing a client, I always go to the joint committee and at least inform the Treasury Department. You have got to go to the joint committee staff. With rare exceptions, if the staff doesn't agree with you, you're not going anywhere. Sometimes they don't agree with you technically, sometimes they think it's the wrong result, and sometimes they think the committee wouldn't accept it. They have awfully good judgment about what is logical and sensible within the code. In something as complex as the tax code, you have to be very careful or you could end up with some screwball results.

Staffs that play a similar role on other committees are almost always portrayed as obstacles by lobbyists, who at least want the members to consider proposals before they are rejected. Significantly, no tax lobbyist interviewed for this study expressed resentment about the joint tax staff's gatekeeping. On the contrary, they tended to see themselves and the staffs as technicians speaking the same language, and accepted the staff's role even if disagreeing with some specific decisions. They realized that without this kind of a staff, the members would be open to endless lobbying from every special interest in the country. As another Washington tax lawyer said: "the members of the Ways and Means and Finance Committees like the arrangement. They are subject to an awful lot of lobbying, and they can always respond to a lobbyist by asking him what the joint committee staff thinks."

The reliance of the members on staff filtering is shown by their relationships with the Treasury as well as with lobbyists. Members want to know what the Treasury Department's position is on an amendment for *political* reasons, but when the joint committee staff and Treasury produce different estimates of a specific proposal's impact, the members generally believe the joint committee. "The Treasury is in partisan hands," a former assistant secretary for tax policy noted.

The members' preference for the joint tax staff over Treasury colors every aspect of the committee's work. For example, until recently the administration never would have thought of sending a tax bill to Congress as it would on almost any other subject: a memorandum perhaps, but not a bill. The Ways and Means Committee generally would begin by taking testimony on some *ideas* that had not yet been put into legislative language. After testimony, the committee would begin deliberations, usually still without a bill in hand. Only after a series of votes would the joint committee get around to putting the political intentions of the committee into the technical language of a bill. The committee then would go through the bill again to adopt the specific language it would send to the House floor. The procedure clearly reflected the faith members had that their often imprecise verbal expressions would be translated accurately by the staff. Not by accident, it also helped the House preserve its dominant position over Treasury in setting national tax policy. (The detailed nature of the code also helped, by leaving the executive branch with less room for interpretation than it had in most other areas.)

Where people sit in the committee room is another indication of the relationship between the joint committee staff and Treasury. When Woodworth was staff director, he and his staff would sit at the witness table during markups, directly in front of the Ways and Means and Finance Committees. Treasury representatives would be seated off to the side. Then, when Woodworth went to the administration, he was invited to join his successor, Bernard M. (Bob) Shapiro, at the table, where his advice and interpretations seemingly were given equal weight with his protégé's. After Woodworth's death, Treasury representatives stayed at the table but found themselves being shunted aside again, as members let Shapiro explain not only the joint committee staff's views but Treasury's as well.

The member's use of the staff as a filter evolved imperceptibly during Woodworth's tenure into its use of him to formulate compromises. One liberal Democrat on Ways and Means described how Woodworth translated members' political problems into technical language. The example he gave was a provision in the 1976 Tax Reform Act that increased the amount that could be exempted from estate taxes.

> Woodworth would anticipate and define the political problem. The problem for members in 1976 was that we had to find some relief for farmers. That was the *political* problem. So Larry said that what we had to do is substantially increase the $60,000 exemption. So the questions became how do we do that without a raid on the Treasury.

Thus, Woodworth sensed the members' *political* needs and cast them in technical terms. Conable likened Woodworth's skill to that of Wilbur Mills:

> Wilbur Mills' leadership was based on shrewd psychology: knowing what we thought before we knew it ourselves, understanding our preju-

dices and our interest in our home districts, having a personal relationship with us.

Larry was much the same. He was interested in what made us tick.
I've had him say to me, "Mr. Conable, you wouldn't approve of that
proposal because it doesn't fit with the other things you believe." That
was part of his strength: his ability to fit people together and know what
their views were as a result of a long viewing of how their positions form
and come apart on different items. It wasn't just a matter of listening
to their posturing on a given issue. He knew what made them tick. You
don't get that without a lot of experience.

Once Woodworth perceived a possible ground for agreement
among the members, he often facilitated the process by suggesting
different ways the members might want to handle an issue. Far from
being resented, Conable noted that the members welcomed it because Woodworth "always persuaded people he was offering them
options and not giving them solutions."

There was some criticism of the results of all of Woodworth's effort.
Some have argued that his very skill at finding technical language to
facilitate compromise ended up producing a tax code that was more
complex than it might have been with a less proficient staff. Edwin
S. Cohen, a Washington lawyer who was assistant treasury secretary
for tax policy from 1969 to 1972 and undersecretary from 1972 to 1973,
felt this way about the "minimum tax" provisions enacted in 1969.
Interviewed in 1977, Cohen said:

> Frequently the staff has to decide whether they are dealing with some-
> thing that requires a general provision or something specific. Wood-
> worth was particularly adept at doing this—at trying to reach a solution
> that would deal with the particular problem without a more general
> revision.
>
> One of the difficulties with this is that it leads to a tax code that is filled
> with specific provisions and adds to its complexity.
>
> Take the minimum tax. People complain about loopholes and shel-
> ters, but the minimum tax is a monstrosity that does not do anything.
> It is basically a compromise, and a poor compromise, that tries to deal
> with a lot of conflicting views.
>
> It really was a response to the annual news stories about the number
> of people with more than $200,000 in income who paid no tax. I don't
> mean to say that there are not a lot of things wrong with the tax laws.
> There *are* too many tax shelters, but you don't solve this with a Rube
> Golberg minimum tax. If you have 300 cases like this in a year out of
> 25 million returns, you really ought not to mess up the law just because
> the Congressmen don't like the stories that are coming out.

Conable agreed that many of the code's more complex provisions were first suggested by Woodworth but said that the real reasons for these resulted as much from the working relationship between Wilbur Mills (the Ways and Means chairman through 1974) and John Byrnes (the ranking minority member through 1972) as from Woodworth's technical skill. According to Conable:

> Wilbur and John weren't the best of friends, but they worked together very well. Larry would set out the options and Wilbur and John would chew them over. Then Wilbur would say, "well Larry, we don't want to do either A or B, but can you figure out a way to get a kind of A— or B+ that would do thus and so." And Larry of course was bright enough to do it. But he always was carrying out instructions to achieve conclusions that were the results of political compromises.
>
> Larry was sensitive to the charge that he was the great complexifier. He wasn't. The complexities arose from the fact that Larry was bright enough to figure out a compromise between two positions and the chairman and the ranking minority member didn't care how you got there as long as you did. He was sensitive about the charge nonetheless and saw his opportunity to go down to Treasury as a chance to cut some Gordian knots. The great tragedy of his brief service down there was that the two things he came up here to explain—energy and the earned income credit—were not his products at all.

Conable's statements appear to acknowledge the validity of Cohen's criticism by suggesting that Mills' and Byrnes' requests may have come partly because they knew "Larry was bright enough to do it." However, Conable also pointed out two other facts that are crucial to any full understanding of the way the staff fit into its environment. First, Mills and Byrnes wanted to achieve a bipartisan compromise where possible and they knew enough about the code and about the characters of the other members on their respective sides of the table to make the choices among the options themselves. Second, Woodworth's nonpartisan professionalism was not an apolitical neutrality. He did not end up advocating one policy over another, as Stam did toward the end. But he did try to move the legislative process forward. He may have laid out pros and cons before the committees reached their decision, but once that decision was reached, he did not continue to trot out the opposing arguments and thus undermine the committee on the floor. In other words, he was the servant of the committee majority. On different issues, the majority might or might not include the ranking minority member. On both Ways and Means through 1974 and Finance during his whole tenure, that majority always included the committee chairman.

In effect, therefore, even though Woodworth was not the "chairman's man," he naturally ended up devoting more of his time to the two chairmen's needs than to others'.* When things got busy at the end of a session, this more than occasionally led other committee members to feel shortchanged. No one ever criticized Woodworth for this. He and his staff often worked through the night, and members realized that one person could only do so much. But they did want some staff of their own to supplement the joint committee's.

In the Ways and Means Committee, this feeling was expressed primarily by the Republicans. John Byrnes, in an interview, said "the minority, even the ranking member, always took second place. There was a recognition that, what the hell, the chairman had the responsibility to lead the committee and the staff was there to serve the committee." While Byrnes said he would *not* have changed the joint tax committee staff if the Republicans had a majority in Congress—and this is probably the clearest sign of the staff's nonpartisanship—he nevertheless felt he needed a substantive minority staff on the Ways and Means Committee to prepare amendments and write minority reports. (Essentially, Mills's Ways and Means staff handled administrative matters.)

In the Senate, the complaints came more often from junior and middle-rank members in both parties than from the senior Republicans. An aide to Senator Gaylord Nelson described some problems he had in getting information from the joint committee staff on a tax amendment Nelson wanted to offer.

> If it is a very simple question that's going to be public information in the newspaper tonight anyway, they'll give you that. But if it is something pretty esoteric, some new issue you're pushing, that can be different. Take the job creation tax credit we finally got through the committee. We had a hell of a time. We never got any information from anybody over there: from Treasury, the joint committee or Finance. We just did it on the seat of our own pants with the help of the Small Business Committee. Then, when we brought up the amendment, they said how much it was going to cost.

*The author regrets that he did not get Woodworth's own views on these matters. An interview request was pending at the time of his death.

Tensions and Advantages of Nonpartisanship

This aide was not objecting to the joint committee's cost estimate, which was higher than he expected, or to the compromise the estimate forced Nelson to accept. But he did question the timing—that he could not get an estimate or other help out of the staff until it suited the chairman.

This sort of criticism largely died down in the Senate with the 1975 resolution that gave junior members of a committee staff aides of their own. Even at its peak, however, the Senate criticisms were not nearly as serious as the ones raised about the relations between the staff and the House Ways and Means Committee in 1975–1976—Woodworth's last two years as staff director and Al Ullman's first two as chairman.

House Democrats had imposed a number of important changes on the Ways and Means Committee at the end of 1974. First, they took away the power committee Democrats had held for more than fifty years of serving as their party's Committee on Committees. Second, the committee was forced to establish subcommittees. (Mills had disbanded them.) Third, the committee was expanded from twenty-five to thirty-seven members, and the new members were chosen without the old concern for finding people with a proven willingness to compromise. And finally, Mills resigned the chairmanship under pressure, to begin his successful battle against alcoholism.

Al Ullman thus became chairman of a committee that politically was not at all the same as the one on which he served the year before. With a dozen new Democrats and only thirteen old ones (one of whom, Mills, did not attend committee meetings), it would have taken Ullman considerable time under the best of circumstances to get to know what to expect from the new members. Moreover, the new members were chosen with an eye toward making the committee more partisan. For the first time in anyone's memory a significant bloc on the committee, almost a majority of the Democrats, were willing to use the Democratic Caucus to instruct the committee on policy and were willing to support floor amendments to committee drafted bills. As political scientist John Manley, a student of the committee, said in an interview at the time: "I can't imagine anything that would amount to a fundamental change that has not been done. . . . Everything important about the committee when I looked at it in 1969 is changed. . . . It's almost a blank slate."[10]

When committees become blank slates, it should come as no surprise if their staffs are forced into new roles. Most of the same people continued to serve on the joint tax committee staff and the relationship between the staff and the Finance Committee remained unchanged. But Ways and Means was another matter. Ullman could not have used the staff as Mills did even if he wanted to. Less familiar with the code than Mills and forced by internal committee dynamics to work out, in closed meetings of committee Democrats, deals that later would fall apart in the full committee, Ullman turned more and more to Woodworth for solutions. Wilbur Mills, who had studiously avoided criticizing Ullman since 1974, nevertheless was unhappy about the way the staff was being used. "Larry preferred to give several options, not to tell them which one to pick," Mills said in an interview. "That could turn the staff into czars."

Republicans on the committee were not as concerned about the staff gaining dominance, but they were bothered because the way Ullman used the joint committee was compromising its nonpartisanship. Texas Republican Bill Archer voiced a point made by a number of his colleagues in 1975–1976 when he said:

> We are dealing with an area that is not black and white. I think the members of the staff try very hard to be nonpartisan, but they have to face the reality of life, which is—who is the boss. And the reality of life is that we are not in the same political situation as we were in four years ago. I don't think it's just the difference between Mills and Ullman. There has been a dramatic change in the pressures on whomever would be chairman of that committee. So, there is a much greater degree of partisanship on the committee and the staff has got to reflect this. . . . Still, this staff, even at its most partisan, is nothing like any other staff I have seen. It's the best staff I have worked with.

The late William Steiger (R–Wis.) saw the problem as an outgrowth of the staff's desire to serve the chairman:

> The problem we perceived was that the joint committee staff had spent an extraordinary amount of time putting together whatever Ullman was putting together. It was more a function of the way Ullman operated than anything else. The result was that the staff in effect acted exclusively as the staff of the majority. They were under constraints to act that way.

Ullman, in an interview, acknowledged that the joint tax staff had been placed in a "terrible spot" when he became chairman. But he insisted that "the chairman of the committee should have a tax expert at his shoulders" who works specifically for him. Ullman has been able to serve his own needs while reducing the tensions placed on the joint tax committee staff by increasing the size of the Ways and Means staff markedly.

As the figures in table 1 show, the staffs of the Ways and Means, Finance, and Joint Tax Committees all have grown considerably over the sixteen years covered. Finance went from a miniscule staff with only one professional to a modest-sized staff similar in size to the staffs of the Senate Agriculture and Senate Armed Services Committees. (It probably is no coincidence that the three committees are chaired by Southerners who prefer to work in full committee.) The joint tax staff almost doubled under Woodworth and has continued to grow under Shapiro. But much the more explosive growth was on Ways and Means, where the staff more than tripled in five years.

Even this does not fully indicate the growth in congressional tax staffs. At the same time as the committee staffs have grown, members have been assigning more personal staff aides to work on issues before the Ways and Means and Finance Committees. Every senator on Finance except Long and ranking minority member Robert Dole has one personal committee staff position funded originally under the provisions of SRes 60, and most assign a second person, paid from their personal staff funds, to follow the committee's activities. In the House, almost every member of the committee has one legislative assistant working exclusively on Ways and Means Committee business. Because of the 1973–1975 open committee rules in both the House and Senate, the personal staff—normally excluded from closed committee meetings—have been more effective as well as more numerous. "We didn't even know each other in 1972," said one aide to Ways and Means member Charles Vanik (D-Ohio). Now the aides for like-minded members work together on strategy which enhances the members' relative effectiveness.

Taken together, the growth in Finance, Ways and Means, and personal staffs has meant an obvious downgrading of the joint tax committee staff. Although still the largest tax staff in Congress, it no longer is a monopoly. In a strange way, this seems to have helped the staff regain much of what it lost in Ullman's first years. Woodworth's successor, Bob Shapiro, deliberately stepped back from some of what Woodworth had been doing at the end. In the process, he seems to have reestablished and solidified members' acceptance of the contribution a staff of nonpartisan professionals can make.

TABLE 1

Number of Staff People Employed by the House Ways and Means, Senate Finance, and Joint Tax Committees

(Chairman/ranking minority members' and Joint Tax Committee staff directors' names are indicated. Number of designated minority staff in parentheses.)

	Ways and Means	Finance	Joint Tax
	Mills/Byrnes	Byrd/Williams	Stam
1963	20 (2)	6 (0)	28 (0)
			Woodworth
1965	22 (3)	6 (0)	27 (0)
		Long/Williams	
1967	22 (4)	12 (0)	34 (0)
1969	22 (5)	15 (0)	31 (0)
		Long/Bennett	
1971	24 (5)	16 (0)	31 (0)
	Mills/Schneebeli		
1973	29 (6)	20 (0)	37 (0)
	Ullman/Schneebeli	Long/Curtis	
1975	46 (6)	25 (2)	47 (0)
1976	80 (11)	29 (2)	50 (0)
	Ullman/Conable		Shapiro
1977	88 (11)	29 (4)	54 (0)
1978	92 (14)	33 (4)	63 (0)
		Long/Dole	
1979	96 (18)	38 (9)	64 (0)

Source: Charles Brownson, *Congressional Staff Directory,* 1963, 1965, 1967, 1969, 1971, 1973, 1975, 1976, 1977, 1978, 1979.

Shapiro had worked for the joint tax committee ever since he was graduated from Georgetown Law School in 1967 at the age of twenty-seven. Also a certified public accountant with a master of laws degree and an adjunct professor of law at Georgetown, Shapiro —like Stam and Woodworth before him—came to the staff early and stayed. But he does not intend to match their longevity records:

> I didn't ask for this job. In fact, I had resigned from the staff when it was offered to me. Before the election I had told Larry I was leaving. I had had ten years up here and it was enough. After the election Larry said he wanted to go down to Treasury if he could and told me he wanted me to stay. Some members also said they wanted me to stay. I told him that I would stay if he got the job he wanted at Treasury. If not, I would leave in January [1977] even though he was planning to retire in June. That would give him six months to find a new staff director.
>
> Working here is a tremendous financial sacrifice for me, but that was not the reason I wanted to go. It's tough to be in a situation where you can't plan a vacation or you miss your kids' birthdays. [Shapiro's secretary said he took one week of vacation during his first two years as staff director.] When Larry's children were the age mine are now [eleven and eight], Congress was not in session all year round and tax bills would go through the committee one at a time. It's nice to be able to take a Saturday or a Sunday off, or get home for dinner. I feel a home life is very important. I don't want to miss my kids growing up. I don't want to work until midnight every night. I like to be home for dinner by 7 or 7:30 when Congress is not in session. I'll bring work home, but it's entirely different when you can read with your shoes off for a couple of hours after everyone is in bed.

Shapiro expanded on this in a subsequent interview:

> I loved Larry like a father, but his work habits killed him. He was one of the most dedicated public servants this country has ever had on a long-term basis. He came here when Congress was not in session year round. But for the last ten years, instead of a few tough periods, it has lasted the whole year. He was not trying to be a martyr, but how much can a body take? I've seen his example and I just don't have his stamina. I can't be here until midnight six nights a week. So I delegate a lot more than he did. . . .
>
> I am not looking to the future. . . . I don't want people to think they're going to retire from here. . . . I don't think that's healthy.

Shapiro's "father-son" relationship with Woodworth was probably a closer one than Woodworth had with anyone except his own family, the new staff director said. For that reason, Shapiro emphasized at several points in our interviews that he did not want anything he said about Woodworth to be construed as a criticism. Different people just do things differently, he said.

But those differences may prove to be institutionally as well as personally significant. Shapiro is generally thought to be a better organizer than Woodworth, while his political skills at this stage are less finely honed. That combination seemed to serve the joint committee's needs in 1977–1978.

Shapiro's own description of the staff's job made it sound as if little has changed. On the job of facilitating compromise, he said:

> That's the major thing in this job—putting together consensus compromises. As I see them arguing, I try to come up with proposals to fit the positions they express. The role of the joint committee staff is not to advocate. But we do feel strongly that the staff should lay out additional options for consideration. We will use our discretion to present viable alternatives—ones that the members would consider seriously given the revenue costs and administrative problems.

On partisanship:

> I feel we are not here to represent the administration or the Democratic majority on the committee. We're here to provide assistance to the whole committee. The chairman is the chairman and he sets the agenda, but I try to clear things with the Republicans. When we go through a bill, I will brief the Republicans. I will not divulge any confidences, but I will tell them where the pulls and tugs are. I just feel our staff is there to provide assistance without pushing policy.

On staff advocacy and taking the initiative:

> We don't mind taking the initiative in developing technical revisions. We don't like to be advocates, but I think of advocacy as where you take a side. I'd like to think there's no side in technical revisions.

On pulling back from the role played by the staff in 1975–1976:

> I think you'll give a different picture of the joint committee staff now. I am consciously aware that there was some disenchantment with our role. I thought it was a dangerous path.

Shapiro pulled back from the "dangerous path" in a number of different ways, all of them subtle. For example, Woodworth used to take a position on behalf of the staff on public sessions on minor issues, such as saying the staff saw no problem with an amendment. In part, the difficulty here stemmed from the new open meeting rules. Shapiro vowed never to say he was for or against an amendment in a public session. When House committee members wanted the staff's views on the hundreds of Senate amendments added to the 1978 tax bill, they had to hold closed caucuses to get them. (Members on both sides wanted closed sessions for another, more basic reason: they were at the very end of the Ninety-fourth Congress and public sessions would have forced all of them to make lengthy defenses of amendments they knew had to be dropped.)

However, the changes in Ullman by 1977–1978 were more important than the changes wrought by Shapiro. More sure of himself as a chairman and with a staff of his own on Ways and Means, Ullman simply did not have to ask Shapiro for the same things he asked Woodworth. As a result, the joint committee staff was free to do what it did best: analyze technical complexities, educate members and the press, filter special interest amendments, and serve as a bridge between the House and Senate. Moreover, Shapiro appeared to be gaining the confidence of members for what he was doing. Conable, liberal Democrat Abner Mikva (D–Ill.), and others still talked in 1978 and 1979 about the staff's lessened influence, and the theme was picked up by a national magazine.[11] But others saw the staff coming back. William Steiger, for example, said that the problems he saw with Woodworth's last years were corrected by Shapiro. And several Senate aides said their bosses thought well of the way Shapiro handled the tax bill at the end of the 1978 session. According to one aide to a Republican senator:

> He impressed people. Whenever anyone had a question about the bill, he always seemed to know the answers. And he always looked fresh and well groomed—even on the last day, when we went from 10:00 A.M. one day to 4:00 A.M. the next, and everyone else was dragging.

It will take years before Shapiro builds up the level of respect members held for Woodworth—if he ever can. However, his desire for nonpartisanship might be better served if he never does reach that level. By doing a competent job without developing Woodworth's sophisticated political sense, Shapiro avoids the danger of being misused. As long as the members see some benefit in having a nonpartisan technical staff, they are likely to give it greater latitude if its skills are more technical and less political. Moreover, since political judgment and insight into people's characters take time to develop, Shapiro's belief that people should not spend too long on the staff (assuming he and his successors act accordingly) should minimize the danger of future members treating future joint committee staff directors as Ullman did Woodworth in 1975–1976. It may well be that only extraordinary chairmen, like Mills and Long, can work with extraordinary aides like Woodworth without becoming too dependent on them.

What benefits do the members gain from having a nonpartisan professional staff available to help them on tax legislation? These are considerable, as the members on both Ways and Means and Finance all testify. The staff gives them much more help understanding complex tax issues than they could possibly get from their ever changing cadres of legislative assistants. The staff may have to give more time to the chairman than to other members, but the other members know that the information they do get has not been distorted to meet the chairman's or anyone else's political needs. Moreover, since the members believe they can rely on the staff to keep sensitive points confidential—even from the chairman if necessary—they have no qualms about getting the staff's expert advice as they work on their own amendments. This advice is more than technically expert. The joint tax committee gives the members a neutral institutional memory of the sort political appointees in the executive branch get from the better career civil servants. When an idea is floated, the joint tax staff is likely to remember whether a similar idea came up in the past and to what political effect. Unlike the typical civil servant, however, the joint tax staff shows little inclination to use its institutional memory to support its own bureaucratic inertia. Whether that would apply to other nonpartisan staffs, should Congress try to increase their number, is open to question.

While Congress clearly gains something by having staffs like those of the Joint Taxation and Appropriations Committees, there are limits to their utility. We saw that the pressures put on the staff compromised its position in 1975 and 1976. Had they continued for much longer, we may well wonder whether the staff ever could have come back.

The political pressures that temporarily compromised the tax staff are far from unique. In fact, their near universal presence is what makes most members and their staffs doubt the utility or even the possibility of nonpartisan staffing. That may be going too far, but the skepticism has some basis. We shall turn briefly now to examine the staff of the House Budget Committee to test the possibilities and limits of nonpartisan professional staffing. A deliberate effort was made there to recreate the Joint Taxation Committee's nonpartisan professionalism, but two different factors worked to limit what could be done. First, the partisanship of the committee's members markedly affected the climate within which the staff worked—as it did on Ways and Means in 1975. Second, the committees deal with different subjects. There may be something about the substance of tax or appropriations bills, either intrinsically or as they are defined by member *and* staff, that may make them more conducive to a nonpartisan staff structure and outlook. The benefit other committees might gain from nonpartisan staffs must be weighed against these same two factors.

House Budget Committee

The House Budget Committee did not even exist until long after the trend away from nonpartisan professional staffs had been firmly established.[12] The committee was created, together with its Senate counterpart and the Congressional Budget Office, by the Budget Reform Act of 1974. The two committees are very different. The Senate sponsors of budget reform wanted a permanent budget committee whose members would serve continuously and develop an institutional stake in the process. The concerns of the House were very different. In a compromise that simultaneously met the wishes of the Ways and Means and Appropriations Committee members who feared too strong a Budget Committee and budget reform advocates (such as Richard Bolling, D–Mo., the architect of the House bill) who wanted to increase the role of the party in Congress, the House opted for a Budget Committee with rotating membership. In fact, the House deliberately institutionalized the conflict between the money committees, legislative committees, and party by specifying the number of people from Appropriations and Ways and Means who would serve on Budget and by giving the party caucus a greater voice in choosing the members and chairman of the committee than was the practice at the time.

The conflicts began making themselves felt quickly. Brock Adams (D–Wash.), a liberal member of the Committee on Interstate and Foreign Commerce who supported stronger congressional parties, wanted to be the committee's first chairman. He had the public support of Speaker Carl Albert and Majority Leader Thomas P. (Tip) O'Neill, but that was not enough. In the week before the August 7, 1974 caucus vote, Wilbur Mills put Al Ullman forward as his candidate. Mills won, as he usually did before his celebrated fall from grace later in 1974. His 113 to 90 victory was treated at the time as if it would make a big difference to the congressional budget process. It did not, primarily because Ullman left Budget in December to chair Ways and Means, before the Budget Committee had done anything substantive. The caucus then named Adams chairman for the Ninety-fourth Congress (1975–1976).

However, Ullman's short tenure did affect the make up of the Budget Committee's staff. According to Walter Kravitz, who took a leave from the Congressional Research Service for a year to be the committee's first staff director:

> There's nothing in the law or legislative history that said there should be a professional nonpartisan staff. It was a decision that had to be made and it was one that was hotly argued, even bitterly argued, within the committee.
>
> To put it simply, you had a conflict between the Democrats and Republicans from the Appropriations and Ways and Means Committees, who were joined by the rest of the Republicans and a few other Democrats, versus all of the others from the legislative committees. To some extent, people were trying to replicate the staffs they were used to.
>
> But in addition, people like Brock Adams, [James] O'Hara, and others had long been supporters of a stronger congressional party. They were the people who had built the Democratic Caucus [in the late 1960s and early 1970s]. Generally, they were liberal members who believed very strongly in party control of the legislative process and particularly the budget process. They argued that the Budget Committee should produce a Democratic budget and they argued—with some justification—that this is why the rotation of members was set up in the first place. In their view, the Budget Committee was to be an "arm" of the Democratic Party and therefore the staff should be a Democratic staff. They did want people who had knowledge, but only secondarily. Primarily they were looking for loyalty.

Tensions and Advantages of Nonpartisanship

> When I was hired, I told Ullman that the only kind of staff I knew anything about was a nonpartisan staff. If the committee wanted a partisan staff, I did not know anything about them. Ullman said that he would not want anything other than a professional staff operation.
>
> But you really can't separate the fact that Ullman came from the wing of the party that does not believe in caucus control of the Congress. It believes in independent committees that negotiate with the leadership, not in a leadership with total control.

As should be obvious from what Kravitz said, Ullman was given the authority to put together the kind of staff he wanted. He eventually hired about sixty professionals supplemented by four partisan Democratic aides and two partisan Republicans.* The staff, many of whom had budgeting experience in the executive branch, was divided into two unequal-sized units: one to review proposed expenditures that was headed by former Appropriations Committee staffer Bruce Meredith and another to review tax policy and broad economic issues that was headed by Nancy Teeters, previously an economist with the Congressional Research Service. In 1977, the partisan staffs were expanded to fourteen Democrats and eight Republicans. The Democrats used their allotments to hire personal committee staff aides, each serving an individual member of the committee. The Republicans pooled their resources to build up a common minority staff. These decisions reflected the way each party viewed the core staff: the Democrats were obviously a lot happier with the nonpartisan professionals than the Republicans were (see figure 1).

The Republicans' unhappiness traces back to some very early decisions relating to the committee. First, the Democratic Caucus's initial committee appointments looked to Republicans like an attempt to stack the committee with big-spending liberals from left of the party's center. In retaliation, the Republicans appointed people from their party's right who were inclined to view the budget process in adversary terms. The situation was not purely adversary during the first months, when Ullman was chairman and House Minority Leader John Rhodes was the ranking minority member. But it deteriorated quickly in 1975, with Adams the chairman and Ohio's Delbert Latta the ranking Republican. Latta has been described as an "unfortunate" choice by some because of his stridency, but the selection had

*The Senate Budget Committee has a partisan staff and relies on the Congressional Budget Office for nonpartisan economic and policy analysis.

FIGURE 1

The 1977 Organization Chart
of the House Budget Committee's eighty-two Person Staff
Core Staff (60)

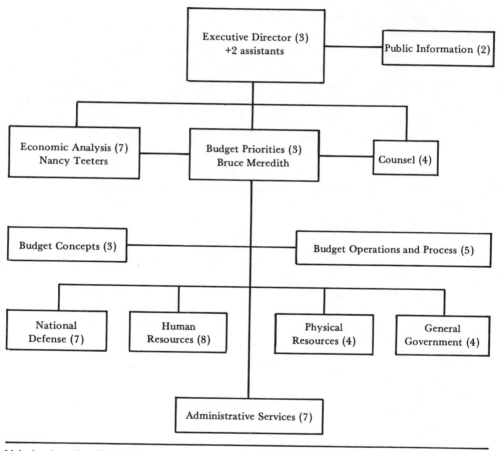

little to do with fortune, whether good or bad. Latta, like Adams, got the job because his party wanted a partisan budget process.

Shortly after the new chairman and ranking Republican were named in January 1975, President Ford sent Congress the first budget to be subjected to the new process. Since the law called for Congress to adopt a budget resolution by May 15, the committee had to make some procedural decisions very quickly. Many members felt that if they worked by modifying Ford's budget they would be conceding too much of the initiative to the executive branch. But, because budgets are too complex to be built from the ground up in committee, the only realistic alternative to working from the president's budget was to prepare an alternative from scratch that the committee would modify in markups. Partisanship among the members made it impossible even to consider the idea of a bipartisan starting point. A "current services" budget might have worked, but was not available in early 1975. The staff might have prepared its own budget, as the Senate staff did, or it could have started from what came to be called the "chairman's mark" (as in benchmark). The committee chose the last alternative, with far-reaching consequences. Kravitz described the decision in this way:

> It was essentially a decision made by the top staff people. There were long arguments within the staff, and Adams had to be persuaded. My own feeling was made up of several considerations. First, there was no other source to which to turn. Second, there was a reluctance to start with the president's numbers as prejudicial. The whole point was to come up with a congressional budget. Third, we felt it was the chairman's responsibility to take a leadership role. The Senate took a different view and started with a mark from the staff. I felt that starting with the staff mark would be too far removed from the House's traditions. I do not think staff should have that kind of prominence in the House. Also, using a staff mark would open the staff to all sorts of attacks for its partisan leanings when we were trying to establish a nonpartisan tradition. If you build a budget from the bottom, that involves making thousands of political decisions. Who would make them? The staff did not want to. There was some talk about having a common Democratic mark, but there was no time for that. So, Adams thought it over and decided this was the way he would have to go.

Thus, preparing a "chairman's mark" was preferred by the staff as a way to protect their nonpartisanship. Undoubtedly preferable to a staff mark from this point of view, the device did not give the staff all of the protection it might have wished. Latta's suspicious nature, his lack of interest in the technical details of budgeting, and the existence of a perfectly good "Republican" budget for him to defend in committee—President Ford's—led him to avoid the technical staff on all but rare occasions. As a matter of fact if not policy, Latta permitted Adams to take up most of the core staff's time while he got what he needed from the Office of Management and Budget.

This situation did not change after President Carter took office. The committee staff's time and priorities still were dominated by the chairman to a degree never experienced by the Joint Taxation Committee. The Republicans continued to acquiesce in the situation and simply beefed up their own staff. Barber Conable has been on the Budget Committee since 1975. When he was asked to compare the Joint Taxation and Budget staffs, he said: "I think it is unfair to make the comparison because the Republican role on the committee has been a very partisan role. We have made very little effort to get together with or use the Budget Committee staff."

Walter Kravitz's relationship with Adams reportedly never was as comfortable as it had been with Ullman, even though Ullman had never met Kravitz before he recruited him for the job. After his year's leave, Kravitz decided to go back to the Congressional Research Service. He was succeeded by his assistant staff director, George Gross, who had worked as a professional staff member on a partisan subcommittee staff before he came to the Budget Committee. Gross resigned in early 1978 to work for the National League of Cities. He was succeeded by Mace Broide, who ran his own public relations firm for ten years before being hired to run the staff by Robert Giaimo, the chairman in the Ninety-fifth (1977–1978) and Ninety-sixth (1979–1980) Congresses. For the decade before going into business for himself, Broide worked on former Senator Vance Hartke's personal staff. Thus, if we look at the personal background of the three staff directors, we apparently see a steady movement away from nonpartisan professionalism and toward the hiring of someone with partisan ties and personal loyalties to the chairman. Kravitz, although a registered Democrat, made his career as a nonpartisan professional. Gross was a committee professional on a partisan staff before his Budget Committee job, but his promotion from within, on Kravitz's recommendation, is within the pattern one expects from a staff that sees itself as professional. Broide's appointment was different in that he had neither the technical skills nor prior service on the committee that one would expect from a professional staff member. However, while the appointment of such a person might have scandalized the Joint Taxation or Appropriations Committees, it should not be confused with the way staffs are appointed by chairmen on most other committees. John Dingell and John Moss did not have to clear their appointments with anyone, except in a most perfunctory way. Broide and the other candidates for the job were interviewed by a succession of members, including Latta.

Broide acknowledged in an interview that the Budget Committee core staff "is a more partisan operation here" than the Joint Taxation Committee's. However, he denied that the difference came solely from the partisanship of the members. "The staff is partisan on the Senate side too, where Muskie [the chairman] and (Henry) Bellmon [the ranking minority member] get along famously." While less partisan Republican members might have tried to use the core staff more, the real barrier to serving both sides, as the tax staff does, seems to come both from the intricacies of budgeting and from the decision to use a chairman's mark. These conditions have remained constant, even as the staff directors' backgrounds have become more partisan. For example, Gross defended the staff's professionalism by saying that it would be happy to work up a budget for the minority if it were asked to do so, but the Republicans do not ask. (This was said in 1978, the first year the Republicans had no budget from President Ford to use as a reference.) Republican staff aides also said that their members did not ask the core staff for help. However, the minority staff frequently asked the program analysts for answers to technical questions: what impact would an x-billion cut have on this program, and so forth. But, while the core staff would prepare a minority budget if asked, and while it does give technical help to the minority staff, it does not routinely share with other members the hundreds of options and political decisions that go into making up the chairman's budget. "The real problem is time," Gross said. "What we give the chairman is the bottom line."

Neither Gross nor Kravitz saw any conflict between this and the claim of nonpartisan professionalism, even if the staff is more dominated by the chairman than the Joint Taxation Committee's staff. Kravitz said:

> When you talk about nonpartisan staffs, you must use the word "nonpartisan" in a special way. It's not the same as it is in a support agency.

Everything is political in Congress. Given an environment that is deeply paranoid, where everyone suspects plots and counterplots and nine times out of ten they are right, the word nonpartisan takes on another meaning. It is a relative term.

Let's not kid ourselves. Staffs work for chairmen and chairmen have their own policies and ideologies. You are nonpartisan in the sense that you will work for any chairman who comes along, but you have got to work with the chairman you have.

In the end, the job of the staff is to help the committee do what it wants to do—to help it come to a decision and to help it implement a decision once it is reached. The staffs are nonpartisan in the sense that (1) they are not trying to play politics with the issue but are trying to help the committee come to a decision; (2) whoever comes along, they will try to give the same devoted service; and (3) they will not start from a political premise in their work but will start from a professional premise.

Kravitz's last point raises a very different kind of issue from the ones relating to the chairman's domination of the staff's time. Republicans found some of the budget analysts helpful, but had considerably more problems with the economics staff headed by Nancy Teeters. Some of these problems stemmed from Teeters' personality. As a staff economist for the Federal Reserve Board (1957–1966), Office of Management and Budget (1966–1970), Brookings Institution (1970–1973), Congressional Research Service (1973–1974), Budget Committee (1974–1979), and then as a governor on the Federal Reserve Board (1979 ff.), Teeters always has been known for being assertive and occasionally abrasive. These qualities are far from being rare among congressional staff. It takes a little bit of both to act with elan, on one's own, in the name of one's senator or representative. However, these character traits can cause problems when one is expected to serve people with whose professional judgments one disagrees. Here, the Republicans have found Teeters' immediate successor much more helpful and easy to approach.

However, the differences between budget analysts and economists are professional ones that transcend personalities. One thoughtful Republican staff aide spoke of the program analysts' conception of nonpartisanship in this way:

Nonpartisanship is understood by the staff in budgetarian terms— that is, there is a professional way of putting together a budget. Many of the staffers came from OMB [Office of Management and Budget] where they were used to putting together a budget under Democratic or Republican administrations. They are used to taking what they have been given by the agencies and trimming it to fit the overall figures. The budgetarians may have policy preferences, but they do not have any business talking about whether a program is desirable. Their professionalism comes in when it comes to strictly budgetary questions: for example, how much will this cost? Is the buildup contemplated in this program feasible in the time frame given? The proper approach of a professional budget staffer is to tighten costs where possible and not to avoid the issue of future costs. These should be the kinds of things Democrats and Republicans can agree on.

The professionalism of the budget analyst, in other words, is a kind of professional skepticism that leads the analyst to behave much like the professionals on the Joint Taxation Committee. Since the issues raised by the committee's use of these analysts are essentially the same as those raised by the tax staff, there is no need for us to dwell on them here—even though they did outnumber the economists thirty-four to seven in 1977. The economists, in contrast, raise an issue that is different in principle. Consider Nancy Teeters' definition of professionalism:

> I view my job to be that of giving them the economic information and projections straight, without any partisan tinge. If I say I think there should be a tax cut, it will not be because of the politics of it.

Teeters, in other words, saw her job as going well beyond that of asking questions or laying out options. She gave the members her projections and even made policy recommendations. What made her a professional, in her eyes, was that she recommended what she believed would be good for the economy, and not what she thought would win votes at election time.

Members were compelled to see this distinction fairly quickly. In early 1977, when Congress was working on its first budget resolution, Teeters was projecting an unemployment rate of 7 1/2 percent for fiscal 1978. Since higher unemployment rates mean lower tax revenues coupled with higher expenditures for employment programs, predicting one in the budget automatically means either a higher deficit or lower spending for controllable programs. Adams, unhappy with either prospect, asked Teeters if she could not get her prediction down. She responded by sayng that if Congress decided to do a few things not contemplated in the budget, it might be able to get the rate down to 7 1/4 percent. Adams said that was still unacceptable and asked if she couldn't get it down to around 6 percent. Teeters said that she could not do so without doing things even some Democrats would not accept and that even then there would be circular effects pushing the rates back up over 7 percent. Adams eventually accepted the argument and used it with other Democrats who were unhappy with the budget's figures. Her fidelity to her economic professionalism in this example and her ability to educate members in the finer points of economics should be contrasted with the frankly partisan approach of economists on such committees as the Joint Economic Committee, who have been known to write reports for politically desirable bills (such as the original Humphrey-Hawkins Full Employment Bill) containing numbers no respectable economist could justify on professional grounds.

Teeters' view of professionalism is a typical one among economists. Few would dispute her view that the role of the economist *qua* economist is to make predictions and recommendations. Before we let this definition go by unnoticed, however, we ought to be aware of what it means for Congress as a body made up of noneconomists.

Think of the situation facing Congress as it prepared for President Carter's January 1978 message on the fiscal 1979 budget. At the end of 1977, *Business Week* published a compendium of predictions and statements on the outlook for the U.S. economy for 1978 from nine different econometric models and twenty-seven privately employed economists.[13] In the survey, the twenty-seven private economists said the real gross national product would grow in 1978 at predicted rates ranging from 2.9 to 4.7 percent. The rates predicted by the nine models ranged from 2.8 to 4.7 percent, with Chase Econometrics at 2.8 and Wharton and Data Resources (DRI) at 4.5. (Chase, DRI, and Wharton have cornered the government's business for models.) The predicted rate of inflation ranged from 4.9 to 6.5 percent for the private economists and 5.9 to 6.4 percent for the models, with Wharton at 5.7, DRI at 6.1, and Chase at 6.2. Predictions of the 1978 rate of unemployment varied from 6.4 to 7.3 percent among private economists and 6.5 to 7.4 percent among the models, with DRI at 6.6, Chase at 6.7, and Wharton at 6.8. These variations may not seem like much: on the whole the economists were agreeing with each other. Nevertheless, the quantitative differences were enough to cause big problems for a person charged with writing a budget. As a standard rule of thumb, budgeters estimate that a 1-percent difference in the unemployment rate means about $15 to $20 billion in federal revenues and $2 to $3 billion in outlays.

When economists differ in this way, what should a nonpartisan professional staff do to help Congress deliberate about the budget? It might want to try to act as the Joint Taxation Committee does by laying out all of the estimates and letting the politicians choose the ones they like best. This may not comport with Teeters' definition of "professionalism," but it is the more common one among most traditional nonpartisan staffs. Picking one set of numbers from among many would be a troublesome task for a traditional staff concerned about its nonpartisanship. But although choosing may be troublesome, it may not be avoidable. No tentative budget can be written unless its authors have settled on some figures for the predicted gross national product (GNP), inflation and unemployment, and interest rates. Components of the GNP are needed to estimate tax revenues, inflation to calculate outlays for indexed expenditures (such as social security, civil service pensions, and food stamps), and unemployment to estimate outlays for programs such as unemployment compensation. Then, to the extent one believes that fiscal policy affects the economy, one has to recalculate the entire budget each time a number is changed in a program that could affect one or another major economic indicator. For this reason, it is not only inadvisable but literally impossible to construct a meaningful federal budget using a range of figures for each economic indicator. At some point, the economists must settle on something and use it.

Unfortunately for the nonpartisan purist, there is no way for an economist to arrive at a single prediction for any indicator on purely economic grounds. George Gross described how the economists from the House Budget Committee, Senate Budget Committee, and Congressional Budget Office arrived at a common set of predictions one year: "The three sets of economists simply got together and hammered out a consensus, just as if they were politicians. I was very upset by that." The practice of reaching a common congressional economic consensus was ended in 1978 when the three sets of players could not agree, but that did not make the intellectual problem any simpler. Each one still had to use its own economists' judgments to pick a single starting point from the conflicting econometric predictions. Teeters talked about how she handled it:

Frankly, I think the personality of the person who builds a model has a lot to do with what comes out of it. What I will do is put a program through different models and then judgmentally decide what the cost estimate should be. . . .

I am caught in the middle here. I think the administration is over-projecting economic growth and CBO is underprojecting. In the past, we usually settled this at the staff level. [The Senate Committee relies on CBO projections.] This time, the estimates had to go to conference. At one point, the senators treated it as if they were numbers in a spending bill in conference. They were going to take one from CBO, one from us and split the difference on a third. We adjourned for the evening, and the economists pointed out that they were being inconsistent. . . .

I had picked a number for the House resolution which, if split with CBO, would yield the number I thought was right. I don't know the reason CBO's and our projections always differ. We're all using the same models, but nobody really takes a forecast right off the machine.

Thus, the economists have to use a kind of informed intuition mixed with political horse sense to inform their economic starting points for budgeting. Then, as the political art of budgeting moves forward, the judgments become even more noneconomic. Kravitz talked about this:

If you come within 5 percent accuracy in your estimates of government expenditures or receipts you are considered grand and glorious. As the budget gets bigger the absolute dollar amount of the possible error gets larger too.

But you have to choose. You have to make assumptions. We don't have to do that at CRS and that's a luxury. *We don't have to prepare something for action.*

What happens in a congressional committee is that even though you know you are building a house of cards, you cannot as a matter of practicality reiterate that all the time. As the dialogue goes on, what was tentative and judgmental begins to take on a concrete form and then absoluteness. You begin to get arguments about whether you should have a 70 or 72 billion dollar deficit even though any deficit estimate has to be plus or minus 5, 10 or even 20 percent. You've got to believe there is a difference between 498 and 502 billion dollars in projected spending even though it is absurd in budgeting terms, playing games with sand. In political terms it is meaningful of course. I guess it is within the adversary nature of Congress that it cannot deal with sand. In a way, I got the feeling I was not dealing with a real world. [Emphasis added.]

Tensions and Advantages of Nonpartisanship

So far, what we have been talking about is the way economists who share common economic assumptions and use common economic models end up playing with sand to force their judgments into a shape suitable for political action. However, not all economists share common assumptions. Moreover, the differences in assumptions among economists directly parallel the partisan differences among politicians on economic issues. As a result, economists who make recommendations on professional economic grounds will almost always find their recommendations more acceptable to some politicians than others. Therefore, even though they may be acting professionally, their professional judgments are likely to have partisan implications and for that reason are not likely to be accepted as nonpartisan. Kravitz explained this in his interview by comparing the views of nonpartisan professionalism held, on the one hand, by most economists, and those held, on the other hand, by noneconomists at CRS and by the staff of the Joint Taxation Committee.

> I had this experience with Nancy [Teeters] and other economists in CRS. I would find something they wrote objectionable from CRS's standards of objectivity and they would be astonished. [Kravitz had administrative responsibilities at CRS both before and after his work for the Budget Committee.] I would say "how do you know such and such to be true? You haven't offered any proof." The answer I would get would be "you take it to any economist in the country and you'll get this same answer." That was no answer to me, but it was the answer I got.
>
> Eventually, I had to think about this more deeply. It seemed to me that what was at stake here were assumptions held by 90 percent of the economists in the country but not the other 10 percent. Once you accepted the assumptions, everything else followed. But it was at precisely that basic point that the real argument occurred. In a sense, that is the difference between conservative and liberal ideology on economic issues. Once you accept it as given that the government can and should be used to tune the economy, everything after that follows.

Of course, the distinctions among economists are much more precise than they are among politicians who think about economic issues. While politicians may think of themselves as liberal or conservative, economists may be Keynesians who believe the government can fine tune the economy (generally liberal), Keynesians skeptical of fine tuning who prefer to rely on market forces (generally conservative), Monetarists (generally conservative, but not always), supply side theorists, and a host of others who seem to be proliferating as economists become less confident about Keynesianism. A nonpartisan professional staff in Teeters' sense would be one that hired competent economists and let them make their recommendations. If most competent economists happen to be Keynesians who believe in fine tuning, so be it. Kravitz's notion, in contrast, would seem to require a staff director to recruit people from different economic schools to offer competing estimates to politicians based on their different approaches. It should be no surprise that Teeters' view prevails in Washington, as liberal Democratic politicians hire compatible chief economists who are told to hire others based on the chief economist's professional standards. Teeters' staff on the Budget Committee, like Alice Rivlin's at the Congressional Budget Office, was almost entirely made up of Keynesian fine tuners. (Rivlin, like Teeters, a former Brookings Institution economist, was named the first head of CBO in 1975.) When Rivlin was challenged on this by conservative Republican senators, she said that she could not find any other kinds of economists to work at CBO.[14]

The battle over economic assumptions moved to center stage during the debate over the most politicized economic issue of 1978: the Republican effort to cut personal income tax rates by one-third over a three-year period. (Ronald Reagan proposed a similar tax cut in his 1980 presidential campaign.) Led by Delaware Senator William Roth and New York Representative Jack Kemp (an advisor to Reagan in 1980), supporters claimed that income tax *cuts* would *increase* total federal revenues by stimulating economic growth. The original sponsors differed over whether the described "feedback" would begin immediately, but most expected a net increase within a few years at most. The idea was drawn from the controversial economic theories of Arthur Laffer, popularized by the energetic editorializing of the *Wall Street Journal*'s Jude Wanniski, author of the grandiosely titled, *The Way the World Works: How Economies Fail—and Succeed.*[15] Wanniski's proselytizing was helped by the strategic placement of another young Lafferite—Paul Craig Roberts, the first economist hired for the House Budget Committee's minority staff. (Roberts— living proof that entrepreneurial staffers work not only for liberals but for any new-style, activist, media-oriented politician—left the Budget Committee in 1977 to work for Senator Orrin Hatch, R–Utah, and then replaced Wanniski at the *Wall Street Journal.*)

Kemp's and Roth's (and Wanniski's and Roberts') ideas received only slight attention until most members of Congress were convinced by California's Proposition 13 in June 1978 that the people really wanted their taxes cut. The so-called "Kemp-Roth tax cut" did not pass, but it carried a large number of people along on its bandwagon and was made the major focus of a fall 1978 Republican National Committee whistle-stop campaign tour. Many Republican economists who supported Kemp-Roth did so for their own reasons after publicly disavowing Laffer's economic theories. Yet, the theories remained the public justification for the concept.

In light of the obvious partisan implications of Laffer's theories, it is interesting to see how the different nonpartisan professional staffs responded. Teeters disputed the theories and opposed the tax cuts vigorously, in private. Rivlin did so publicly, in testimony.[16] (Roberts, a key figure on the other side of the debate, published a trenchant critique of the way Keynesian models treat tax cuts, with particular emphasis on the CBO.[17]) Finally, the Joint Taxation Committee's Shapiro refused to take a position.

Shapiro's situation may be the most interesting. The Joint Committee on Taxation is responsible for preparing estimates of the gain or loss in treasury revenue likely to be produced by any proposed change in the tax laws. All of the joint committee's estimates are "static"—that is, they ignore any effect a proposed tax cut or increase might have on the economy that in turn would have a second-level effect on tax revenues. This put Shapiro in an awkward position. Everyone knew that a tax cut would have *some* positive effect on the economy: the debate between the supporters of Kemp-Roth and its opponents was over how much and how soon. An almost identical debate took place over a William Steiger proposal to cut capital gains taxes (a compromise version of which was enacted in 1978). As with Kemp-Roth, the idea stimulated widely varying econometric predictions of the "feedback" effect. In an interview, Shapiro discussed how he reacted to the pressures to drop his static estimates in favor of one that included feedback:

> I wouldn't do it. I told the committee I would give them a range of estimates and the assumptions on which they were based. I was willing to rule out the highest estimate—the one showing a net gain in revenue for the first year. It was generally accepted that the equations were wrong. And I was willing to rule out our static estimate: everyone knew that was wrong too. Except for that, I was willing to give the range of

other estimates, but not to estimate the primary, secondary and tertiary feedback effects on my own.

Eventually, Treasury came up with a figure (on capital gains) and the members did not contest it. I went along with it without endorsing it by referring to it as Treasury's figure. That preempted me from having to do it.

I think it is very difficult for the staff to say it agrees or disagrees with one of a range of assumptions, any of which could be questioned. The economy is too complex to focus on any one change and try to attribute any specific feedback on that one change. . . . I feel the joint committee staff is not here to tell the members what is right and what's wrong but to set forth the issues and to give the members as much background information as they need to assist them in reaching their decision.

Shapiro's views about estimating revenues help us focus on the advantages and limits of nonpartisan staffing. Shapiro wanted the members to weigh their options in light of the available information —including the assumptions underlying the numbers that supported each option. He was convinced that this approach best served the members. Not unimportantly, he also believed it best served the staff's desire to remain nonpartisan. Once the staff started using debatable assumptions to make judgments that had policy implications, he believed it would be exceedingly difficult for the staff to preserve its nonpartisan posture.

The staff's uneasiness about making debatable judgments may be one reason it seemed to limit its agenda to technical tax questions. When the members wanted to think about tax credits for one or another social purpose, the staff would not on its own review the comparative social implications of pursuing similar goals through a direct grant or other means. Neither did the staff oversee these social programs once they were passed. About the only oversight initiated by the staff came on technical issues where the staff felt the tax code could be simplified without affecting the members' policy objectives.

We should compare Shapiro's views on these matters with Teeters'. Teeters felt called upon to decide which set of assumptions, in her professional opinion, was most sound. By doing so, she took within her province some tasks that Shapiro felt belonged to the members. It is easy to prefer Shapiro's style to Teeters', but the choice may not be as straightforward as it seems. Shapiro's staff dealt with a self-contained subject in a self-contained way. When he refused to decide which econometric model best predicted the future effects of a tax cut, it was at a time when the members were thinking specifically about a tax bill. When he analyzed a proposed tax credit for private school tuition, it was only for its revenue impact. Teeters, in contrast, had to deal with the tax cut issue as part of the process of writing a budget. We saw earlier that no budget could be written unless members accepted one prediction of the many put forward. This task of choosing among competing estimates repeated itself hundreds of times in the course of preparing a budget. If budget economists were to follow the Joint Taxation Committee's example scrupulously, they would have to present all of the assumptions on all of the major issues to the members. Are the members prepared to go through that exercise? One might wish they could, but they cannot. Budgets, unlike single, self-contained policy issues, simply contain too many assumptions to be considered fully in a fiscal year. To the extent the member cannot deliberate over the assumptions, however, they have delegated to their professional staff a portion of their authority to make decisions. Perhaps there is no alternative to this. If so, Congress probably would be doing itself a disservice if (contrary to the electoral self-interest of chairmen that would prevent it anyway) committees ever tried to return to 1946 and rely solely on nonpartisan professional staffs. Yet, we have seen in our earlier chapters the problems caused by staffs hired for political loyalty rather than expertise.

The questions being raised here go much deeper than budgets or taxes. They go to some very basic issues relating to the future of representative government in an age of technological specialization. If the members are so overburdened that they need professional staffs not only to point out but to choose among alternative assumptions, we may well ask whether something crucial to democratic government is being lost in the process. Before we explore this much further, however, we should first consider whether the difficulty is more acute in budgeting than in other areas in which Congress uses professional advice. For this, we turn now to a case study of the way members used competing analyses on one subject that was both highly technical and highly political—natural gas price deregulation.

Chapter 9

Policy Analysis and Natural Gas Deregulation: A Parable About Fig Leaves

OUR EXAMINATION of nonpartisan staffs has uncovered a crucial distinction between professional staffs that confine themselves to laying out options or suggesting possible compromises and equally professional staffs that do independent policy analysis and, in some instances, make recommendations. The former have an easier time maintaining their nonpartisan credibility but, however useful they may be, they seem to be unable to serve all of Congress's needs. The latter perform an important service, but at the expense not only of their credibility but also, perhaps, of something more basic to the idea of representative democracy.

Congress clearly has been acting over the past decade as if it felt a need for more policy analysis produced on Capitol Hill.* Congress's

*See chapter 2 for an outline of the growth of policy analysis in the four support agencies (Congressional Research Service, General Accounting Office, Office of Technology Assessment, and Congressional Budget Office).

interest can be traced to at least three distinct causes: its growing acceptance in academia, the desire of congressional Democrats in the early 1970s to have analysts of "their own" to counter analyses provided by the administration, and a sense of caution induced by the cost and mixed performance of Great Society programs. The result was a major growth not only in the number of support agency professionals but also in the number of House and Senate staff members with advanced professional degrees in fields other than law.

What this staff growth means for the level of congressional information depends upon two separate factors: the quality of the analysis itself and the uses to which it is put. Both supporters and critics of policy analysis seem to assume that the increased number of policy analysts on Capitol Hill has meant more influence for their analyses.[1] The assumption has a surface plausibility. Why else keep the analysts around?

But the fact that analysis is produced, or even that it is cited in debate, does not automatically mean that it is used *as analysis*. We all know, for example, that there is a great deal of difference between the ways a scholar and a trial lawyer use material provided by experts. One wants a reasoned argument, the other needs ammunition. To understand how Congress uses the ever-increasing supply of analysis, therefore, one must look at the ultimate point of consumption —at the way the members themselves use and understand the material they cite in the course of their deliberation.

A quick survey of the situation provides support for both the analytic and the cynical view of the way members use the material they cite. The cynical view—by far the more common one in Washington —gains support from the facts that some 45 percent of committee staff professionals hold law degrees and only about 8 percent hold Ph.D.s.[2] The percentage of Ph.D.s is not insignificant, but their work is almost always filtered through staff directors and members of Congress whose professional training leads them to think in adversary terms.

On the other hand, some analyses have had direct and at least occasionally beneficial effects on the legislative process. For example, the original Humphrey-Hawkins full employment bill, calling for the politically attractive goal of 3 percent unemployment by 1980, seemed all but assured of passage in 1976 until Charles Schultze, then of the Brookings Institution, pointed out that its goal would be impossible to achieve without other economic dislocations that Congress was not likely to support.[3] Perhaps more to the point, the failure of the administration's welfare reform package in 1978 can be attributed in part to a Congressional Budget Office analysis of its costs.[4]

In other words, the role of policy analysis in congressional deliberation may be both more complex and more ambiguous than most observers realize. Perhaps we should avoid generalizations at this stage, therefore, and look carefully at one issue on which members of Congress referred repeatedly to policy analyses in their debates.

Natural Gas Pricing

The 1977–1978 debate over natural gas pricing is a good example of the use of analysis in Congress for three reasons. First, the cost to consumers of alternative natural gas pricing schemes and the effect of prices on supplies were studied extensively by economists inside and outside the legislative branch. Each of the four congressional support agencies contributed important material. The principal economic study used by House Democrats was produced by a staff professional on Representative John Dingell's Energy and Power Subcommittee, and the principal counter-study was done by a freshman Republican member on the same subcommittee who previously had been a staff aide. Thus, the debate used studies from both partisan and nonpartisan sources. Moreover, the studies generated within the legislative branch all but dominated the 1977 floor debate, displacing most of the material produced by the administration, on the one side, and industry trade associations, on the other.

The second reason is less straightforward. President Carter and the leaders of Congress concurred in giving the president's energy package top legislative priority for 1977–1978, and they acknowledged beforehand that natural gas pricing would be among the package's most divisive issues. The issue's visibility clearly increased the supply of information available. The four support agencies normally try to avoid duplication in their research effort. However, all four produced analyses of the president's energy plan, each contributing something distinctive to the debate. If ever there were an issue on which the size of congressional staffs affected the amount and quality of information available to members, this was it.

Policy Analysis and Natural Gas Deregulation

Finally, the use of policy analysis in the natural gas debate of 1977–1978 can tell us something about the way Congress's sources of information have changed over the past two decades. When Congress debated the issue of natural gas price deregulation in 1955–1956,[5] virtually all of its quantitative information came from the gas industry and the administration, while all of its arguments about costs and supplies were based on sweeping intuitive judgments and assumptions from these same sources. (The debate, it should be remembered, took place before any of the econometric models used by the analysts of 1977–1978 had been developed.) On the other hand, the 1955–1956 debate was probably more detailed and more sophisticated than the ones of the 1970s on the constitutional questions raised by price regulation and on the issue of potential monopolistic or oligopolistic control in the industry. Thus, the fact that there was more quantitative information available in 1977–1978, and the fact that Congress used its enlarged staff to help it cope with the econometric technicalities of this information, do not settle whether the senators and representatives of 1977–1978 were themselves any better informed than their predecessors.

The pages that follow will present, with apologies to those who have little interest in natural gas, a detailed analysis of the studies most heavily used by members in 1977–1978. Close attention to these studies—closer than that given by all but a handful of members' offices—is necessary before we are in a position to generalize about the way Congress uses policy analysis today. We shall discover that the studies in question, like those of the Keynesian and anti-Keynesian economists, made assumptions that predetermined their conclusions. As a result, the reams of econometric analysis on natural gas matters did little more than divert Congress from the issues it should have addressed—the ones underlying the analyses. Ironically, many of these were precisely the ones debated by the supposedly less well informed Congress of two decades ago.

Not all policy analysis will have exactly the same shortcomings as the natural gas studies, of course. However, the explanation for Congress's failure to recognize the connection between assumptions and conclusions in these studies also explains why Congress, as an institution, cannot be an intelligent consumer of analysis able to sift the good from the bad. Members today are simply too busy and not sufficiently knowledgeable to do that sifting. Hence, they are persuaded of or cynical about particular pieces of analysis for reasons that often have little to do with the merits of the study in question. Instead, they fall back, intuitively, on something they rely on in most of what they do. Unable to judge the substance, members judge people, relying on their sense of an analyst's trustworthiness and (depending on which is wanted) objectivity or political loyalty.

Some of the gas studies used in 1977–1978 were better than others, of course, while some very good ones were not used at all in the congressional debate. The following review is limited to the material actually used by Congress in the 1977 floor debates and the marathon 1977–1978 natural gas conference.

Historical Background

To understand the 1977–1978 deregulation debate, we must go back to 1954, when the Federal Power Commission (FPC) was told by the Supreme Court[6] to regulate the wellhead price of natural gas destined for the interstate market.[7] (The congressional debate of 1955–1956 was a nearly successful attempt to overturn this decision that was thwarted when President Eisenhower vetoed the bill for reasons that had nothing to do with its merits.) Since most natural gas at the time was a waste by-product from oil well drilling, gas prices at the time were low (about 10¢ per thousand cubic feet [mcf] in 1955) and rose very slowly during the 1960s. The period of relatively level prices also was one of steadily increasing production. Natural gas production increased from 4 trillion cubic feet (Tcf) in 1945 to 13 Tcf in 1960 and 22 Tcf in 1970.

The 1970s brought a decline in production together with an increase in the regulated wellhead price of new natural gas. Prices rose to about 34¢/mcf in 1972, 42¢/mcf in 1975 and then took a big jump to $1.42 in June, 1976. But the price increases before 1976 did not forestall growing production shortages. With demand increasing at an annual rate of about 5 percent, production fell from 22.6 Tcf in 1973 to 19.5 Tcf in 1976. Proven gas reserves dropped from 292 Tcf in 1967 to 216 Tcf in 1976, about an eleven-year supply at current rates of consumption.[8]

As production declined, the gas industry argued that the best way to get it back up again would be to end price regulation and let prices rise to market levels, thus offsetting the high cost of drilling and exploration in the areas where gas must now be found. Industry critics said that prices were allowed to increase in the 1970s with no resultant increase in supply. The industry answered that none of the increases amounted to much until 1976, and drilling has increased markedly since then.

President Carter's "National Energy Plan," announced on April 20, 1977, partially accepted the gas industry's view that the price for new gas should be higher than the price allowed by the FPC in 1976. The administration called for a new gas price of $1.75/mcf that would go up with the consumer price index. For the first time, the bill also would have regulated the price of gas produced and sold within the same state. By doing this, the administration hoped to eliminate the incentive producers had under the existing law to keep gas away from the regulated interstate market and sell it at higher, unregulated prices to consumers within the state where the gas is produced. The administration's proposal thus would have meant an increase in the price of gas sold on the interstate market and a decrease in the intrastate gas price.

Just as the administration's proposals of 1977–1978 represented an attempt to go part way toward satisfying advocates of deregulation, so the deregulation proposals offered in Congress in 1977–1978 went part way toward meeting the concerns of those worried about the impact of a sudden price increase on consumers. All recent deregulation amendments with a serious chance of passing have cushioned the impact on consumers by limiting deregulation to newly discovered gas. Since most gas purchased at any one time is covered by existing contracts, this limitation automatically has meant that deregulated prices would be introduced gradually.

The 1977 bills also contained another consumer cushion: incremental pricing. Developed in 1974 by Leslie J. Goldman, then an aide to Senator Adlai E. Stevenson (D-Ill.), incremental pricing was designed to require industrial users of natural gas to bear the full cost of any increase in new gas prices before any of that cost was averaged into the price paid by residential users. The purpose of this was to spread the burden of a price increase to all consumers (purchasers of the industrial goods) before letting it fall on people heating their homes with gas. This concept was embodied in different forms in both the administration's and the Senate's bills in 1977, and became an important point of bargaining during the 1977–1978 conference. (Goldman worked in 1977 for the White House Energy Policy and Planning Office that wrote the administration bill and later became an assistant administrator for Energy Resource Development in the Department of Energy, taking his Senate innovation with him to two executive branch institutions in the energy issue network.)

The issue of gas pricing divided the House and Senate fairly evenly in 1977 with different results in the two chambers. Deregulation was defeated in the House on August 3, 1977 by a vote of 199 to 227, twenty-four votes more than the 1976 margin. The Senate had to break a two-week filibuster-by-amendment before accepting deregulation on October 4. The key vote, coming on September 22, was 52 to 46 for deregulation.

An incredible number of econometric studies were cited in the 1977 natural gas pricing debate. One reason for this was that in 1977, as in earlier years, members of Congress saw the impact of gas prices on gas supplies and consumer costs as the prime issue in the debate. Everyone agreed the deregulation eventually would mean higher home heating prices and that this would create at least some hardship for people on fixed incomes—the question was how much of a hardship and to what avail? If deregulation would mean increased supplies (and, therefore, lessened dependence on foreign fuel and a more productive national industrial capacity) at a modest increase in consumer costs, that would lead to one political conclusion. If, on the other hand, it would mean sharply higher energy costs for consumers, little increase in supplies, higher priced manufactured goods (as manufacturers pass through their energy costs) and a worsening trade deficit (as we import the same amount of oil while putting manufactured goods at a competitive disadvantage), that would lead to quite a different political conclusion. As a result, politicians who asked about costs and supplies before they voted were asking an important question. Economists familiar with the subject recognized its importance and churned out numerous "answers."

While many studies were cited in the floor debates of 1977, a few stood out from the rest. House supporters of the administration's position relied primarily on an analysis produced by the staff of John Dingell's Subcommittee on Energy and Power.[9] Deregulation advocates in the House relied on work done by a freshman member of the subcommittee, Representative Dave Stockman (R-Mich.), for himself and the subcommittee's ranking Republican, Clarence (Bud) Brown of Ohio.[10]

Policy Analysis and Natural Gas Deregulation

In the Senate, administration supporters, led by Senator Henry Jackson of Washington, relied on a study done for him by the Congressional Budget Office.[11] Critics of the administration from a "pro-consumer" perspective, such as Edward M. Kennedy (D-Mass.), Howard Metzenbaum (D-Ohio), and James Abourezk (D-S.D.), tended to cite a study done by Lawrence Kumins of the Congressional Research Service for the Joint Economic Committee.[12] Supporters of deregulation, such as James Pearson (R-Kan.) and Lloyd Bentsen (D-Tex.), used one Professor Edward W. Erickson prepared for the Natural Gas Supply Committee, an industry group.[13] A General Accounting Office study, which took no position on deregulation, was cited by people on all sides of the issue.[14]

Against Deregulation: The Administration

The administration's own studies were given conspicuously short shrift in the 1977 floor debates. The White House Energy Policy and Planning Office, headed by James R. Schlesinger, was responsible for the president's energy package until the Department of Energy opened for business on October 1, 1977. Schlesinger's office produced quantitative analyses of the impact of deregulation that were every bit as detailed as the ones done by Dingell's staff and by the congressional support agencies. White House press aides gave the office's numbers wide currency in the weeks before floor debate when it told reporters that deregulation would be a "$70 billion rip-off" of the American consumer.[15] Nevertheless, the administration's numbers were rarely cited in the floor debate, for two reasons. First, members of Congress prefer to use their own material when they can. Second, and more important, the administration's methodology was seen to be biased and simplistic.

The administration's studies of natural gas deregulation were released in May, 1977. According to the White House Energy Policy and Planning Office, President Carter's proposal to increase the price of regulated gas from $1.42 to $1.75/mcf while imposing controls on the unregulated intrastate market, would result in almost as much increase in supply as would occur under deregulation. The administration argued that costs, on the other hand, would be substantially lower under the president's plan, because $1.75 would be a high enough price to encourage suppliers to tap most known or probable gas from conventional sources. Allowing the price to go higher would only result in the development of smaller, less productive wells at too high a marginal cost.

Since the administration assumed that natural gas prices above $1.75 would have little or no impact on dwindling gas supplies, its notion of distributive equity governed its attitude toward prices above $1.75. The administration feared that without regulation, consumers would bid prices up, yielding economic "rents" to the producers. Since the producers would and could do nothing in return, Schlesinger considered it appropriate to refer in testimony to any earnings they might receive as being unjust.[16]

Schlesinger's views about justice or equity were common among supporters of continued regulation, but the way the administration figured costs was unique. The administration put forward four possible scenarios for deregulation, each one assuming that all uncommitted gas would be decontrolled immediately.[17] This was an accurate reflection of what the industry wanted, but it was not what Congress was considering. The bills adopted by the Senate and narrowly defeated in the House compromised deregulation with incremental pricing, transitional controls over offshore gas until 1982, and more stringent definitions of "new" or "uncommitted" gas than the administration analysis assumed. Undaunted by this discrepancy, the administration concluded that the proposed deregulation measures would produce revenues "somewhere between those of the first and third cases." How this assertion was justified remains unclear to this day, but it was the source of the "$70 billion rip-off" charge. The one figure in the administration analysis fitting that description is the one for case two: 1978–1985 producer revenues of $86 billion more than under present law (called the "base case" by the administration). Subtract the $15 billion producers supposedly would get under the president's bill and one is left with $71 billion.

All of the administration's cost estimates were based ultimately on its estimate of the costs of continuing as is. Unfortunately for the administration's future credibility, it seriously misread this "base case" cost. The errors were spotted at first by Frank Taylor, a University of Houston petroleum engineering graduate student who was working as an intern on the personal staff of Representative Bob Krueger (D-Tex.), a leading deregulation advocate. Taylor's observations took on political weight when they were confirmed by Walter W. (Chip) Schroeder, a young economic modeling specialist on administration supporter John Dingell's subcommittee staff. In a letter to Krueger, Schroeder said the administration had assumed that gas on the unregulated intrastate market would sell for $0.62/mcf in 1978 and $0.70/mcf in 1985 if the law was left unchanged. These estimates were far too low, he continued: "If one assumes a 1978 price of $1.35 and a 1985 price of $2.40 (still below the distillate equivalent price), then the administration analysis understates producer revenues under continued regulation by $4.53 billion in 1978 and a cumulative total of $44.36 billion through 1985. This means that case one deregulation costs $56 minus $44 billion, or $12 billion." Schroeder's own analysis, based on different assumptions, put the cost of deregulation much higher than this. But this weakening of the administration's assumptions punctured one of its key arguments: that the National Energy Plan was a compromise between present law and deregulation from the producer's point of view. Instead, it appeared that the administration bill would mean significantly lower revenues for producers than the *status quo*.

This put the administration in a political box. When its gas-pricing proposal was defeated in the Senate after winning narrowly in the House, it became clear that the administration would have to come closer to the industry's position if it wanted a compromise. However, every time it tried that, it faced the prospect of losing support from people who accepted its original claim that keeping the *status quo* would mean the lowest consumer costs. If it had acknowledged its original errors openly and promptly, the administration still might have been able to play the role of honest broker. Instead, its handling of the technical data throughout 1977 and 1978 aroused suspicions in Congress that the administration was trying to mislead them. Instead of helping the deliberative process, the administration's analysis was part of the political problem the administration had to overcome before it could get Congress to agree on anything.[18]

The administration's "base case" numbers clearly were causing problems in the early months of the marathon 1977–1978 energy conference, when each side thought the *status quo* better for its position than a compromise. One compromise proposal, looking a good deal like the one that was finally adopted, was soundly defeated by Senate conferees in December. (Senator Jackson labeled it a "Christmas Turkey.") The administration then decided finally to jettison its original numbers. Over the Christmas 1977 recess, Secretary Schlesinger and other Department of Energy officials visited Senator Jackson and tried to convince him that a deadlock, continuing the *status quo,* would be a lot worse for the consumers than he realized. The department had just completed a review of its figures and decided it had underestimated the cost of the *status quo* by almost $20 billion.[19]

Jackson was not convinced immediately. Skeptical of economic models in general and aware of the criticism of this model in particular, he wanted to make sure this was not just another politicized analysis designed to fulfill the administration's desire for a bill. Only after Jackson's staff confirmed the new data with Schroeder did the conference make its first glacial movements toward the final compromise.[20]

The situation just described is a good illustration of why Congress feels it needs professionals of its own. If all the analysts do is free Congress from its dependency on politicized or intellectually sloppy administration material, that is no small benefit. Whether Congress's own analyses helped the debate is another question, to which we now turn.

Against Deregulation: The Energy and Power Subcommittee

The two most widely used studies on the administration's side of the deregulation debate were those produced by Dingell's Energy and Power Subcommittee and by the Congressional Budget Office (CBO).

The econometric model the Energy and Power Subcommittee used for its analyses was designed by Chip Schroeder. Schroeder, twenty-seven years old when Dingell hired him in 1975, is a 1972 M.S. graduate of MIT's Sloan School of Management. He had no experience dealing with energy policy, but Dingell and staff director Frank Potter wanted someone who could apply the major econometric models to issues in the subcommittee's jurisdiction. He became enough of a substantive expert, however, to leave the subcommittee in late 1978 for another "network" job as special assistant to his old committee staff colleague, Charles Curtis, chairman of the Federal Energy Regulatory Commission.

Schroeder's technical background convinced him during 1975 that the model the administration used was fundamentally unsound, and he convinced others on Capitol Hill of this conclusion. By early 1976, he had developed a model of his own. Unlike the others then in use, Schroeder's model could analyze the cost of some compromises that might resolve the regulation-deregulation debate because it could predict direct consumer costs for residential users of natural gas, taking account of incremental pricing.

In 1977, Schroeder used his model to estimate probable gas supplies and costs under the House version of the administration proposal and six different deregulation scenarios, three of which were close approximations of bills actively being considered by Congress.[21] (These were supplemented throughout the 1977–1978 conference by unpublished estimates of the cost of one or another compromise proposal.) Thus, Schroeder's definition of "deregulation" was less extreme and less costly than the "deregulation" in the administration analysis.

On the other hand, Schroeder's assumptions about the likely market clearing price of new natural gas were far more pessimistic than the administration's. Where the administration assumed *new* gas would sell for about $2.50/mcf, the cost of substitute industrial petroleum, Schroeder assumed that the *average* price of new and old gas together would be about $2.50/mcf. Thus, new gas prices could easily soar above $5/mcf at first, in Schroeder's view, only to drop off again as unregulated gas became a greater portion of the whole. As a result, Schroeder's final numbers were not so very far below the administration's despite his more realistic definition of deregulation.

Schroeder saw deregulation (under the three realistic definitions) costing consumers $51.8 to $53.7 billion more for the years 1977–1985 than the House bill, with the major cost coming in the first five years. After that, new gas prices under the administration's bill would not differ greatly from those under the deregulation proposals passed by the Senate and defeated by the House, as new gas prices dropped from $5 back down toward the average price for an equivalent amount of energy from oil. (This conclusion lay behind the energy conferees' decision to accept gradual deregulation over a seven-year period instead of accepting or rejecting it outright).

The assumption that the price for deregulated gas initially would soar up to the $5/mcf price range, well above the price of home heating oil at that time, is controversial. Milton Russell (a member of the staff of Resources for the Future and author of the energy chapter in the Brookings Institution's *Setting Natural Priorities: The 1978 Budget*[22]) said in an interview that the high initial price "assumes all these markets bounce around like hockey pucks." If they do not, Schroeder's overall estimates would have to be scaled down dramatically. Russell's objection does not settle the issue, of course. Whether or not gas prices under deregulation would jump this way in the short term would depend primarily on the relative balance of short-term supply and demand and on the relative concentration of power among sellers and buyers. Economic models can build in assumptions about these factors, but they cannot analyze them.

Moving away from the short term, the major long-term dispute relating to Schroeder's work also has to do with supplies. Schroeder, like the administration, believed that deregulating the price of new gas would produce virtually no new gas that would not have been produced with a $1.75 regulated ceiling. For higher prices to produce more supplies, the gas would have to be available in forms that become steadily more recoverable, in economic terms, as the price goes up. A lack of response of supply to price can mean only one of two things: either the resource must be on the verge of exhaustion, or there must be something about the underlying geology of gas to explain the situation.

The relationship between price and supply, which in turn depends on the geophysical characteristics of gas fields and reservoirs, turns out to be the key premise on which *any* conclusion about the long-term "cost" of deregulation must rest. The relationship normally is expressed quantitatively by economists in terms of a *supply elasticity* index. That index is an expression of the percentage change in supply brought about by a given percentage change in price. If a 100 percent increase in price would double the supply of any given commodity, the supply elasticity index for that commodity would be 1.0. If the same 100 percent increase in price would increase supplies by only 10 percent, the index would be 0.1.

Much of the difference between the administration's supporters and the supporters of deregulation can be understood in terms of their different assumptions about supply elasticity. The administration took the position that the supply elasticity of natural gas was different at different prices. Prices up to $1.75 would bring about a significant response, but above $1.75 the response would drop off to practially nothing. The studies supporting deregulation, in contrast, assumed the supply response to price would remain constant, and substantial, as prices went up.

Schroeder, like the deregulation advocates, used a supply elasticity index that did not change as the price went up. He disagreed with them, however, by using a very small index (0.1). Despite his use of a level index for the years 1978–1985, Schroeder endorsed the administration's basic policy conclusion by saying that most of the supply bonus to be gained from deregulation could be achieved if the controlled price were pegged at $1.75 instead of $1.46. His reasoning, however, had little to do with the quantitative assumptions of his model. Schroeder thought producers had been withholding gas from the market because they did not want their new discoveries to be controlled at the old price. He was convinced that as soon as Congress settled with certainty on a new price, whatever it might be, producers would release the gas they had been holding. (Schroeder believed that the gas glut that appeared after Congress finally passed the energy bill in 1978 confirmed his assumption, but Milton Russell believed there were less malevolent explanations.[23])

Schroeder expected little to come from higher prices before 1985 except for the withheld gas. Higher prices probably would stimulate new drilling and lead to new discoveries; however, it usually takes a few years for a new discovery to find its way to market. Therefore, the main supply bonus from higher prices would be likely to occur after the eight-year period (1977–1985) covered by his analysis.

Schroeder's decision to cut off the analysis in 1985 is puzzling. By his own account, this means ignoring the main benefits while maximizing the costs. Ending off the analysis at 1985 may help members compare closely related compromise alternatives within a time frame to which they can relate politically, but it does seem to bias any effort to think about the fundamental policy questions in the regulation-deregulation debate.

This difficulty is compounded when we start thinking about gas from unconventional sources. One of the industry's arguments for deregulation was that it would give them an incentive to develop technologies for recovering gas from unconventional sources, such as geopressurized methane, Devonian shale, tight formation gas, and the like. Geologists acknowledge that there is much more of this unconventional gas in the earth than there is gas from conventional sources. The question is how to extract it economically.*

Schroeder gave two reasons for ignoring unconventional gas in his analysis: the technologies were largely hypothetical, and even if they were developed, it appeared unlikely that much unconventional gas would get to market before 1985. While these reasons make sense, they indicate serious conceptual problems with predictions based on a quantitative elasticity index, whatever the index's size and whoever constructed it. Indexes based on historical performance are an inadequate guide to the future; on the other hand, any effort to get away from historical data necessarily involves highly speculative assumptions which make any resulting numerical index too artificially precise. The seemingly precise indexes are conceptual dead ends that beguile members away from the more basic supply issues Congress should have been debating.

Against Deregulation: The Congressional Budget Office

The other important study used on the administration's side was produced by the Congressional Budget Office (CBO) and cited repeatedly by Senator Jackson in floor debate. As has often been the case in the CBO's short history, its study, more than any other on either side of the debate, tried to explain and present arguments for its important assumptions in terms the members of Congress would find accessible. It was the only study, for example, that took the reader through all the steps leading from predicted supplies to estimated costs.

The study was clear on all but one point—a point that is crucial for understanding the role of congressional staff policy analysis. CBO Director Alice M. Rivlin ended her preface to the study with a sentence that can be found in just about everything the CBO publishes: "In keeping with the CBO's mandate to provide objective analysis, the paper offers no recommendations."[24] Rivlin's posture was politically understandable, but misleading. CBO may not say outright,

*Ultimately the industry won almost immediate deregulation of unconventional gas, as was noted in our discussion in chapter 6 of the efforts some on Dingell's staff were making to hold hearings on information brought to them by *National Geographic's* Bryan Hodgson.

Policy Analysis and Natural Gas Deregulation

"Congress should do X," but many of its studies contain statements similar to these from the natural gas pricing study:

> This paper concludes that the size of consumer expenditures at risk under deregulation is large and that the likelihood that increased production will be substantial by 1985 is small. If these findings are right, then the question of natural gas deregulation becomes primarily one of income distribution and, to a lesser extent, one of reducing and reallocating the demand for natural gas in response to higher prices. With regard to income distribution, deregulation would transfer large amounts of money from consumers to producers. Thus a value judgment is necessary regarding whether national goals are better served by the income remaining with consumers or being passed to producers.
> . . .
> Although the expected higher cost to consumers, as well as the lack of substantial production, arouses considerable skepticism about immediate deregulation, it is attractive in some respects because it bears the promise of being a simple, sweeping solution to a complex and exasperating problem. There are, however, several alternative remedies, some of which can modify deregulation in a manner that lowers the costs but preserves most of the benefits. These alternatives include incremental pricing, a phase-in of deregulation, alternative price ceilings, and deregulation with a wellhead tax.[25]

As these statements show, the CBO may not have said which of several compromise possibilities it was *for,* but it sure let you know what it was *against.* Fortunately, most members of Congress are familiar enough with official disclaimers to ignore them; they are aware of the implied recommendations in a discussion of "costs" and "benefits," and they recognize a policy conclusion when they see one.

The CBO's premises, reasoning, and conclusions about prices were similar to Schroeder's, with the same strengths and weaknesses. The CBO study estimated that immediate deregulation would bring producers $76 billion more through 1985 than the administration bill. Much of this, it said, would stem from a rapid surge in the price of deregulated gas to about $4/mcf. This price would go down to about $2.80/mcf by 1985.

The CBO's supply estimates, however, were not based on elaborate and necessarily imprecise, supply elasticity assumptions. Instead, CBO's analysis was based on drilling rates, a figure that is related to, but easier to handle, than elasticity. Unlike the other studies, the CBO's contained a clear statement of its reasoning on this question. The CBO assumed that higher prices would stimulate drilling—specifically that the rate of drilling would increase 5.5. percent more quickly per year under the administration plan than under a continuation of present policy. Deregulation, the study assumed, would result in a 9.0 percent per year more rapid growth in drilling. Next, the CBO study assumed a constant rate of discovery for each exploratory foot drilled. (The rate of discovery actually has been declining in recent years, so this probably was an overestimate.) From these two assumptions, the study concluded that deregulation would result in total production levels of about 19.8 Tcf in 1985, compared to 18.9 Tcf under the administration plan.

The CBO's assumptions about drilling rates were obviously crucial to its conclusions about the costs and benefits of immediate deregulation. CBO analyst Lawrence Oppenheimer, who did most of the work on gas for the study, said the assumption of a 9-percent annual increase under deregulation was an optimistic consensus estimate from people in the industry. His estimate of a 5.5-percent annual increase under the administration's plan was shakier, he acknowledged. It was based on his view that the proposal would decrease drilling incentives in the less productive onshore fields, where new finds are committed now to the intrastate market, while increasing incentives to develop more productive offshore fields.

These assumptions and conclusions reflect some of the same problems as Schroeder's analysis. First, Oppenheimer ignored unconventional gas because his analysis went only through 1985. Second, he acknowledged that 5.5 percent—and consequently the $76 billion figure—were rough estimates. Yet, all through the 1977 floor debates, Senator Jackson and others used the $76 billion figure without qualification, ignoring the more fundamental and more uncertain supply issues. Furthermore, they used the figure as a bludgeon against an amendment to which it did not apply. Oppenheimer was careful to state that the "deregulation" of his study did not include incremental pricing or any other compromises with immediate deregulation, many of which were included in the actual deregulation provision against which Jackson used the figure.

Some of the analysts at CBO are aware of the false impressions created by their seemingly precise numbers, but they do not feel they are in a position to correct the situation. One person at CBO (who asked not be be identified) described a situation that illustrates the problem. After the outline of the conference report became known, Edmund Muskie, the chairman of the Senate Budget Committee, asked CBO to prepare a memorandum analyzing the compromise. CBO's initial draft response was not quantitative. It described *in words* and in rough percentage terms how the compromise would stimulate production and increase costs. The draft was rejected within CBO. Some people there thought members of Congress would not pay attention to an analysis without numbers. So, the memo was redrafted to make its rhetorical point quantitative, even though the numbers were more misleading than the words they replaced. (Muskie, incidentally, was persuaded to support the compromise, a decision that swayed other liberals who had been thinking of opposing it.)

The Other Support Agencies: GAO and CRS

The natural gas studies produced by the Congressional Research Service (CRS) and General Accounting Office (GAO) in 1977 were not as influential as the others examined here. However, they do help illuminate some important features of the politics of policy analysis on Capitol Hill.

Of the four support agencies, the GAO has the most ambitious conception of its role. It is the only one, for example, that openly states that its job is to recommend legislation to Congress "from an economic or efficiency standpoint."[26] Despite this, it took no stand on deregulation—thus reversing the position of the CBO, which recommended against it while saying it made no recommendations. The GAO's unwillingness to make a specific recommendation on gas prices was based on its pessimism about supplies. It thought deregulation *would* mean significantly more supplies than continued regulation, but thought future supplies were likely to be depressed under any federal pricing policy. It therefore deferred to Congress, stating in a 1976 study that the issue "requires a political judgment based on a careful weighing of the trade-offs."[27] Taking a similar position in 1977, the GAO asserted:

> The 1985 production levels estimated by the Administration with and without the plan's initiatives would require sustained reserve additions

which, we believe are unreasonably high based on historical experience. . . . On the basis of our previous report [of 1976], we would
conclude such reserve additions and resulting production to be too high
to be used for planning purposes.[28]

These pessimistic conclusions did not enter the 1977 deregulation
debate directly, but they indirectly helped increase doubts about the
administration's analysis. In addition, they were cited by several of
the staff people who did their own studies opposing deregulation. For
example, Energy and Power's Schroeder mentioned the GAO as one
source for his intuitive feeling that deregulation would not increase
supplies dramatically.

Two comments are in order about the GAO's conclusion. First,
GAO's pessimism came down to an assumption that the future would
look like the past. This was not an unreasonable assumption for planning purposes, but, like the CBO's drilling assumptions, it did not
seem the sort of foundation that would permit elaborate computer
models predicting costs and supplies out to decimal points. Second,
it is worth noting that those who favored deregulation explicitly
assumed the future would *not* repeat the past. Their entire policy
argument rested on the assumption that deregulation would create
a new climate for exploration, replacing the restrictive climate of the
past twenty years.

The GAO did not limit itself to noting its disagreement with the
administration's technical predictions. It went on to recommend
eleven major legislative proposals, not in the administration bill, that
together would improve the prospects for achieving the administration's energy savings objectives. While this fit within the GAO's
stated understanding of its responsibility, it did not stop there with
an assessment of the adequacy of the means proposed by the administration to achieve its stated ends. Reaching well beyond the traditional role of support staff, the GAO proceeded to comment on the
administration's ends themselves.

GAO agrees with the basic concepts of the Administration's plan, an
effort long overdue. . . . It firmly believes that the prompt passage of
effective legislation is essential if this country is to deal with energy
problems in the remainder of this century.[29]

Thus, the GAO may have avoided the partisan thicket of deregulation, but it showed no hesitancy about stating what the nation's goals

for the century ought to be. Congress's reaction to this was interesting. It was absolutely silent. People on both sides of the debate praised the GAO's fairness while using isolated sentences from its critique to support their case. No one, however, seems to have followed the GAO's reasoning, or done anything with its legislative proposals. And no one suggested that unelected GAO bureaucrats have no mandate to determine the goals of national policy.

The Congressional Research Service is much more modest about its mission than the GAO. Yet, it seems to have gotten itself into more trouble with Congress on this issue. A study prepared by the CRS's Lawrence Kumins in December 1975 was used extensively by the supporters of continued regulation when the subject was debated in the House in February 1976, but the study probably brought the service as much public criticism as anything else it has done in recent years. Statements against it by deregulation supporters went far beyond criticisms of its arguments. Kumins's and the service's competence and objectivity were questioned directly in a legislative appropriations hearing[30] and on the House floor,[31] and the study was the subject of an internal CRS review of its procedures.[32] Without entering here into the merits of those accusations, suffice it to say that they directly affected the way Kumins's 1977 material was used.

Kumins produced two studies of the cost of deregulation in 1977, both at the specific request of some of Congress's most strident opponents of compromise with deregulation. Representative Andrew Maguire (D-N.J.), who serves on the House Commerce Committee, asked for one that came out in the weeks between the Energy and Power Subcommittee's narrow acceptance of deregulation and the full committee's reversal of that position.[33] The second, mentioned earlier, was produced for Senator Kennedy's Energy Subcommittee on the Joint Economic Committee on the eve of the Senate floor debate. In both cases, the members deliberately asked for the analysis to be done by someone who they knew would oppose deregulation. They were looking, in other words, for material to use in their speeches, not for analysis to help them make up their minds.

Kennedy is an interesting example of how people who are not specialists in a field judge analysis. Kennedy may be one of the most active legislators in the Senate. On the issues he knows best, he is in command of the facts and can call upon respected people to support his point of view with high quality material. On other issues, he also likes to use analysis to support his position, but he is too busy to judge what he is getting. His speech on the Senate floor citing Kumins—obviously written by a staff person who did not go over the details with Kennedy—is a good case in point.

In his speech,[34] Kennedy cited Kumins' conclusion that the administration plan would cost $51 billion more through 1985 than existing law. He then cited the CBO's conclusion that deregulation would cost $162 billion more than the administration's proposal and added the two together to say that deregulation would cost some $200 billion more than existing law. The problems with using this $200 billion figure are staggering, for two reasons. First, if someone were going to cite the CBO's figure about how much more deregulation would cost than the administration bill, how could he fail to mention that the same CBO study, disagreeing with Kumins, said that the administration plan would cost *less* than a continuation of existing law? The failure to mention this seems particularly important, since the point of Kennedy's speech was to urge the Senate to adopt no new law rather than either the administration plan or deregulation. Second, Kennedy's $200 billion was reached by adding Kumins's estimate of the administration plan's cost through 1985 to the CBO's estimate of the cost of full deregulation (with none of the compromises in the pending Senate bill) through 1990! Furthermore, the speechwriter took the 1990 number from a small table, half of which was devoted to 1985 costs.[35] While it seems unlikely that Kennedy personally took the time to check his statistics, the way he uses staff—setting aides in competition with each other to see who can best advance the senator's interest[36]—creates an atmosphere in which some on his staff seem to feel that shoddy work is acceptable, as long as it is not caught, and it supports the position the boss wants to take.

But let us get back to Kumins to consider why his studies were cited so often in 1975 but not in 1977. The work Kumins did for Maguire in June 1977 was not important at all in the House floor debate of that year. The Joint Economic Committee report was used in the Senate debate, but only by those, like Kennedy, whose position on gas prices was uncompromising. Perhaps even more tellingly, the lengthiest Senate rebuttal of the proregulation analyses by a deregulation supporter went out of its way to add an *ad hominem* attack of Kumins to its brief critique of the Joint Economic Committee print.[37] In addition, the two leading supporters of the administration, Jackson in the Senate and Dingell in the House, both deliberately asked others in the support agencies to do the work they wanted. Jackson used the CBO and Dingell, when not relying on his own staff, asked others in CRS (such as Herman Franssen) to work on natural gas. Staff aides to both said they did not ask Kumins because there was no point getting an analysis that would be dismissed out of hand by members who had not made up their minds.

What happened to Kumins's 1977 studies—which on their merits, were weightier than the more heavily used 1975 study—illustrates in an extreme form a political problem the four support agencies must face constantly. Congress says it wants the support agencies to do objective policy analysis. However, policy analysis necessarily involves the agencies in taking positions, at least implicitly, on political issues the members properly like to reserve for themselves. Hence, if the agencies want their work to be used as analysis, they must be concerned about the reputations of their analysts. When one gets tarnished, even unjustly, his or her work may continue to be used as ammunition, but not as analysis. This creates a danger for others in the organization. Therefore, when one of its analysts' work is questioned, as Kumins's was in 1975, an agency concerned about how its material is received might be expected to protect itself by transferring the analyst to another subject where he or she would be less controversial. But that is not as easy to do as it sounds. Whenever an analyst's work becomes controversial, it is because it deals with an issue that divides the members. For every member upset, another will be pleased. The support agencies are in no position to take people away from a subject when powerful members specifically request their work.

They can limit the organizational damage in other ways, however. A long CRS study on energy done for Jackson by CRS contained a section on natural gas costs by Herman Franssen that disassociated itself from Kumins's conclusions. Kumins was cited as only one analyst among several and one of the more serious criticisms of his work (the failure to account for the cost of replacement fuels) was acknowledged. Franssen concluded that "not enough is known about the price elasticity of natural gas supply to support either the claims of much of the industrial sector that price elasticity is high, nor is there enough evidence to claim the opposite."[38]

For Deregulation: Brown-Stockman

The quantitative studies favoring deregulation were no less problematic than those on the administration's side of the debate. They were intended primarily as ammunition to combat those who were similarly armed on the other side. Still, if read carefully, they may serve to sharpen our understanding of the dispute.

The study done by Representative Stockman for himself and Representative Brown was the most widely used study on the deregulation side of the House debate. In an interview, Stockman was candid about why he did the study:

> I started to look at the administration's numbers and realized how phony they were and that motivated me to a counterstudy. It seemed better to have a study of our own instead of just taking pot shots at theirs.
>
> We only had about one and a half or two weeks before markup to do the job, so there was no time to farm it out. I basically did it at my desk with my hand calculator.

Since the purpose of the study was admittedly partisan, it is not surprising that it did no better than its opposition at examining its own assumptions. The crucial first assumption for Stockman, as for everyone else, concerned the amount of gas that would be produced under deregulation. Instead of attempting to assess the supplies on his own, Stockman simply assumed that the quantitative elasticity index the administration used for prices of $1.45 to $1.75 would apply for prices above that as well. The assumption was made with literally no analysis of the underlying geology. Stockman might as well have been analyzing soy beans or any other commodity whose supplies are not strongly limited by physical constraints. As was true for the administration, Schroeder, and the CBO, everything else in Stockman's analysis followed from these basic assumptions about the supply elasticity of the resource base.

Representatives Stockman and Brown predicted that 207.4 Tcf of natural gas would be produced from 1978 through 1990 if present policies were to remain unchanged, 214.0 Tcf if the House (administration) bill was passed and 238.8 Tcf if new gas prices were deregulated. The cumulative wellhead cost of the gas through 1990 would

226

Policy Analysis and Natural Gas Deregulation

be $207.0 billion under the *status quo*, $249.7 billion under the House bill, and $414.2 billion under deregulation. But for Stockman this was only the beginning of the analysis. Instead of concluding that this difference of $164.5 billion between the House bill and deregulation would be the "cost" of deregulation through 1990, he added all of the indirect costs of regulation coming from lower supplies before totaling the bill. The result was dramatic. Instead of deregulation costing $164.5 billion, Stockman's study concluded it would save $47.2 billion—more than a $200 billion turnaround!

The elements that went into this accounting were almost mirror images of the ones that went into the studies on the other side. For example, the price of deregulated new gas was figured at $2.50 in 1978, rising gradually to $2.99 (in constant 1975 dollars) by 1990. Stockman rejected Schroeder's argument that new gas prices would shoot well above $2.50, asserting that the new gas would get tied up in long-term contracts at lower rates.

On the benefit side of the equation, Stockman estimated that production under deregulation would exceed production under the House bill by about 2 Tcf per year in the early 1980s and 3 Tcf in the late 1980s. This would be enough of a difference to affect residential users, for whom the substitute fuels are not oil, selling at $2.50 per million BTUs, but liquid natural gas, synthetic natural gas, and electricity, the average cost of which was figured at approximately $6 per million BTUs. The savings to those who would not have to buy substitute fuels Stockman calculated to be $168 billion. The rest of the savings came from transportation costs: if pipelines carry more gas, their fixed costs can be spread over more units, resulting in lower transportation costs for the end users. This would amount to a $44.2 billion savings from 1978 through 1990. Taken together, transportation and replacement fuel savings more than wipe out the extra wellhead cost of new gas, given Stockman's assumed wellhead price.

It is obvious that Stockman's elasticity assumption was the driving force behind his other numbers. When he was asked where his assumptions came from, Stockman admitted that he had no idea what the production levels would be under either proposal. "I do happen to know some geology and I believe there are enormous supplies out there," Stockman said. Even if there were not, his views about economics convinced him that continued regulation would mean steadily decreasing supplies and that, therefore, deregulation would be the best approach whatever the absolute production levels.

> I don't really know how much conventional natural gas will come from deregulation, but I do know deregulation will give us a more sensible price structure. If supplies are low, prices will go up and people will switch to more plentiful fuels. From my point of view, I think the economic price structure is just as important as the incremental supplies we might get if we deregulate. The problem is that when we debate natural gas in the Energy and Power Subcommittee, we debate gas in isolation from other fuels or other segments of the economy. The legislative process inevitably separates systemic variables into isolated ones and whenever that happens, the debate will be phony.

Despite those views, Stockman felt the political realities required a counterstudy treating gas as an isolated variable. So, he produced one. To do it he had to assume his conclusions about gas supplies, just as his opponents did. Like his opponents, his views about other matters convinced him his assumptions were right. But the "other matters," it will become evident, were really what the debate was about.

For Deregulation: Erickson

All of the other studies used on the deregulation side of the debate essentially were variations on the themes in the Stockman-Brown analysis. The study used most often in the Senate debate was done by Edward W. Erickson, professor of economics and business at North Carolina State University in Raleigh. It was commissioned by the Natural Gas Supply Committee, an industry trade association, and published in September, the same month the bill came up on the Senate floor.[39] Since it was produced outside Congress, it will be treated only briefly here.

Erickson said the net savings from deregulation would be $123.3 billion through 1990, instead of the $47.2 billion Stockman predicted. Furthermore, Erickson included no transportation savings from increased pipeline use in his study; his savings all came from the avoidance of expensive replacement fuels. The crucial difference between Erickson's views and Stockman's (or anyone else's) involved his supply assumptions. Erickson's model assumed that the administration bill would depress production levels to 15 Tcf per year for 1985–1990, whereas deregulation would increase production to 20 Tcf per year over the same period.

Senators who cited Erickson's study in debate used it in the same way they used the other studies: they looked for the "bottom line" number in the report ($123.3 billion) and cited it without qualification. No one quoted or even seemed to have noticed these sentences: "Too much emphasis should not be placed upon the apparent numerical precision associated with the output of a computer model. A common sense evaluation of the result is most appropriate."[40] The study also warned the reader, "It is critical that the judgment basis of the Benefit Cost Estimation Model be clearly understood. The Natural Gas Supply Committee does not pretend to have a computer model which will predict to the nearest tenth of a Tcf the quantities of natural gas forthcoming under alternative pricing policies."[41]

When asked how his committee concluded that about 20 Tcf would be produced under deregulation, Executive Vice-President David H. Foster said it was based on an informed, intuitive judgment based on conversations with people from five of the largest gas producing companies. Erickson confirmed this, saying that the assumption was "casual, not systematic, but thought out." "What we did," Erickson said, "was ask, 'Suppose we could go back to 20 Tcf, what would the effect on the economy be?' Maybe we won't get back to 20 Tcf but if not, whatever causes an erosion under 20 Tcf would bring about a similar erosion under the Administration bill." Asked how he arrived at 15 Tcf for the administration bill, and thus a 5 Tcf gap between that bill and deregulation, Erickson said it was based on his view that deregulation would create more incentives than present policy, whereas the administration bill would be a rollback. Thus, Erickson's methodology and quantitative supply conclusions about the effect of deregulation essentially paralleled the CBO's. The difference between them lay in their analyses of the Administration bill. Needless to say, none of the senators citing either of these studies brought this out in the Senate debate.

The Real Issues

It should be fairly clear by now that all of the supposedly precise numbers on both sides of the deregulation debate rested on intuitive assumptions about production from which everything else followed. Harrison (Jack) Schmitt (R-N. M.), the Harvard Ph.D. geologist-astronaut-turned-freshman senator, was one of the very few members of Congress to address this point. Schmitt noted in Senate debate[42] that natural gas resources, considered apart from the economics of production, exist in quantities that for practical purposes can be considered infinite. (This point is *not* in dispute.[43]) Whether these physical resources are turned into recoverable reserves will depend upon four factors, Schmitt argued: price, technology, geology, and the availability of risk capital. The response of supply to price depends at any given time on each of the other three factors. "The fact is that we do not really know what happens to the supply curve above $1.45 mcf," Schmitt said.[44]

The world, in other words, is an uncertain place. One example can be used to illustrate this point. In the early 1970s, the federal government sold an extraordinarily expensive lease in the Gulf of Mexico to a joint venture that included some of the world's largest oil companies. The companies were eager to go to work because all of the available geophysical data suggested this might be one of the biggest finds in the history of the country. The result: eleven dry holes and a loss of about a quarter of a billion dollars.

This costly failure should serve as a warning to people who treat even well-informed guesses about the earth's subsurface resources as anything other than guesses. If one example does not make this point, anyone in the petroleum industry can recount stories of companies giving up on an area after drilling thousands of feet only to have a competitor move in, drill a little deeper, and make a find. (This is how Occidental Petroleum's huge Libyan oil discoveries of the 1960s were made.)

When one considers that estimates of the world's potential resources are based on information no better than what was available to the oil companies, it becomes clear that all estimates are probabilistic at best. Projecting the estimates into a future with changing economic conditions, unknown technologies, and an uncertain international climate is even more problematic. Yet, all econometric studies must do precisely this before they can begin.

None of this settles the deregulation argument, but it does transform it. The real debate over production turns out to be far less precise than the quantitative estimates out to decimal points seem to suggest. It is, instead, a debate between those on one side, who are optimistic about what is economically recoverable under foreseeable technologies, and those on the other, who are pessimistic.

With the issue thus transformed, one is freed from the tyranny of numbers and can begin seeing the other political assumptions that went into the econometric models. For example, the models all focused on the consumer costs of deregulation to consumers (or on the revenues it would bring producers) with disagreements over how to define and quantify those costs or benefits. Any study that looks at consumer costs obviously does so because the person asking for the study thinks that issue important. In this case, James Schlesinger made it clear in the testimony cited earlier that the administration's main, indeed sole, reason for keeping regulation was because it thought it would be *unjust* to make consumers transfer huge amounts of money to producers while getting little in return. This same concern has motivated all the studies commissioned by liberal Democrats since 1975. Those favoring deregulation were left in a defensive posture on the question—always reacting, always working on "counterstudies"—because they did not share the same ideas about justice. Representative Stockman voiced this alternative view of justice when he said that if production were going to decline, the modest aim of federal policy should be to let the market encourage conservation and a smooth transfer to other fuels by forcing consumers to face the real cost of energy.[45]

A second crucial set of political assumptions underlay all of the econometric studies. Whether optimistic or pessimistic in their supply estimates, the models all assumed a free market. Those who think the gas industry is not competitive (primarily liberal Democrats) thus were operating from a premise inconsistent with the models, even though they probably cited the models' quantitative conclusions more often than any other single voting bloc. And the political implications of assuming a free market were vitally important to the deregulation side of the debate: if the natural gas industry is an oligopoly in which a few companies can collude to withhold supplies from the market, all predictions about deregulation resulting in greater production might have to be thrown out the window.

The assumption of a free market also involved less obvious under-lying political assumptions. First, all of the arguments for deregula-tion assumed that selling gas at the market clearing price would produce incentives for reinvestment in gas exploration, but the deregulation bills offered did not require companies to reinvest, and producers in the past had refused to commit themselves to reinvest-ment in return for higher prices. Second, the market clearing price for natural gas was assumed to be the BTU equivalent price of No. 2 oil. This price was set only in part by market forces and partly by the actions of an international cartel. Those advocating deregulation argue that the cartel's oil prices are so high that letting gas sell at the price of oil will produce enough of an incentive for exploration. They may be right, but the economic assumption rests in turn on four political ones: (1) that the United States will not use military force or vigorous economic measures to force a break in the cartel's price; (2) that the cartel will not revise its prices sharply downward; (3) that a major new producer will not come along (for instance, Mexico) and refuse to join the cartel; and (4) that political instability in the oil-producing states will not blow the cartel apart in a way that ends up reducing prices. (Instability would be more likely to increase prices, of course, but a scenario involving price cuts is not impossible.)

Thus, the models all had to assume answers to questions that were really ones of geology, international relations, antitrust law, and po-litical philosophy. I would maintain that if members had understood, debated, and at least tentatively answered all of those questions, they would have had all they needed to decide how to vote—without the models. The models may have added some new information to the debate, but it came with a heavy price: the imposingly technical material flooded the system, intimidated the members, and beguiled them away from debating some important matters they had consid-ered in greater detail two decades before.

The Limitations of Policy Analysis

It seems unlikely that this conclusion applies only to natural gas deregulation. In fact, I would submit that the enterprise of analyzing policy *at its heart* is the art of asking the right questions, and that framing questions always embodies assumptions that limit political choices. On this level, the essence of policy analysis—not its tools, but its essence—is identical to the art of the politician.

This observation is not an argument against the political use of economics, econometrics, or cost-benefit analysis. It *is* an argument against using them to answer questions outside their competence. It is also an argument against letting "policy analysts," or their politician-employers, claim that political questions can be reduced to technical ones. Only after the political questions are resolved, or at least exposed and held constant for the sake of analysis, can policy analysis then help politicians evaluate programs.

This brings us back to the original questions: Of what use were the natural gas studies and to what use were they put? To answer this accurately, we first must specify the context. Schroeder's model helped members in conference compare the relative (not the absolute) costs of various compromise possibilities. Neither his nor any other model, however, led the members to address the assumptions that underlay the political choice between regulation and deregulation. As a result, the members misused the studies in two different ways. Some were cynically playing to the press galleries, throwing numbers around but making up their minds on other grounds. Others looked sincerely to the models for answers. Those members who honestly relied on the quantitative studies were misleading themselves, while those who used them cynically were misleading the public. In neither case did the massive staff effort behind the studies serve to clarify the real issues.

Why then did the representatives and senators use the studies as heavily as they did? Part of it was public relations, but there were two deeper reasons as well. First, some members hid behind the studies: even though they may have made their decisions on other grounds, they felt more comfortable knowing that if something should go wrong, they would be able to say they simply went along with the experts. In this respect, the political use of studies on Capitol Hill is no different from their use anywhere else in government or business.

The second reason is evident from something Representative Stockman said. Asked by this author why he and other members preferred debating the quantitative conclusions of opposed econometric studies to debating the basic assumptions that went into them, Stockman answered:

> Nobody wants to say it's all based on a basic value. My position is that
> the free market does work, but that is a pretty thin fig leaf for something
> as important as this.

A fig leaf! Members of Congress apparently are ashamed to discuss public issues without hiding behind the numbers provided by
economists. In a post-Weberian world, where "facts" and "values"
are thought to have distinct cognitive foundations, politicians are
embarrassed about basing political choices on principles of justice
or "basic values." Or, they are ashamed to acknowledge it when
they debate the issues in public. What the staffs did for Congress
in this case, therefore, was to cover the fig leaf with the em-
peror's new clothes.

This conclusion surely is not limited to the natural gas controversy.
The natural gas analyses seem more complex, in principle, than ones
evaluating military hardware, and less complex than the seemingly
infinite circularities of budgeting considered in chapter 8. In all
cases, however, members of Congress seem to prefer using the new
quantitative rhetoric of social science to discussing the unquantifia-
ble but more informative assumptions on which the numbers rest. If
members are to get anything useful from quantitative analysis, however, they have to be in a position to uncover, compare, and evaluate
these assumptions. However, even if a few members have the pa-
tience and skill to do this, none has the time. As is true in so many
of the ways Congress uses its staff, the members want people to do
work they do not have the time to do themselves. But once the work
is done, it creates more work the members do not have time to do.
Staff analysis does free Congress from its dependency on the administration's or other outsiders' conclusions, but it fails in its more basic
task of informing deliberation.

Is there a way out of this dilemma? I believe there is, in principle,
but implementing it would be extremely difficult. In principle, members should direct analysts to provide clear statements of their assumptions at the beginning of their reports. These statements should
not be mere lists, or else members will assume—as Senator Jackson
and others did in debate—that all assumptions sound equally valid,
and they are incapable of debating the alternatives rationally. This
attitude, shared widely among elected officials, is flatly wrong. Members often are in a *better* position to debate and then choose among

the assumptions than analysts are.* What the members cannot do is tell what quantitative results flow from a given set of assumptions. Therefore, the most important service an analyst can render would be an elaboration of each assumption underlying a quantitative conclusion, together with a discussion of the competing assumptions considered by the analyst and the arguments for (and against) preferring the assumption over its competitors.

Unfortunately, there are two practical impediments to achieving this goal. First, members may hesitate to debate assumptions for political reasons. Second, very few analysts are capable of identifying all their assumptions, let alone articulating them clearly to their political superiors. This weakness, particularly apparent in the way analysts treat their assumptions about what is just or equitable, is a direct result of their education. They are trained, in economics and policy evaluation courses, to churn out endless tables about the "equity impact" of a given policy choice. By "equity impact," the analysts mean, with only rare exceptions, the way a given program distributes benefits and costs to the poor, the middle class, and the rich. Certainly this is one important consideration in determining the justice or equity of a particular proposal. It may not be the only one, however, as the underlying disagreement between Schlesinger and Stockman should have made clear. Whether it should be the dominant factor in any particular instance is something politicians should debate, not let the analysts assume. Most analysts, however, are incapable of presenting that sort of issue in a form that permits deliberation. If one argues that equity or justice may be more than a question of distribution, they shrug off the statement as a "value preference," a prejudice not subject to rational deliberation. All values are perceived ultimately as fig leaves, and the only thing left for members to debate are the numbers. Never mind that the premise forcing the debate into the realm of numbers leaves the numbers themselves on a foundation of quicksand. The numbers sound more solid and, therefore, if not questioned too closely, seem more persuasive.

---

*This arguably may not be true of budgeting, but the complexities of budgeting are unusual.

Conclusion

This brings us back to a consideration of the relative utility of professional staff analysts and nonpartisans of the type found on the Joint Committee on Taxation. Congress seems to have gotten strong and weak analyses of natural gas questions from both partisan and nonpartisan sources. There are people with axes to grind in the nonpartisan support agencies and there are competent professionals working for subcommittees whose staffs are wholly under their chairman's control. The odds that one will get an analyst who at least tries to be unbiased may be better in a support agency than a subcommittee, but the members understandably are leery of relying on odds when they have to make politically tough choices. Even the best of the analyses from CBO or GAO do not seem to explain themselves in a way that will be most helpful to the members. Nor can members rely on personal staff legislative aides to bare the analytic assumptions for them. These staffs—busy with other things and not hired for their substantive expertise—are simply not up to the task.

This is where the kind of work done by the Joint Committee on Taxation becomes most useful. As a staff with expertise that refuses to do substantive policy analysis, the Joint Committee on Taxation does not supply everything the members need. But by its very reticence, it enhances its credibility as a staff that can lay out competing assumptions, without prejudice, in a way that members can understand. In principle, there is no reason why this job could not be done by the professional policy analyst. In practice, however, the analyst tends to be hired precisely because he or she is a professional committed to one or another set of professional assumptions. In a less than perfect world, therefore, it probably makes sense to separate the tasks and give at least one set of professionals some institutional and career incentives for remaining above the battle.

PART 4

Conclusion

Chapter 10

Congressional Staffs and the Future of Representative Government

WHAT can we conclude from all this? Has the staff explosion of the past three decades helped or hurt Congress? We grant without question that senators and representatives are better able to do their own jobs as individuals by having professional legislative staffs accountable directly to them. But our question, as we have pointed out many times, is an institutional one: how well does the system that helps the members as individuals serve the legislative branch as a whole?

Our previous chapters have shown that the answer to this question is not the same at every point of the legislative process. If we take Congress's workload as given and focus on negotiations, we see that the staffs, acting as surrogates for their "bosses," do as creditable a job of representing their interests as any attorney would for a client in a parallel situation outside Congress. With loyal surrogate-lawyers carrying out their wishes, the members are able to follow more issues than they could if they had to attend all meetings personally. Institutionally, this means that both the members as individuals and Congress as a whole are able to manage a heavier workload with the staffs than would be possible without them. To some extent, therefore, the staffs do seem to help Congress do its work.

But, as we have seen, the surrogate-lawyers are generally expected to be more than just passive representatives of their clients: they are also expected to go out and drum up new business. The increased use of personalized, entrepreneurial staffs has helped Congress retain its position as a key initiator of federal policy, despite the growing power of the executive branch. The relationship between this use of entrepreneurial staff and Congress's power seems almost obvious. Most other national legislatures do not give individual members similar staff resources; most legislatures depend on their cabinets for almost all policy initiatives. Congress is not so passive today, thanks largely to its staff.

The system of individualized staff control seems also to be responsible for much of the oversight that gets accomplished outside of the General Accounting Office. Having a substantial number of staff people with appropriate investigative authority seems a necessary condition for congressional oversight of the executive branch and the independent regulatory commissions. But it is not a sufficient condition. Oversight also depends on chairmen and staffs who consider the effort worthwhile. For some reason, collegial nonpartisan committee staffs have not provided much oversight. Perhaps it is because their accessibility to all members of a committee leaves them with little time for anything else; perhaps because committees that are willing to retain nonpartisan staffs try to restrain their partisanship and maintain close relationships with their counterparts in the executive branch. Thus, the movement away from a system of collegial nonpartisan committee staffing to a more personalized one has been associated with an increase in congressional oversight activity, largely because a personalized system lets chairmen have activist staff entrepreneurs, and chairmen who use entrepreneurial staffs tend to be more interested in maintaining their independence from the executive branch.

Yet, while the growth and use of staff has produced these beneficial results, there is a gloomier side: the effect of staffs on Congress' ability to act as a deliberative body. To see the importance of this issue, we need to consider some of the basic functions Congress was meant to perform in our constitutional scheme of government. Congress, we learn from *Federalist* No. 52, was meant to serve as a substitute for direct meetings of the citizens.[1] Direct meetings are physically impossible in a large commercial republic, and such a republic—James Madison argued in *Federalist* No. 10—was the best mechanism consistent with democratic principles for guarding against a tyranny by a majority faction. Increase the nation's size and complexity sufficiently and you make it all but impossible for a single interest to dominate, for it must be subjected to a process of accomodation, moderation, and compromise with the interests of others.

But the physical impossibility of direct democracy in a large republic was not the only reason for preferring a representative system. We can easily imagine how to overcome the physical problems by using modern communications. Even so, the framers of the Constitution would not have thought modern technology an acceptable substitute for a system of representation. Representation was likely to produce not only a more manageable process than direct democracy, but better results. A representative system would require elected members from one district, with one set of needs and interests, to talk to members from districts with different needs and interests, if the members hoped to achieve anything.[2] Indirect communication, such as we see today, was not what was envisioned: direct communication among elected members was considered essential to informed deliberation.

Why are direct conversations important? Why is it not sufficient for members to rely on indirect staff mediation and communication by memorandum? The reason is that while indirect communications can convey a great deal of information, it cannot help a member *feel* or *sense* his colleagues' reactions to his own or each other's arguments. To use an example from an earlier chapter (chapter 9), information about who would bear the cost of national gas deregulation is something staff could convey in principle—as long as we bear in mind all the caveats from earlier chapters about the information gaps that inevitably develop in an overloaded system. But only the members can decide who *ought* to bear what cost. When people's views about the justice or equity of an issue differ—as they did on natural gas and almost always do on other controversial legislative issues— the apparent persuasiveness of an argument becomes crucial. For one thing, members need information about each other for tactical reasons, to help them achieve what they want. Less obviously a member's decision about whether to support a bill may be affected by his colleagues' reactions. In a democratic government based on the acceptance and presumed trust of the people, whether a program (or the rhetoric used to support a program) induces massive resentment, passive acceptance, or warm endorsement may be every bit as important as any of its other effects.

Direct conversations among the members are so important to the legislative process that facilitating them had been, until recent years, a primary objective behind many of Congress's otherwise incomprehensible procedures. Most people are inclined to avoid conversing or debating with people with whom they disagree. One of the most important strengths of Congress has been the way its structure has encouraged people to engage in a process that most people naturally prefer to avoid. While party discipline has tended to stifle this process in other countries, Congress's procedures have been designed to encourage, inform, and structure communication among the members in ways that both promote deliberation and discourage long-standing resentments. That was the real reason for allowing closed committee meetings[3] and for the elaborate rules of personal courtesy governing debate.[4] In recent years, however, the members have weakened the procedures designed to protect their ability to debate and deliberate freely. Debate and discussion have lost their central place in the legislative process and that loss has produced serious consequences. The growing importance of staff is but one reflection of the new situation.

For a process of legislative deliberation to function reasonably well, at least three distinct requirements must be satisfied. The members need accurate information, they need time to think about that information, and they need to talk to each other about the factual, political, and moral implications of the policies they are considering. The new use of staff undercuts each of these.

The first, and simplest way relates to the flow of information. We saw in our chapters on oversight (chapters 6 and 7) that the growing dominance of large "chairmen's staffs" has produced management problems that result in uncertainties in the flow of information from staffs to chairmen and from chairmen to others in the Senate or House. Most of the information reaching members may well be reliable, but it would take an expert to sort out the reliable from the unreliable, and even an expert cannot possibly know about material that has been stifled to serve a staff's or chairman's own interests.

This problem is probably the easiest of the three major problems associated with the growing role of staff to resolve in principle. If every committee had a nonpartisan professional staff core, there would be fewer occasions on which Congress would receive intentionally partial or distorted information from its staff. To the extent that nonpartisan professional staffs are inadequate in providing all that Congress asks of its staff, Representative Ullman's solution on the House Ways and Means Committee has much to recommend it. Let every committee have a dual staff: a nonpartisan professional core to do the kind of work done by the staff of the Joint Committee on Taxation and a personalized chairman's (or ranking minority member's or junior member's) staff to be more entrepreneurial, investigative, or political.

Still, this does not seem to get at the heart of the issue. Improving the accuracy of the information flow would not, for example, have created more time for the members to wade through the kind of complex material they were given on natural gas deregulation. The reason members rely on staffs to do their negotiating, and the reason they are not able to be critical consumers of the information they receive, is that they have more to do than time in which to do it. The second problem with the use of staff, therefore, is that it has not left the members with more time to concentrate on their legislative work. If anything, the use of entrepreneurial staffs has meant an increase in the numbers of hearings and amendments considered every year.*

One by-product of this indicates the net effect on congressional life: while representatives as recently as 1965 spent almost one full day every week on "legislative research and reading,"[5] by 1977 the time spent on reading was down to an average of eleven minutes per day.[6] In other words, instead of freeing the members to concentrate, the staffs contribute to the frenetic pace of congressional life that pulls members in different directions, reduces the time available for joint deliberation, and makes concentration all but impossible. With the pressure of business thus created, it should be no surprise that members are beguiled into looking at issues as technical problems instead of political ones. Overburdened and somewhat intimidated by the material the "experts" throw at them, they are delighted when issues can be resolved in apparently noncontroversial, techno-

---

*The data on Congress's workload over the past three decades show that Congress is spending more hours in session, holding more committee and subcommittee meetings, and taking more recorded votes while passing fewer public bills of somewhat greater than average length. Thus, the work *product* of Congress is not going up; only the workload. For details, see appendix A–8.

cratic terms. The situation feeds on itself. The members need staff because they have so little time to concentrate, but the new work created by the staff takes even more of the members' time, indirectly elevating the power of the Washington issue networks in which the staffs play so prominent a role.

About the only way Congress could improve this part of its present condition would be to reduce its agenda systematically and substantially. However, this solution raises further problems—one practical and the other more basic. The practical problem is that Congress's fractionalized workload results partly from recent procedural reforms that strengthen the subcommittees and partly from the advantages that entrepreneurial staffs bring to chairmen and other members who seek to gain credit for new policy initiatives. If a majority of the members were willing to forsake their political self-interest to give the parties or other bodies in Congress the authority to limit the agenda, it would not be difficult to implement that decision. But it is difficult now to imagine members voluntarily giving up control over the agenda, when they fought so hard to get that control less than a decade ago.

More fundamentally, it is not even clear that a reduced congressional agenda would be desirable under present circumstances. The reason for reducing the agenda, we should remember, would be to improve Congress's ability to deliberate and thereby make it able to function better as a body that represents the needs of all the people. It is true that reducing the legislative agenda would probably improve deliberations on the items that remain, but it would hardly improve the representative character of the government as a whole. If one accepts the present role of government, reducing Congress's agenda would simply let more of what happens in the other branches go without congressional review. As an answer to a problem of democratic representation, that cure seems worse than the disease. But whether desirable or not, it may not even be possible to reduce Congress's agenda substantially, given the present role of government. The bureaucracy finds itself compelled repeatedly to come back to Congress to clarify vague delegations of authority from the legislative branch—delegations that generally are vague because specificity might have endangered the chances for getting anything through Congress. But even if Congress managed to delegate with perfect clarity, the bureaucracy would have an interest in coming back repeatedly to protect or expand its role.

Congressional Staffs

Congress, in other words, would have a hard time ducking out of much of its workload without taking the unlikely step of dealing with that workload's root sources. About the only way to reduce Congress's workload without vastly increasing the discretionary power of the less representative branches of the government would seem to be to reduce the size and complexity of government as a whole. However, the size of the bureaucracy is itself only an intermediate reason for the size of Congress's agenda. The growth of government has come about partly because the nation has become more complex, but even more, as James Q. Wilson has pointed out, because people have changed their ideas about what government should do.[7] People in government have *chosen* to respond to more of the demands being made upon them, and these responses in turn have generated more demands. In fact, elected officials, their staffs, and bureaucrats often do not even wait for someone to articulate a demand before they get to work on the response: given the chance, they look for problems to solve, encouraging demand as much as responding to it (see chapter 3 for examples).

Thus, there is a connection between the world of ideas, the size of the government's agenda, and the way Congress does its work. That connection helps us understand the third, and most basic, problem with the new role of congressional staff—the use of staff negotiations as a substitute for direct conversation and deliberation among the members. Direct conversations and deliberation still take place, of course.[8] But there can be no question that in recent decades there has been an increase in indirect negotiation and a decrease in direct deliberation.[9] This should come as no surprise. After all, that is precisely what members expect most of the committee staffs and legislative aides to be doing. The staff of the Joint Committee on Taxation does mediate and supply information without negotiating, but few others limit themselves in this way. To the extent, therefore, that the legislative process would be improved by retaining some sort of a significant staffing system while increasing the emphasis on direct deliberation, it would be yet another reason for Congress to try to use this staff as a model for other committees. (Unfortunately, as we mentioned in chapter 8 on nonpartisan staffing, the political conditions for achieving this are rarely present today.)

Perhaps the importance of deliberation can be put in clearer focus by distinguishing deliberation from negotiation. Negotiation and deliberation are related activities, but there is a fundamental difference between them that generally is lost in contemporary figures of speech. One useful way to get at that difference might be to begin with Henry Kissinger's *White House Years,* [10] in which he argued that presidents should not negotiate personally with other heads of state. Some congressional staff people have suggested privately to me that they wish their bosses would follow this advice. Their comments reveal that they fail to comprehend the nature of their bosses' work.

What makes a senator or representative different from a president in this regard? First, the president, as the only chief executive, obviously has to delegate the task of detailed negotiation to others because the breadth of his duties makes it impossible for him to do anything more than set broad policy guidelines on most of the matters for which he is responsible. Members of Congress face a similar problem keeping up with details, of course, but Congress can resolve that difficulty by delegating responsibility to elected colleagues who act as committee specialists.

The second, and more important, difference is the one that helps us understand the distinction between negotiation and deliberation. Negotiation involves discussion in which each party is trying to achieve the best deal for his own side. When the president negotiates with another head of state, he represents the whole nation in his own person. There is no distinction between the "side" that the president represents and the interests of the nation. Therefore, the national interest generally is best served when the chief executive does not expose himself to the danger of face to face negotiations in which he may inadvertently bargain away more than is necessary.

Negotiations designed to achieve the best deal for one's "side" also take place in Congress—logrolling is one classic form—and as we have shown, staffs are just as able to handle this task as a lawyer who represents a private client's self-interest or a diplomat who represents the president. But deliberation, even if it may grow out of negotiation, is a different activity in which the aim is to arrive at a decision as to the common good. In contrast with the situation when two heads of state are involved, members of Congress each represent a part of the nation's interest, while the whole nation's interest requires interaction between the people representing its parts. It is true that a member may end up inadvertently giving away more of his own or his district's interests in direct conversation with a colleague than he might in staff negotiations. But if he should, the worst that would happen would be that another member, representing another part of the nation, would end up with more of what he wanted. In the best of circumstances, the direct confrontation between two elected people—each with his own political instincts and constituencies, and each starting from his own interests—will transform initial perceptions and desires into a more "enlightened self-interest" as the members become more informed through their deliberations.

It is important to point out that, while a process of deliberation may have the national interest as its end, it does not require legislators to begin by thinking in terms of general principles. (If anything, debate that concentrates excessively on all-inclusive principles poses the very dangers of faction Madison most wanted to avoid.) As Richard Fenno has observed, members of Congress:

> . . . are inductive thinkers. That is to say, they start with specific instances—very frequently constituency-related instances—to get a handle on what is going on. . . .
>
> The notion that oftentimes is conveyed—that somehow or other legislators ought to deal in broad policy and leave the details to the civil servants—robs the legislator of precisely what he does best in the process of scrutiny, which is to grasp some detail and work out from there.[11]

The deliberative process is not well served when members of Congress avoid what they do best. On the contrary, it is helped when they use their concrete knowledge about the specific impact of a program to help them see what the general words of a statute or regulation mean in practice. The deliberative process does not require the members to avoid thinking about their own or their districts' interests; on the contrary, it requires different members informing each other about their separate districts and then working out something that seems to make practical sense.

This inductive deliberative process gets short circuited when Congress relies on staff-to-staff negotiations. Instead of judgments made by politicians in light of their experience, we see members relying on staff technocrats whose self-interest is not the same as their bosses', and whose knowledge of the world is limited to what they learned in school or from other participants in the specialized Washington issue networks. Instead of politicians thinking about the detailed practical impact of the programs they are about to pass, we see politicians taking general positions, leaving the details to staff, claiming credit, and learning about the impact afterwards from their constituents. No wonder we see such public cynicism about the government's competence. Instead of thrashing it all out before the fact, the members too often do not know enough of the details they would need to deliberate until after a program is implemented. By then, the program will have developed a constituency of its own that will resist the changes that could more easily have been demanded in advance.

We have been talking so far about the ways in which the use of staff has affected Congress procedurally. Has there also been a discernible effect on the sutstance of public policy? Staffs clearly do influence policy in thousands of little ways in any given year, as we saw in our three chapters tracing the path of a bill through Congress (chapters 3, 4, and 5). But has the dependence on staff had any *systematic* impacts on policy? Our answers here must be more tentative than they were for procedural matters, but at least two kinds of effects suggest themselves—one relating to the role of the Washington issue networks, and a second relating to the naturally narrow focus and inertia of staff negotiations.

The most direct impact of the role of staff has to do with the reception Congress gives the ideas put forward by groups or individuals that have no identifiable constituency, such as some of the smaller issue groups on the right and left, academicians, and issue specialists in think tanks and consulting firms. Senators and representatives are too busy to see every lobbyist who comes their way and must depend on their staffs to screen them. Organizations and individuals with real political or economic power have little difficulty getting in the door to make their case, but people who have nothing to offer but their ideas have a tougher time. If it were not for the staffs, the latter could easily be frozen out, given the members' limited time for sifting worthwhile ideas from worthless ones. The staffs give these people their chance. But the staffs generally do not go out actively to seek the broadest range of opinion on the subjects within their responsibility. Rather, like members, they tend either to rely on friends and acquaintances or wait passively for people to make themselves known to them. Thus the staffs, like the members, tend to favor people from organizations that have the staff resources to keep up with issues as they develop. However, since the staff people are not themselves elected, and since their future careers in the Washington community often depend on their gaining reputations as innovators, it is to their interest to spend time listening to people whose ideas may help them put something new on the oversight or legislative agenda, even if those people have no political constituencies of their own. The interwoven interests of the participants in the various issue networks lead them to work together to identify problems they can then use their expertise to solve. The future interests of the staff flow directly from the changes in career patterns that we discussed earlier, in which staff jobs are stepping stones for ambitious young lawyers instead of places where mid-level bureaucrats and political cronies end their careers.

The tendency of the staffs' future career interests to enhance the power of experts without constituencies is reinforced by the staffers' backgrounds. The new staffs tend to be young lawyers who came to Washington because they had been political activists and wanted to "make a mark" on "the system." In addition, their undergraduate and law school training has tended to make them more sympathetic to arguments based on general ideological principles (from the left for Democratic aides and from the right for Republicans) than either their classmates with "real jobs" or the elected members. They thus tend to draw members toward precisely what Fenno said members do least well. The technocratic and ideological staffers may be distinct (such as the technocratic Schroeder, chapter 9, and ideological Sroka, chapter 5) or the same staff person may embrace both attitudes (such as Lemov, chapter 7). Moreover, both may work side by side with other staff people whose legal specialization and future ambitions tie them more closely to traditional economic interests (such as Demarest, chapter 6), or whose past experience and background similarly lead them to act as interest group advocates (such as Cherkasky, chapter 3). But major corporate, trade association, and labor union interests would have little difficulty being heard in a Washington that had no staffs, nor would an issue-based organization that had developed a deliverable political constituency. Where the staffs make a difference, therefore, is in their openness to, career interest in, and institutional need for ideas and slogans whose main political support initially comes only from the fact that staff people and journalists are interested in listening to them.

While the first systematic substantive impact of staff on policy comes out of its entrepreneurial role, the second comes from its role in negotiations. Both have the net effect of increasing the amount of legislation that gets passed and the kinds of interests served by that legislation. The job of a staff negotiator is to help move the process ahead toward a resolution. While a member may pull him back, it almost always is in the interest of the staff negotiator to see a set of negotiations through to a successful conclusion. This is particularly true if the program contains some section the staff member can think of as his own. The program—or the planned hearing, if the person is an investigator—may represent a major investment of time for a staff person whose future may depend on gaining recognition in Washington for having made a difference. As a result, the process of staff negotiation tends to lend practical weight to the view that the purpose of the legislative process is to fashion agreements behind which the greatest number of self-appointed interested parties can unite.[12] The impetus of staff, in other words, is to build coalitions by having programs respond, at least symbolically, to more demands, rather than let them die their natural death. The result is increasingly inclusive, increasingly complex legislation that can only be understood by an expert. Needless to say, this increases the power of permanent Washingtonians with the necessary expertise, such as former staffers.

In the course of building the coalitions just described, programs are considered in isolation from each other. It is not normally in the interest of staff to question how a program affects the budget, the overall structure of government, or the ability of citizens to understand what their government is doing. Of course, members themselves have this same inclination to see programs in isolation from each other. If they did not, they would scarcely tolerate the way staffs negotiate in their name. But a member who serves on several different committees, directly communicates with constituents, and sits down with other members to share the results of their composite experiences, is far more likely than an aide to have a basis for getting beyond the inclinations to think about the relationships between policies in ways that cross lines of issue specialization.

It should be obvious by now that one cannot fully discuss the growth and use of Congressional staff without confronting fundamental questions about the nature of representation in an era of governmental complexity. On the one hand, dependence on Congressional staff has, as we have seen, increased the relative power of technocratic issue specialists and of groups with no economic or political constituency. This both reflects and reinforces the complexity of government. On the other hand, Congress has reacted to the governmental complexity it has created by building up its staffs defensively to preserve an important role for itself. But the size of those staffs and the way they are used has reinforced a situation in which the deliberative aspect of representation gets short shrift on all but the broad outlines of a few issues.

The weakening of deliberation is serious for a Congress that works best when it responds to constituents' needs and interests in a setting that encourages the members to think more broadly. The process no longer forces members to talk to each other to resolve the tough issues; the agenda keeps them busy with other things. The trouble Congress had in leading the country to a national consensus on energy policy during the 1970s was but one side effect of this, and the complexifying role of staff must bear a partial responsibility. If Congress is to play its crucial representative role on whatever replaces energy as the key issue of coming decades, it must find some way to limit its agenda and reinforce the role of direct deliberation. While it is hard to imagine what that might be, the future of representative government depends on it.

APPENDIX

TABLE A-1

Number of Congressional Staff, 1979

House	
Committee Staff[1]	2,073
Personal Staff	7,067
Leadership Staff[2]	160
Officers of the House, Staff[3]	1,487
Subtotal, House	10,787
Senate	
Committee Staff[1]	1,217
Personal Staff	3,612
Leadership Staff[2]	170
Officers of the Senate, Staff[3]	1,351
Subtotal, Senate	6,350
Joint Committee Staffs	138
Support Agencies	
General Accounting Office	5,303
(30 percent of above)	(1,591)
Library of Congress	5,390
(Congressional Research Service)	(847)
Congressional Budget Office	207
Office of Technology Assessment	145
Subtotal, Support Agencies	11,045
(Subtotal, only CRS in Library, 30 percent of GAO)	2,790
Miscellaneous	
Architect	2,296
Capitol Police Force	1,167
Subtotal	3,463
Total	31,783
(Total, only CRS in Library and 30 percent of GAO)	(23,528)

Notes

1. Includes Select Committee Staff
2. Includes Legislative Counsels' Offices. House Republican Conference, Democratic Steering Committee, Majority and Minority Policy Committees, Office of the Vice-President.
3. Doorkeepers, Parliamentarians, Sergeants at Arms, Clerk of the House, Senate Majority and Minority Secretaries and Postmasters.

Sources: Report of the Clerk of the House, July 1, 1979 to September 30, 1979; *Report of the Secretary of the Senate*, April 1, 1979 to September 30, 1979; Workforce Analysis and Statistics Branch. U.S. Office of Personnel Management. *Federal Civilian Workforce Statistics*, Monthly Release, October 31, 1979.

Appendix

TABLE A-2

The Growth of Committee Staffs; 1891-1979, Selected Years

Year	House	Senate
1891	62	41
1914	105	198
1930	112	163
1935	122	172
1947	167	232
1950	246	300
1955	329	386
1960	440	470
1965	571	509
1970	702	635
1971	729	711
1972	817	844
1973	878	873
1974	1,107	948
1975	1,433	1,277
1976	1,680	1,201
1977	1,776	1,028
1978	1,844	1,151
1979	1,959	1,098

Sources: 1891-1935: Harrison W. Fox Jr. and Susan Hammond, *Congressional Staffs: The Invisible Force In American Lawmaking* (New York: Free Press, 1977), p. 171. 1947-1978: Judy Schneider, "Congressional Staffing, 1947-78," Congressional Research Service, 24 August 1979, reprinted in U.S. Congress, House, Select Committee on Committees, *Final Report*, 96th Cong., 2nd sess., 1 April 1980, p. 539. Schneider's figures are only for the statutory and investigative staffs of standing committees. They do not include select committee staffs, which have varied between 31 and 238 in the House and 62 and 172 in the Senate during the 1970s. 1979: *Report of the Clerk of the House*, July 1, 1979 to September 30, 1979; *Report of the Secretary of the Senate*, April 1, 1979 to September 30, 1979.

TABLE A-3

Ranking of Senate Committees by Size of Staff in 1979

	1947	1960	1970	1975	1978
Judiciary	19	137	190	251	200
Governmental Affairs	29	47	55	144	178
Labor and Human Resources	9	28	69	150	123
Commerce, Science and					
Transportation	8	52	53	111	96
Budget	*	*	*	90	93
Appropriations	23	31	42	72	78
Environment (Public Works)	10	11	34	70	62
Foreign Relations	8	25	31	62	61
Energy & Natural					
Resources (Interior)	7	26	22	53	49
Banking, Housing &					
Urban Affairs	9	22	23	55	48
Finance	6	6	16	26	45
Agriculture, Nutrition					
& Forestry	3	10	7	22	34
Armed Services	10	23	19	30	30
Rules & Administration	41	15	13	29	30
Veterans Affairs	*	*	*	32	24
Aeronautics & Space Science	*	10	12	22	*
District of Columbia	4	7	18	33	*
Post Office & Civil Service	46	20	31	25	*

*Committee not in existence.

Source: Schneider, "Congressional Staffing, 1947-1978"; *Report of the Secretary of the Senate*, April 1, 1979 to September 30, 1979.

TABLE A-4

Ranking of House Committees by Size of Staff in 1979

	1947	1960	1970	1975	1978
House Administration[1]	7	4	25	217	269
Interstate & Foreign Commerce	10	45	42	112	149
Appropriations	29	59	71	98	129
Banking	4	14	50	85	110
Education & Labor	10	25	77	114	103
International Relations	10	14	21	54	101
Ways & Means	12	22	24	63	93
Public Works	6	32	40	88	83
Judiciary	7	27	35	69	82
Government Operations	9	54	60	68	82
Science & Technology	*	17	26	47	80
Merchant Marine & Fisheries	6	9	21	28	79
Budget	*	*	*	67	77
Interior	4	10	14	57	68
Post Office & Civil Service	6	9	46	61	65
Agriculture	9	10	17	48	58
Armed Services	10	15	37	38	45
Small Business	*	*	*	27	40
Standards of Official Conduct	*	*	5	5	37
District of Columbia	7	8	15	43	35
Veterans Affairs	7	18	18	26	34
Rules	4	2	7	18	25
Internal Security	10	46	51	27	*

[1] Since 1972, figures include employees of House Information Systems, the House of Representatives central computer facility.

*Not a standing committee for years in question

Source: Schneider, "Congressional Staffing, 1947-1978"; *Report of the Clerk of the House,* July 1, 1979 to September 30, 1979.

TABLE A-5

The Growth of Personal Staffs, 1891-1979, Selected Years

Year	House	Senate
1891		39
1914		72
1930	870	280
1935	870	424
1947	1,440	590
1957	2,441	1,115
1967	4,055	1,749
1972	5,280	2,426
1976	6,939	3,251
1977	6,942	3,554
1978	6,944	3,268
1979	7,067	3,612

Sources: Through 1976: Harrison W. Fox, Jr., and Susan W. Hammond, *Congressional Staffs: The Invisible Force in American Lawmaking* (New York: Free Press, 1977), p. 171. For 1977 and 1978 Senate: Judy Schneider, "Congressional Staff, 1947-78." For 1977, 1978, and 1979 House: *Report of the Clerk of the House.* For 1979 Senate: *Report of the Secretary of the Senate.*

TABLE A-6

Mean Number of Personal Staff With Legislative Designations, By Party and Region*

House of Representatives					
Year	Sample Size	All Representatives	Southern Democrats	Other Democrats	Republicans
1972	100	1.3	1.1	1.7	1.2
1979	435	2.2	1.8	2.4	2.1

Senate					
Year	Sample Size	All Senators	Southern Democrats	Other Democrats	Republicans
1973	98	3.9	3.1	4.4	3.7
1979	100	5.5	4.9	5.4	5.8

*The table compares an analysis of the number of legislative aides working in the House and Senate in 1972 and 1973 done by political scientist Norman Ornstein with a comparable 1979 analysis done by this author, after consultation with Ornstein to make sure the same criteria were used to decide who should and who should not be counted.

Sources: Figures for the House in 1972 and Senate in 1973 come from Norman J. Ornstein, "Legislative Behavior and Legislative Structures," in James J. Heaphey and Alan P. Balutis, *Legislative Staffing: A Comparative Perspective* (New York: John Wiley and Sons, 1975), p. 169. The figures for 1979 were derived from U.S., Congress, House, *Report of the Clerk of the House from Jan. 1, 1979 to March 31, 1979,* 96th Cong., 1st sess., H. Doc. 96-136 and U.S., Congress, Senate, *Report of the Secretary of the Senate from Oct. 1, 1978 to March 31, 1979,* 96th Cong., 1st sess., S. Doc. 96-21, parts 1 and 2. Staff titles derived from these sources were cross-checked with Charles Brownson, ed., *1979 Congressional Staff Directory* and Congressional Monitor's *Bimonthly Directory of Key Congressional Aides.*

Appendix

TABLE A-7

Development of the Support Agencies, Selected Years, 1947-1979

Year	Library of Congress	(Congressional Research Service only[1])	General Accounting Office[2]	Congressional Budget Office	Office of Technology Assessment
1946			14,219		
1947	1,898	(160)	10,695		
1950	1,973	(161)	7,876		
1955	2,459	(166)	5,776		
1960	2,779	(183)	5,074		
1965	3,390	(231)	4,278		
1970	3,848	(332)	4,704		
1971	3,963	(386)	4,718		
1972	4,135	(479)	4,742		
1973	4,375	(596)	4,908		
1974	4,504	(687)	5,270		10
1975	4,649	(741)	4,905	193	54
1976	4,880	(806)	5,391	203	103
1977	5,075	(789)	5,315	201	139
1978	5,231	(818)	5,476	203	164
1979	5,390	(847)	5,303	207	145

Notes: 1. Legislative Reference Service through 1970.

2. The GAO's job changed after World War II. Before 1950, the GAO was responsible for auditing all individual federal transactions and keeping record of them. 1950 legislation transferred these responsibilities to the executive branch. The staff reductions through 1965 result from this 1950 change. See Frederich C. Mosher, *The GAO: The Quest for Accountability in American Government* (Boulder, Colo.: Westview Press, 1979), p. 124.

Sources: Library of Congress: *Annual Reports of the Librarian of Congress.* GAO (1946-65): *Annual Reports of the Comptroller General of the United States.*

OTA (1974-76): *Appendixes of the Budget of the United States* for Fiscal 1976 (p. 18), 1977 (p. 18) and 1978 (p. 40).

CBO (1975): Joel Havemann, *Congress and the Budget* (Bloomington, Ind.: Indiana University Press, 1978), p. 109. Figure is as of October, 1975. The CBO's director took office on 24 February 1975.

GAO (1970-78), CBO (1976-78) and OTA (1977-78): Judy Schneider, "Congressional Staffing, 1947-78," Congressional Research Service, 24 August 1979.

For 1979: U.S. Office of Personnel Management, *Federal Civilian Workforce Statistics*, Monthly Release, October 1, 1979, p. 6.

TABLE A-8

Congress's Workload, 80th through 95th Congress

Congress (Years)	House			Senate			Congress	
	Hours in Session	Committee, Subcommittee Meetings[1]	Recorded Votes	Hours in Session	Committee, Subcommittee Meetings	Recorded Votes	Number Public Bills Enacted	Pages of Public Bills Enacted
80 (1947-48)	1,224	NA[2]	169	1,462	NA	248	906	2,236
81 (1949-50)	1,501	NA	275	2,410	NA	455	921	2,314
82 (1951-52)	1,163	NA	181	1,648	NA	331	594	1,585
83 (1953-54)	1,033	NA	147	1,962	NA	270	781	1,899
84 (1955-56)	937	3,210	147	1,362	2,607	224	1,028	1,848
85 (1957-58)	1,147	3,750	193	1,876	2,748	313	936	2,435
86 (1959-60)	1,039	3,059	180	2,199	2,271	422	800	1,774
87 (1961-62)	1,227	3,402	240	2,164	2,532	434	885	2,078
88 (1963-64)	1,251	3,596	232	2,395	2,493	541	666	1,975
89 (1965-66)	1,547	4,367	394	1,814	2,889	497	810	2,912
90 (1967-68)	1,595	4,386	478	1,961	2,892	595	640	2,304
91 (1969-70)	1,613	5,066	443	2,352	3,264	667	695	2,927
92 (1971-72)	1,429	5,114	649	2,294	3,559	955	607	2,330
93 (1973-74)	1,487	5,888	1,078	2,028	4,067	1,138	649	2,361
94 (1975-76)	1,788	6,975	1,273	2,210	NA	1,311	588	2,963
95 (1977-78)	1,898	6,771	1,540	2,510	6,656	1,156	634	NA

Notes: [1] Figures do not include the House Appropriations Committee for the 84th through 88th Congress. House Appropriations, included in the subsequent Congresses, numbered 584 in the 89th Congress, 705 in the 90th, 709 in the 91st, 854 in the 92nd and 892 in the 93rd.

[2] NA = Not readily available.

Sources: Arthur G. Stevens, "Indicators of Congressional Workload and Activity," Congressional Research Service, 30 May 1979, and U.S. Congress House, Select Committees on Committees, Task Force to Review Congressional Changes in the 1970's, Final Report, July 11, 1979, typescript.

NOTES

Chapter 1

1. Spencer Rich, "An Invisible Network of Hill Power," *The Washington Post,* 20 March, 1977, A. E5.

2. For two eloquent statements reflecting this point of view, see Additional Views of Senator Daniel P. Moynihan (D–N.Y.) in U.S. Senate, Committee on the Budget, *Report on the First Concurrent Resolution on the Budget, FY 1980,* S.Rept. 96–98, 96th Congress, 1st Session, April 12, 1979: 330–333 and James L. Buckley, *If Men Were Angels: A View From The Senate* (New York: G.P. Putnam's Sons, 1975), pp. 117–149.

3. See, for example, Warren E. Miller and Donald E. Stokes, "Constituency Influence in Congress," *The American Political Science Review,* 57 (March, 1963): 45–57.

4. This was described as an "outsider's" strategy by Ralph K. Huitt in "The Outsider In the Senate: An Alternative Role," *American Political Science Review,* 55 (September 1961): 566–75. For a perceptive article on the modern Senate that shows how the "outsider" style has become dominant, see Nelson W. Polsby, "Goodbye to the Inner Club," *The Washington Monthly,* August 1969, pp. 30–34. No one has yet written a similar article on the House of Representatives, but it is clear that the House is taking the same direction the Senate did in the 1960s with more members developing issues on their own and using the media to sway both national public opinion and their colleagues.

Chapter 2

1. Richard E. Cohen, "The Hill's Building Boom," *National Journal,* 12 August 1978, pp. 1294–95.

2. Harrison W. Fox, Jr. and Susan W. Hammond, *Congressional Staffs: The Invisible Force in American Lawmaking* (New York: The Free Press, 1977), p. 15.

3. Judy Schneider, "Congressional Staffing, 1947–78," A study prepared for the Congressional Research Service of the Library of Congress, 24 August 1979. Reprinted in U.S. Congress, House, Select Committee on Committees, *Final Report,* 96th Cong., 2nd sess., 1 April 1980, pp. 531–32.

4. Fox and Hammond, *Congressional Staffs,* p. 171.

5. Kenneth Kofmehl, *Professional Staffs of Congress* (West Lafayette, Indiana: Purdue University Press, 1962), p. 4. My thanks to Andrew Linehan (of the Carnegie Endowment for International Peace's Project on Executive-Congressional Relations) for drawing my attention to the importance of this passage in Kofmehl's book.

6. P.L. 79–601, 60 Stat. 812.

7. Kofmehl, *Professional Staffs of Congress,* p. 52.

8. Ibid., p. 58.

9. Ibid., p. 67.

10. Clem Miller, *Member of the House: Letters of a Congressman* (New York: Charles Scribner's Sons, 1962), p. 13.

11. Randall B. Ripley, *Power In the Senate* (New York: St. Martin's Press, 1969), pp. 201–02.

12. P.L. 91–510, 84 Stat. 1140.

13. See Norman J. Ornstein, "Causes and Consequences of Congressional Change: Subcommittee Reforms in the House of Representatives, 1970–73," *Congress in Change,* ed. Norman J. Ornstein, (New York: Praeger, 1975), pp. 88–114, especially p. 106.

14. Fox and Hammond, *Congressional Staffs,* pp. 15–16.

15. See Morris P. Fiorina, *Congress: Keystone of the Washington Establishment* (New Haven: Yale University Press, 1977), pp. 56–60.

16. James D. Carroll, "Policy Analysis for Congress: A Review of the Congressional Research Service," in U.S. Congress, Senate, Commission on the Operation of the Senate, 94th Cong., 2d sess. *Congressional Support Agencies: A Compilation of Papers,* Committee Print, p. 6.

17. See, for example, Michael J. Malbin, "CRS—The Congressional Agency That Just Can't Say No," *National Journal,* 19 February 1977, pp. 284–89; and Richard E. Cohen, "The Watchdogs for Congress Often Bark the Same Tune," *National Journal,* 8 September 1979, pp. 1484–88.

18. Martin J. Fitzgerald, "The Expanded Role of the General Accounting Office," part of a "Public Policy Forum on the New Congressional Bureaucracy," *The Bureaucrat* 3, no. 4 (January 1975): 385. For two recent book length treatments of the GAO, see Frederick C. Mosher's history, *The GAO: The Quest for Accountability In American Government* (Boulder, Colo.: Westview Press, 1969), and a companion book by Erasmus Kloman, *Cases in Accountability* (Boulder, Colo.: Westview Press, 1979).

19. U.S. General Accounting Office, *1976 Annual Report of the Comptroller General of the United States* (Washington, D.C.: Government Printing Office, 1977), p. 221.

20. Joseph Pois, "The General Accounting Office as a Congressional Resource," in Commission on the Operation of the Senate, *Congressional Support Agencies,* p. 40.

21. Technology Assessment Act of 1972 P.L. 92–484, 86 Stat. 797; Congressional Budget and Impoundment Control Act of 1974, P.L. 93–344 88 Stat. 297.

22. Dick Kirschten, in "The Misplaced Mission of OTA," said the OTA's staff had been "divided for the most part into political fiefdoms. . . . Now in its fourth year, OTA never has been able to shake the reputation—whether wholly deserved or not—of functioning as little more than a joint committee, serving the whims of its 12-member congressional board." *National Journal,* 12 November 1977, p. 1777. See also, D. Kirschten, "After the Bash, the Crash," *National Journal,* 4 February 1978, p. 202 and "OTA Patronage—At A Reduced Price," *National Journal,* 11 March 1978, p. 404 and Richard E. Cohen, "Taking Control of the Troubled OTA," in "The Watchdogs of Congress," *National Journal,* 8 Sept. 1979, p. 1485.

23. See Michael J. Malbin, "Where There's A Cause There's A Caucus," *National Journal,* 8 January 1977, pp. 56–58.

24. U.S., Congress House Select Committee on Committees, *Final Report,* pp. 70–71.

25. Fox and Hammond, *Congressional Staffs*, p. 173.

26. Ibid., p. 178; Robert H. Salisbury and Kenneth A. Shepsle argue that Fox and Hammond overstate the degree of turnover, some of which may be due to such factors as the creation of new committees. Nevertheless, even their more modest numbers suggest a career pattern that is quite different for most committees from the pattern one impressionistically has of the 1940s through early 1960s. See "Congressional Staff Turnover: Its Causes and Consequences," A Paper Presented at the Annual Meeting of the Southern Political Science Association, November 1–4, 1979 and available through the Center for the Study of American Business, Washington University, St. Louis.

27. Harry McPherson, *A Political Education* (Boston: Little, Brown, 1972) p. 8.

28. Hugh Heclo, "Issue Networks and the Executive Establishment," in Anthony King, ed., *The New American Political System* (Washington: American Enterprise Institute, 1978), pp. 87–124. See also Laurence Leamer, "Networks," *The Washingtonian*, November 1979, pp. 158–60 and 202–18.

29. Nicholas Lemann, "Survival Networks: Staying in Washington," *The Washington Monthly*, June 1978, pp. 23–32.

30. Linda E. Demkovich, "The Cautious Approach of Cannon's Commerce Committee," *National Journal*, 27 May 1978, p. 849.

31. Nicholas Lemann, "Protégé Power: The Wonderful World of Special Assistants," *The New Republic*, 7 April 1979, pp. 10–13.

32. James W. Singer, "Practicing Law In Washington—An American Growth Industry," *National Journal*, 7 April 1979, pp. 10–13.

33. Malmgren, Inc. sent a five-page memorandum to prospective clients in 1978 pointing out that two of its top people, Harald B. Malmgren (the president) and Jeffrey Salzman, used to work for Senator Abraham A. Ribicoff, (D-Conn.), a member of the Finance Committee. The memo was sent specifically to firms likely to be hurt by the controversial increase of U.S. taxes on income earned abroad. "It is well known," the memo said, "that the likely pattern of compromise of the best basis for a new solution, is the proposal introduced by Senator Ribicoff and Salzman has been the principle (sic) drafter of all variations of the approach. (He was, of course, formerly Legislative Assistant to the Senator.)" The memo also advertised Malmgren's credentials in similar terms. See George Lardner Jr., "Hill Expertise for Sale: $200,000" *Washington Post*, 10 April 1973, A1 and A14.

Chapter 3

1. See Ronald C. Moe and Steven C. Teel, "Congress as Policy-Maker: A Necessary Reappraisal," *Political Science Quarterly* 85 (September, 1970): 443–70 and Nelson W. Polsby, "Strengthening Congress in National Policymaking," *The Yale Review* (Summer 1970) reprinted in N. Polsby, ed., *Congressional Behavior* (New York: Random House, 1971), pp. 3–13.

2. David E. Price, "Professionals and 'Entrepreneurs': Staff Orientations and Policy Making on Three Senate Committees," *Journal of Politics* 33 (May 1971): 316–36.

3. David E. Price, *Who Makes the Laws: Creativity and Power in Senate Committees* (Cambridge, Mass.: Schenkman Publishing Co., 1972), p. 29.

4. See Paul Halpern, "Consumer Politics and Corporate Behavior" (Ph.D. diss., Harvard University, 1972).

5. Harold M. Schmeck, Jr., "8-Volume Record of Hearings That Were Never Held Is Published, With Full Quotations, By Senate Panel," *New York Times*, 4 October 1976, p. 15:3.

6. U.S., Congress, Senate, Select Committee on Small Business, *Annual Reports*, 1970–75.

7. U.S., Congress, Senate Select Committee on Small Business, *Annual Reports*, 1976–79.

8. For a more complete discussion of recent changes in product liability law, including ones the committee did not investigate, see Richard A. Epstein, "Product Liability: The Gathering Storm," *Regulation*, 1, no. 2 (September/October 1977): 15–20.

9. Peter F. Drucker, *The Unseen Revolution: How Pension Fund Socialism Came to America* (New York: Harper & Row, 1976).

10. Spencer Rich, "An Invisible Network of Hill Power," *Washington Post*, 20 March 1977, pp. E1, 9.

11. Richard Harris, *The Real Voice* (New York: Macmillan, 1964), pp. 4–20.

12. Burton Hersh, "The Survival of Edward Kennedy," *The Washingtonian*, February 1979, pp. 91–103 at 97–98.

13. Roger H. Davidson and Walter T. Olaszek, *Congress Against Itself* (Bloomington, Indiana: Indiana University Press, 1977), p. 165 ff.

Chapter 4

1. See David R. Mayhew, *Congress: The Electoral Connection* (New Haven: Yale University Press, 1974).

2. For an account of Muskie's role as a sponsor of budget reform and as Budget Committee Chairman, see Joel Havemann, *Congress and the Budget* (Bloomington and London: Indiana University Press, 1978), pp. 27–29.

3. Bernard Asbell, *The Senate Nobody Knows* (Garden City, N.Y.: Doubleday and Co., 1978), pp. 249–50.

4. Ibid., p. 250.

5. Ibid., pp. 405–07.

6. Ibid., pp. 346.

7. Ibid.

8. For more on the committee under Ribicoff, see Michael J. Malbin, "Senate Governmental Affairs—The Committee with a Consensus," *National Journal*, 27 August 1977, pp. 1344–47.

9. The Congressional Budget Office said tax expenditures were worth $150.1 billion in fiscal 1979. They projected an increase to $191.2 billion in fiscal 1981 and $296 billion in fiscal 1984. See Richard E. Cohen, "Can Congress Close Spending's Back Door," *National Journal*, 14 July 1979, pp. 1167–68.

10. See David Hess, "Deserted, Glenn Does Slow Burn Over Tax Bill Flop," *Akron Beacon Journal*, 4 July 1977.

11. For the committee report, see U.S., Congress, Senate, Committee on Governmental Affairs, *Program Evaluation Act of 1977*, S. Rept. 95–326, 1 July 1977.

12. U.S., Congress, Senate, Committee on Rules and Administration, *Hearings on Program Evaluation Act of 1977 (S.2) and Federal Spending Control Act. of 1977 (S.1244)*, 28 Sept. 1977, 19 April and 8 June 1978, p. 10. The second bill in the above title, S.1244, was introduced by Senator Joseph Biden (D-Del.). No committee had held hearings on the bill before this. Giving it equal billing with S.2 was considered to be an insult to S.2's sponsors although Rules Committee people defended it by noting that S.1244 had been referred directly to their committee. Biden's bill, like Muskie's, would have required periodic reauthorization and would have used budget authority as the basis of its termination mechanism. The Biden bill would not have terminated tax expenditures, but it would have required comparative evaluations of similar tax expenditure and direct spending programs. It was also much more explicit than S.2 about

the questions to be answered in a program evaluation. The bill is reprinted ibid, pp. 485–99. S.2 is printed ibid., 412–84.

13. Ibid, p. 17.

14. Ibid, p. 18.

15. See Joel Havemann, "Budget Reform Legislation Calls for Major Procedural Change," *National Journal*, 18 May 1974, pp. 734–42, especially p. 739: "Staff Cooperation Helped Produce Legislation." The budget staff working group of 1974, as the 1977–78 Sunset group, was created after hearings in the Rules Committee revealed deep opposition to a Government Operations Bill by the chairmen of the authorizing and appropriations committees. As with Sunset, the ranking Government Operations sponsors (Senator Sam J. Ervin Jr., D-N.C., then the committee's chairman and Percy) asked for a staff group to rework the bill.

16. See note 12.

17. U.S., Congress, Senate, Committee on Rules and Administration, *Hearings*, p. 69.

18. Ibid., p. 118.

19. For an example, see ibid., p. 127.

20. For an outline of these last weeks, see Ann Cooper, "Muskie's Sunset Odyssey, How He Finally Got A Vote," *Congressional Quarterly*, 14 October 1978, pp. 2951–52.

21. See Richard E. Cohen," Sunset Proposals In Congress—Sinking Below The Horizon?" *National Journal*, 24 November 1979, pp. 1978–81.

Chapter 5

1. U.S., Congress, House of Representatives, Committee on Veterans' Affairs, *Hearing before a Select Subcommittee on Granting Veterans' Status to WASPs*, 20 September 1977, pp. 29–32.

2. *Congressional Record*, daily ed., 19 October 1977, S. 17322.

3. *Hearing before a Select Subcommittee on . . . WASPs*, p. 430.

4. Quoted in Colman McCarthy, " 'Tiger' Teague and the Veterans Compromise," *Washington Post*, 19 November 1977, A19:1.

5. Juan Cameron, "The Shadow Congress The Public Doesn't Know," *Fortune*, 15 January 1979, p. 40.

6. *Hearings Before A Select Subcommittee on . . . WASPs*, pp. 266–68.

7. *Congressional Record*, daily ed., 3 November 1977, H. 12139–48.

8. Ibid., H. 12149 (Edgar) and 12158–59 (Heckler).

9. Ibid., H. 12149 (especially William Ford of Michigan).

10. Ibid., 4 November 1977, S. 18812–21. The two objections were from Senators Durkin of New Hampshire and Javits of New York.

Chapter 6

1. Howie Kurtz, "FERC Inaction on Natural Gas Cases Rouses Critics," *Washington Star*, 25 May 1979, D11:2, reported an instance when Curtis persuaded Dingell not to press a request for information that would have embarrassed FERC before its 1979 authorization hearings. The article quoted a "spokesman for Dingell" as saying: "They are friends. When Charlie calls up and pleads that he's got troubles, he's got a better chance of getting agreement than a total stranger."

2. For a critical look backward at that successful campaign, see William Tucker, "Environmentalism and the Leisure Class," *Harper's,* December 1977, pp. 49–56 and 73–80.

3. For a description of the many formal and informal ways Congress does oversight, see Morris Ogul, *Congress Oversees the Bureaucracy* (Pittsburgh: University of Pittsburgh Press, 1976), *passim.*

4. Gregory G. Rushford, "Why Senator Eagleton Fired Me," *The Washington Monthly,* December 1977, pp. 21–25, 25.

5. This is the statement from which Dingell actually read in the hearing. It was softened in: U.S., Congress, House, Committee on Interstate and Foreign Commerce, Subcommittee on Energy and Power, 94th Cong., 2nd sess., *Hearing on "The Natural Gas Story" Investigation,* 17 September 1976, pp. 150–51. Serial 94–148.

6. See U.S., Congress, House, Committee on Science and Technology, Subcommittee on Fossil and Nuclear Energy Research, 95th Cong., 1st sess., *Hearings on Market Oriented Program Planning Study,* 12 July 1977.

7. Bryan Hodgson, "Natural Gas: The Search Goes On", *National Geographic,* November 1978, pp. 632–52.

8. "Former FEA Administrator Frank Zarb Is Assessing Supplemental Natural Gas Supplies," *Inside DOE: An Exclusive weekly report on the Department of Energy,* 1 January 1979, p. 2.

9. Jack Anderson and Les Whitten, "High Oil Prices Trigger Scandals," *Washington Post,* 1 February 1977, B12:4.

10. Martin Dyckman, "Energy Agency Whistleblower May Lose His Job," *St. Petersburg Times,* 26 February 1978, pp. I–A and 7–A.

11. *Washington Post,* 30 March 1978, E23:4.

12. Sheila Hershow "Energy Department Whistleblower Out of Luck," *The Federal Times,* 5 June 1978, pp. 1, 5.

13. Martin Dyckman, "Truth-Teller Fights For His Job and His Life," *St. Petersburg Times,* 2 June 1978. Dyckman's article also said that Rohweder learned in May that he was suffering from chronic lymphocytic leukemia.

14. James P. Herzog, "DOE Boat Rocker Finds His Reward," *The Knoxville News-Sentinel,* 3 June 1978, p. 8.

15. Phillip Shandler, "He Blew the Whistle—Now He's Fighting to Keep His Job," *Washington Star,* 18 June 1978, F6:1.

16. Sheila Hershow, "Dingell Wants Answers on Atlanta Sex Case: Did Top Energy Official 'Cover-up'?" *Federal Times,* 6 February 1978, pp. 1, 5.

17. John Hill confirmed this in an interview with Sheila Hershow, "Conflict Cloud Over Energy Aide," *Federal Times,* 6 January 1978, p. 5.

18. Sheila Hershow, "Bardin Belittles Criticism of Aide," *Federal Times,* 20 January, 1978, p. 6.

19. U.S., Congress, House, Committee on Interstate and Foreign Commerce, Subcommittee on Energy and Power, 95th Cong., 2nd sess., *Hearings: Department of Energy Authorization—Fiscal Year, 1979,* vol. 3 (of 4), pp. 662–65, (8 March, 1978) and 892–95 (10 March 1978).

20. For the best article on the importance of the staff's 1976 "white collar crime" memo to subsequent events, see William Nottingham, "Indictments Were a Long Time Coming," *St. Petersburg Times,* 15 September 1978, pp. A1:1 and A19:1. The article was one of several in that day's newspaper on the so-called "Daisy Chain" indictments.

21. U.S., Congress, House, Committee on Interstate and Foreign Commerce, Subcommittee on Energy and Power, 95th Cong., 1st sess., *Hearing: FEA Compliance Programs* 95th Cong., 6 April 1977, (H.R.2788), Serial 95–62. The staff memo of February 28 is printed in the hearing, pp. 40–51.

22. Federal Energy Administration, *Task Force on Compliance and Enforcement: Final Report,* 13 July 1977.

23. U.S., Congress, House, Committee on Interstate and Foreign Commerce, Subcommittee on Energy and Power, 95th Cong., 1st sess., *Hearing on FEA Compliance Matters,* 28 September 1977, pp. 18ff.

24. See Richard Corrigan, "Righting Oil Pricing's Wrongs," *National Journal,* 5 August 1978, p. 1256.

25. For press coverage of this investigation of crude oil resellers, see: William Nothingham, "Energy Aide Reportedly 'Pressured' Oil Probe News," *St. Petersburg Times,* 27 June 1978, pp. 1–A and 4–A; Sheila Hershow, "Possible 'Oil-Swindle' Cover-ups Under Study," *Federal Times,* 10 July 1978, p. 3; "Spreading Oil Scandals: They could involve billions of dollars," *Time Magazine,* 24 July 1978, p. 51; J.P. Smith, "U.S. Hunts Fraud in Oil Prices," *Washington Post,* 23 September 1978, A1 and A18; Walter Mossberg and Jerry Landauer, "Energy Agency Alleges Oil-Price Manipulation by Middleman Firms," *Wall St. Journal,* 28 September 1978, p. 4; Sheila Hershow, "Did Energy Fumble: Oil Swindle Said to Cost $2 Billion," *Federal Times,* 18 December 1978. The last of these articles is the most complete on the Dingell subcommittee's role in 1978.

Chapter 7

1. For a history of Staggers' chairmanship see David E. Price's "The Impact of Reform: The House Commerce Subcommittee on Oversight and Investigations," (Durham, N.C.: Duke University Institute of Policy Sciences and Public Affairs, 1978), Working Paper No. 4782. An abridged version appears in Leroy Rieselbach, ed., *Legislative Reform: The Policy Impact* (Lexington-Heath, 1978), pp. 133–57. In general, I am more critical of the Moss subcommittee than Price is.

2. Ward Sinclair, "The Man who Perfected Oversight," *Washington Post,* 14 January 1979, inserted in the *Congressional Record,* daily ed., 1 March 1979, E822.

3. *Congressional Record,* daily ed., 3 August 1977, H8394.

4. Price, in Rieselbach, ed., *Legislative Reform,* p. 142.

5. Inderjit Badhwar, "Moss Says Its Change, Not Reform," *Federal Times,* 13 March 1978, p. 1.

6. "Suspend 2 Top CSC Officials, Says Moss," *Federal Times,* 7 November 1977, p. 3.

7. Badhawar, "Change, Not Reform," p. 6.

8. Inderjit Badhwar, "Telephone Tap Contract Hit By Rep. Moss," *Federal Times,* 8 May 1978, p. 6.

9. Judith Miller, "Taxes and Accounting/S.E.C.'s Report on Profession," *New York Times,* 11 July 1978.

10. Jack Anderson, "Jordan's Distaste for Rep. Moss," *Washington Post,* 8 August 1978, D25.

11. U.S., Congress, House, Committee on Interstate and Foreign Commerce, Subcommittee on Oversight and Investigations, 95th Cong., 2d sess., Business Meeting of Aug. 16, 1978, *Contempt Proceedings Against Secretary of HEW Joseph A. Califano, Jr.,* Committee Print 95–76. The proceedings were dropped in September after Califano surrendered the subpoenaed material.

12. U.S., Congress, House, Committee on Interstate and Foreign Commerce, Subcommittee on Oversight and Investigations, *Preliminary Staff Report Concerning Delays In Natural Gas Production By Cities Service Oil Company,* 94th Cong., 1st sess., 18 July 1975, Subcommittee Print.

13. U.S., Congress, House, Committee on Interstate and Foreign Commerce, Subcommittee on Oversight and Investigations, *Report on Federal Regulation and Regulatory Reform.* Available either as a Subcommittee Print, 94th Cong, 2d sess., October 1976, or as House Document 95–134, 95th Cong., 1st sess. Quotation is from Minority Views, p. 671. For hearings on this case, see U.S., Congress, House, Committee on Interstate and Foreign Commerce, Subcommittee on Oversight and Investiga-

tions, *Hearings on Natural Gas Supplies in the United States*, June 9, 13, 26, 27 and July 14, 21, 1975, vol. 1, in 2 parts, Serial 94–23 and 94–24.

14. U.S., Congress, House, Committee on Interstate and Foreign Commerce, Subcommittee on Oversight and Investigations, *Natural Gas Supplies: Declining Deliverability at Garden City, La., Report*, 94th Cong., 1st sess., October 1975, Subcommittee Print.

15. U.S., Congress, House, Committee on Interstate and Foreign Commerce, Subcommittee on Oversight and Investigations, *Declining Deliverability at Bastian Bay Field, La., Report*, 94th Cong., 1st sess., November 1975, Subcommittee Print.

16. U.S., Congress, House, Committee on Interstate and Foreign Commerce, Subcommittee on Oversight and Investigations, *Mobil Oil Corporation: Failure to Deliver Gas to the Interstate Market, Report*, 94th Cong., 2nd sess., February, 1976, Subcommittee Print.

17. *Regulation and Regulatory Reform*, Minority Views, p. 672.

18. U.S., Congress, House, Committee on Interstate and Foreign Commerce, Subcommittee on Oversight and Investigations, *Gulf Oil Corporation: Failure to Deliver Natural Gas to the Interstate Market, Report*, 95th Cong., 1st sess., February 1977, Subcommittee Print.

19. U.S., Congress, House, Committee on Interstate and Foreign Commerce, Subcommittee on Oversight and Investigations, *Hearings on Allegations of Withholding of U.S. "Behind-the-Pipe" Natural Gas Reserves*, 95th Cong., 1st sess., 22 and 23 February 1977, Serial 95–12.

20. U.S., Department of the Interior, News Release, "Remarks of Secretary of the Interior Cecil D. Andrus At A Press Briefing on Natural Gas Production Opportunities," 27 April 1978.

21. *Natural Gas Supplies: Declining Deliverability of Garden City, La.*, p. 1.

22. *Hearings on Natural Gas Supplies*, June 9, part 1, p. 2.

23. Carole Shifrin, "FTC Suit on Gas Data Urged," *Washington Post*, 10 June 1975, A1 and A9.

24. Carole Shifrin, "Subpoenas Hit Big Oil Firms For Gas Data," *Washington Post*, 17 June 1975, D8 and D10.

25. Carole Shifrin, "FTC Dispute on Gas Reserves Aired," *Washington Post*, 25 June, 1975, D9.

26. Carole Shifrin, "Aides Grilled on Gas Reserves Aired," *Washington Post*, 27 June, 1975, D9 and D11.

27. Carole Shifrin, "Head of FPC Admits Flaws In Gas Data," *Washington Post*, 15 July 1975, D8.

28. United Press International Wirephoto, *Washington Post*, 23 July, 1975, G1.

29. Price, "The Impact of Reform," in Rieselbach, *Legislative Reform*, p. 143.

30. *Hearings on Natural Gas Supplies*, vol. 3, Serial 94–88, 21 January 1976, p. 2.

31. U.S., Congress, House, Committee on Interstate and Foreign Commerce, Subcommittee on Oversight and Investigations, *Questions and Answers About the Nature and Causes of the Natural Gas Shortage, Staff Report*, 94th Cong., 1st sess., February 1976, p. 7.

32. For example, a regulatory reform report, published in October 1976, repeated the Bureau of Competition's charges without mentioning the Bureau of Economics and, without even mentioning that the FTC on 29 July 1975, by a vote of 5 to 0, had decided that the Bureau of Competition had not developed enough information for FTC action. See *Federal Regulation and Regulatory Reform*, p. 405. For the FTC action see Carole Shifrin, "FTC Spurns Action Over Gas Figures," *Washington Post*, 30 July 1975, C9, C11. For Moss's statement that "the subcommittee will issue a comprehensive report on this as soon as possible," see *Federal Regulation*, Additional Views, p. 737.

33. *Congressional Record*, daily ed., 6 December 1977, H 12727–30.

34. "The Moss Cover-Up," *Wall Street Journal*, 7 December 1977, p. 24.

35. *Congressional Record*, daily ed., 15 December 1977, H 13002–06. Representative Collins, still unsatisfied with Moss's position, responded in the same day's *Con-*

gressional Record, Extensions of Remarks, E 7427–28. For a follow-up editorial on the subject, see "Oversights and Insights," *Wall Street Journal,* 20 December 1977, p. 16.

Chapter 8

1. For previous studies of the staff of the Joint Committee on Taxation, see John F. Manley, "Congressional Staff and Public Policy-Making: The Joint Committee on Internal Review Taxation," *Journal of Politics* 30 (November 1968): 1046–1067, and *The Politics of Finance: The House Committee on Ways and Means* (Boston: Little, Brown, 1970), pp. 307–19; David Price, *Who Makes the Laws: Creativity and Power In Senate Committees* (Cambridge, Mass.: Schenkman Publishing Co., 1972), pp. 194–98., and "Professionals and Entrepreneurs: Staff Orientations and Policy Making on Three Senate Committees," *Journal of Politics* 33 (May 1971): 316–36.

2. E. W. Kenworthy, "Colin F. Stam: A Study in Anonymous Power," *Adventures in Public Service* ed. D. and F. Kuhn, (New York: The Vanguard Press, 1963) p. 116, quoting an article by Stanley S. Surrey from *Harvard Law Review* of May, 1957.

3. Stephen K. Bailey and Howard D. Samuel, "The Excess Profits Tax of 1950," *Congress At Work* (New York: Henry Holt and Co., 1952) p. 342.

4. For these criticisms, see Manley, *The Politics of Finance,* pp. 312–13 and Ralph K. Huitt, "Congressional Organization and Operations in the Field of Money and Credit," *Fiscal and Debt Management Policies* ed. William Fellner et al. (Englewood Cliffs, N.J.: Prentice-Hall, 1963) pp. 452–53.

5. Price, *Who Makes The Laws,* p. 195.

6. U.S., Congress, Senate, *Examination of President Nixon's Tax Returns for 1969–72,* Prepared for the Joint Committee on Internal Revenue Taxation by its Staff, 93rd Cong., 2d sess., 3 April 1974, S. Rept 93–768.

7. John Pierson, "Larry Woodworth: Dulce et Decorum," *Wall Street Journal,* 9, December 1977, inserted in the *Congressional Record* daily ed., 12 December 1977, E7372.

8. For two accounts of the connections between how members were appointed, the committee's compromising "restrained partisanship" and the closed rule, see Manley, *The Politics of Finance, passim.,* and Richard F. Fenno Jr., *Congressmen In Committees* (Boston: Little, Brown, 1973), pp. 1–13.

9. John Pierson, "Larry Woodworth: Dulce et Decorum".

10. Michael J. Malbin, "New Democratic Procedures Affect Distribution of Power," *National Journal,* 14 December 1974, p. 1881, 1884.

11. "A Tax Committee Loses Its Clout," *Business Week,* 7 May 1979, p. 86.

12. Most of the history in these paragraphs is taken from Joel Havemann, *Congress and the Budget* (Bloomington and London: Indiana University Press, 1978).

13. "An Uneasy Balance for the U.S. Economy," *Business Week,* 26 December 1977, p. 55.

14. Havemann, *Congress and the Budget,* p. 106.

15. Jude Wanniski, *The Way the World Works: How Economies Fail—and Succeed* (New York: Basic Books, 1978). An adaptation of Wanniski's argument from the book was published in his article, "Taxes, Revenues and the 'Laffer Curve'," *The Public Interest,* Winter 1978, pp. 3–16.

16. Excerpts of July 11–13, 1973 testimony circulated by the House Budget Committee. The excerpts were approved by the witnesses. Rivlin testified on July 11.

17. Paul Craig Roberts, "The Breakdown of the Keynesian Model," *The Public Interest,* Summer 1978, pp. 20–33.

Chapter 9

1. For a critic who makes this connection, see Edward C. Banfield, "Policy Science as Metaphysical Madness," *Bureaucrats, Policy Analysts Statesmen: Who's Leads?* ed. Robert Goldwin, (Washington, D.C.: American Enterprise Institute, 1980), pp. 1–19. A shorter version of this chapter appears in the same volume, pp. 62–87.

2. Harrison W. Fox, Jr. and Susan Webb Hammond, *Congressional Staffs: The Invisible Force in American Lawmaking* (New York: The Free Press, 1977), p. 175. Fox's and Hammond's numbers are based on 1972 surveys. The percentage of both attorneys and Ph.D.s probably is higher today.

3. James W. Singer, "The Humphrey-Hawkins Bill—Boondoggle or Economic Blessing?", *National Journal*, 12 June 1976, pp. 812–15.

4. For an article on the analyses of welfare reform, see Linda E. Demkovich, "The Numbers Are The Issue In The Debate Over Welfare Reform," *National Journal*, 22 April 1978, pp. 633–37.

5. For the debate in the House on H. R. 6645, see *Congressional Record*, 84th Cong., 1st sess., vol. 101, part 9, pp. 11844–11931 (28 July 1955). For the Senate debate on S. 1853 see *Congressional Record*, 84th Cong., 2d sess., vol. 102, parts 1 and 2, 16 January to 6 February 1956, pp. 418–2096.

6. Phillips Petroleum Co. v. Wisconsin 347 U.S. 672 (1954).

7. The material in this historical overview is based largely on Paul W. MacAvoy and Robert S. Pindyck, *Price Controls and the Natural Gas Shortage* (Washington, D.C.: American Enterprise Institute for Public Policy Research, 1975), pp. 11–16; Robert S. Pindyck, "Prices and Shortages: Evaluating Policy Options for the Natural Gas Industry" in *Options for U.S. Energy Policy* ed. Albert Carnesale et al., (San Francisco: Institute for Contemporary Studies, 1977), pp. 143–77 and Edmund W. Kitch, "Regulation of the Field Market for Natural Gas by the Federal Power Commission," *The Journal of Law and Economics* 11 (October 1968): 243–80.

8. For the production and reserve figures, see: U.S., Congress, Joint Economic Committee, staff study on *The Economics of the Natural Gas Controversy*, 95th Cong., 1st sess., 19 September 1977, pp. 14 and 22.

9. U.S., Congress, House, Committee on Interstate and Foreign Commerce, *National Energy Act*, Report Together with Minority, Additional, and Supplemental Views, (to accompany H.R. 6831), H. Rept. 95–496, pt. 4, 95th Cong., 1st sess., 19 July 1977, pp. 85–124.

10. Ibid, pp. 313–29.

11. U.S., Congressional Budget Office, *Natural Gas Pricing Proposals: A Comparative Analysis*, printed at the request of Senator Henry M. Jackson, chairman, U.S. Senate Committee on Energy and Natural Resources, Publication 95–50, September 1977. Cited by Senator Jackson in floor debate, September 19, 1977. *Congressional Record*, daily ed., S15149. At least fourteen other senators referred to this study in the course of the Senate debate.

12. U.S., Congress, Joint Economic Committee, staff study, *The Economics of the Natural Gas Controversy*.

13. Natural Gas Supply Committee, *The Net Benefits to the American Economy of Deregulation of the Price of New Natural Gas* (Washington, D.C.: September 1977).

14. Comptroller General of the United States, *An Evaluation of the National Energy Plan*, Report to the Congress, 25 July 1977, EMD–77–48.

15. President Carter never used the phrase "70 billion ripoff" himself, but he did refer to a 70 billion cost at a September 29, 1977 press conference during the Senate antideregulation filibuster and he used the word "ripoff" in an October 13, 1977 press conference. The full phrase was used by many others in the administration, however. See *Congressional Quarterly Weekly*, 18 March 1978, p. 713 for Carter's varied statements on deregulation.

16. In fact, when Representative Stockman tried to get Schlesinger to say the administration had resource goals in mind as well as distributive justice, Schlesinger resisted. See U.S., Congress, House, Subcommittee on Energy and Power of the Committee on Interstate and Foreign Commerce, *Hearings on The National Energy Act,* pt. 2, Natural Gas, 95th Cong., 1st sess., 12, 13, 17, and 18 May 1977, Serial 95–23, p. 242.

17. "Producer Revenues and Consumer Costs Under Decontrol," released May, 1977 by the White House Energy Policy and Planning Office, Natural Gas Task Force. This paper was reprinted in: U.S., Congress, Senate, Committee on Energy and Natural Resources, *Hearings on Natural Gas Pricing Proposals of President Carter's Energy Program* (Part D of S. 1469), 95th Cong., 1st sess., 7, 13, 14 and 17 June 1977, publication 95–75.

18. Congressional suspicions were first aroused in the period just before the 1977 floor debates, when it became known publicly that the White House had held up publication of a politically inconvenient Energy Research and Development Administration study, repeatedly asking ERDA to reanalyze and rewrite its material. The study, called the Market Oriented Program Planning Study (MOPPS), concluded that there was far more gas than any present analyses were acknowledging if prices were allowed to rise to, say, $3.00/mcf. It was brought to light in a hearing conducted by Representative Walter Flowers, chairman of the House Science and Technology Subcommittee on Fossil and Nuclear Energy, and was cited repeatedly in the August 3 floor debate on the gas bill. U.S., Congress, House, Subcommittee on Fossil and Nuclear Energy Research of the Committee on Science and Technology, *Hearings on Market Oriented Program Planning Study,* 95th Cong., 1st sess., 12 July 1977.

The administration's credibility received a second jolt in December as conferees were starting their work on natural gas. An interagency Professional Audit Review Team created in 1976 specifically to monitor federal energy information efforts issued a report on December 5, 1977 that accused the administration of changing its computer model to meet preconceived policy objectives. According to the team, the office responsible for producing the administration's estimates "has not been independent of the energy policy function nor was the office managed and operated in a manner conducive to promoting credibility." The team noted that the office made twenty-one changes in its basic predictive energy model, the Project Independence Evaluation System (PIES), under Schlesinger's orders or with his approval. The net impact of the changes, the report said, was to increase anticipated energy demand and decrease predicted domestic supplies. Obviously, more demand and less supply means more need for a legislated national energy program. The twenty-one changes affected virtually all of the PIES forecasts. There had been criticisms of PIES's predictions during the Ford administration, so some changes might have been called for. But these changes were adopted by a White House policy staff without prior public discussion or even subsequent public notification. U.S. Professional Audit Review Team, *Report to the President and the Congress: Activities of the Office of Energy Information and Analysis,* Federal Energy Administration, 5 December 1977, p. 29. The team was chaired by Richard W. Kelley of the General Accounting Office and contained staff level representatives from the Securities and Exchange Commission, Bureau of Labor Statistics, Federal Trade Commission, Bureau of the Census, and Council of Economic Advisors. The team and the Office of Energy Information and Analysis both were established by the Energy Conservation and Production Act dated August 14, 1976 (90 Stat. 1125). For a summary of the report, see Richard Corrigan, "Operation Manipulation," *National Journal,* 17 December 1977, p. 1967.

The critique came out at a bad time for the administration—if any time could be a good one. The conference was stalled over natural gas pricing. While many more basic political factors produced and sustained the stalemate, the base case misestimates were not helping promote a spirit of compromise. Gas producers tended to dismiss the administration's numbers. They thought, as Schroeder did, that they might get more money if the law stayed unchanged than under an administration supported compromise involving regulation of the intrastate market. (The basis for this suspicion was made public March 3, when Charles Curtis, chairman of the Federal Energy

Regulatory Commission said in answer to a question before the Senate Energy and Natural Resources Subcommittee on Energy, Conservation and Regulation that the regulated national rate could go to $2.52/mcf if the rationale and input that led the FPC to approve $1.42 rate in 1976 were applied in 1978.) In contrast, many of the administration's initial supporters, accepting the administration's analysis, thought a stalemate leaving present law unchanged would leave producer revenues and consumer costs below the cost of both the House (administration) bill and Senate (deregulation) bill.

19. The administration revision came in "Base Case Alteration," an unreleased Department of Energy document that put the administration's bill about $5 billion below the base case for 1978–85.

20. Schroeder, in his twenty-five-page "Producer Revenue Impacts of the House Bill Versus Continuation of the Present System" that went to Jackson's staff in February, said the House bill would yield producer revenues of $9 to $18 billion less than the base case during 1978–85.

21. U.S., Congress, House, Subcommittee on Energy and Power of the Committee on Interstate and Foreign Commerce, *Hearings on the National Energy Act.*, pt. 2, pp. 85–124; U.S., Congress, House of Representatives, A report prepared by the staff of the Subcommittee on Energy and Power for use by the Committee on Interstate and Foreign Commerce, *Economic Analysis of Natural Gas Policy Alternatives,* December 1977, Committee Print 95–31.

22. Joseph A. Pechman, ed. *Setting National Priorities: The 1978 Budget* (Washington, D.C.: The Brookings Institution, 1977), pp. 317–53.

23. See Milton Russell, "Suddenly, There's Plenty of Natural Gas," *Washington Post,* 19 January 1979, A21:1.

24. U.S. Congressional Budget Office, *Natural Gas Pricing Proposals: A Comparative Analysis,* p. v.

25. Ibid., pp. xi–xii.

26. See Interview with Comptroller General Elmer B. Staats, "GAO Hopes Efficiency Adds Up," *The San Diego Union,* 7 March 1976.

27. Comptroller General of the United States, *Implications of Deregulating the Price of Natural Gas,* Report to the House of Representatives, Committee on Government Operations, OSP–76–11, p. ii.

28. Comptroller General, *An Evaluation of the President's National Energy Plan,* pp. 418–19.

29. Ibid., p. 1.

30. See Michael J. Malbin, "CRS—The Congressional Agency That Just Can't Say 'No'," *National Journal,* 19 February 1977, p. 287.

31. *Congressional Record,* daily ed., 3 August 1977, p. H8410.

32. Malbin, "CRS—The Congressional Agency That Just Can't Say 'No,'" p. 287

33. L. Kumins, "The Economic Impact of the Energy and Power Subcommittee Natural Gas Amendments to H.R. 6831," Congressional Research Service, undated.

34. *Congressional Record,* daily ed., 21 September, 1979, p. S15251.

35. Congressional Budget Office, *Natural Gas Pricing Proposals: A Comparative Analysis,* p. 23.

36. One senator on Senator Kennedy's Judiciary Committee was quoted as saying that the way Kennedy uses staff results in "the most intense, uncommon competition I've ever seen on a staff. They can be ruthless, a bunch of prima donnas trying to outproduce each other to get his attention." Charles R. Babcock, "Kennedy Touch at Judiciary: Bright, Fractious Staff," *Washington Post,* 20 July 1979, A2.

37. Senator Pete Domenici (R.-N. Mex.), *Congressional Record,* daily ed., 22 September 1977, p. S15334.

38. Congressional Research Service, *Project Interdependence: U.S. and World Energy Outlook Through 1990,* Printed for the use of the U.S. House Committee on Interstate and Foreign Commerce and U.S. Senate Committee on Energy and Natural Resources and U.S. Senate Committee on Commerce, Science and Transportation, November, 1977 p. 203.

39. See footnote 12.

40. Natural Gas Supply Committee, *The Net Benefits to the American Economy of Deregulation of the Price of New Natural Gas,* p. 59.

41. Ibid, p. 3.

42. *Congressional Record,* daily ed., 22 September, 1977, p. S15328–29 and 4 October 1977, p. S16819–22.

43. Government, industry and university estimates of potentially recoverable conventional gas reserves all say there are from thirty-three to seventy years (750 to 1,500) Tcf of gas in the ground. All of these estimates are talking about reserves in soft rock, recoverable at a profit, with known or foreseeable technologies. All similar predictions about oil and gas reserves made over the past seventy-five years have been far too pessimistic. Furthermore, none of the estimates include gas from Devonianshale (perhaps another 600 Tcf), Rocky Mountain tight formation gas (another 600 Tcf), geopressurized methane (500 to 1,000 Tcf more), or other geopressurized resources (yet another 3,000 to 50,000 Tcf!). These resources, if fully developed, could mean up to another one thousand years of supply. The various estimates may be found in the *Congressional Record,* daily ed., 3 August 1977, p. H8400.

44. Ibid., 4 October, 1977, p. S16321.

45. One can go further than this to assert that the different views about fairness that lay behind the New Deal Democratic-Republican party realignment were the key elements in the deregulation roll call votes. The usual interpretation is that the issue was a regional one. However, on the crucial Senate vote on September 22, 1977, twenty-one states saw their two senators voting on opposite sides of the issue. In four of these, senators from the same party disagreed. The other seventeen were Democratic-Republican splits. This compares with eight states with senators from different parties voting together. Six of those eight (Virginia, Arizona, Nebraska, Massachusetts, New York, and New Jersey) had a senator who often voted with the other party. That leaves only Texas and Alaska of the eight. One may add Oklahoma and Louisiana to these as states where producer interests were paramount. Constituencies played an important role in the other states, of course. But Democrats and Republicans generally were free to define their constituencies in ways that fit their economic and moral outlooks.

Chapter 10

1. Alexander Hamilton, John Jay, and James Madison, *The Federalist* No. 52, (New York: Modern Library, 1937), p. 343.

2. Ibid., No. 63, pp. 411–13.

3. For two articles that connect recent reforms to a decline in the deliberative processes on revenue issues, see Catherine E. Rudder, "Committee Reform and the Revenue Process," in *Congress Reconsidered,* ed. Lawrence C. Dodd and Bruce I. Oppenheimer, (New York: Praeger, 1977), pp. 117–39 and I.M. Destler, " 'Reforming' Trade Politics: The Weakness of Ways and Means," *Washington Post,* 28 November 1978, A19.

4. U.S., Congress, House, *Constitution, Jefferson's Manual and Rules of the House of Representatives of the United States, 96th Congress* by William Holmes Brown, Parliamentarian, House Doc. 95-403, 95th Cong., 2d sess., (Washington, D.C.: Government Printing Office, 1979), Secs. 359–73 and 749–52.

5. Survey conducted in the 89th Congress by John Saloma III under the auspices of the American Political Science Association's Study of Congress Project. Findings reported in Donald G. Tacheron and Morris K. Udall, *The Job of the Congressman,* 2d ed., (Indianapolis: Bobbs-Merrill, 1970), p. 303.

6. U.S., Congress, House, Commission on Administrative Review, *Administrative Reorganization and Legislative Management,* 95th Cong., 1st sess., vol. 2 of 2: *Work Management,* House Doc. 95-232, pp. 17–20. My thanks to Roger Davidson for pointing out the significance of this.

7. James Q. Wilson, "American Politics, Then & Now," *Commentary,* February 1979, pp. 39–46.

8. See Joseph M. Bessette, "Deliberation in Congress," a paper presented at the 1979 Annual Meeting of the American Political Science Association, Washington, D.C., Aug. 31–Sept. 3, 1979, *passim.,* for a discussion of this theme. The paper is based on Bessette's *"Deliberation in Congress: A Preliminary Investigation"* (Ph.D. diss., University of Chicago, 1978).

9. For an analysis of a parallel decline in the role of deliberation in party politics see Nelson Polsby, "The News Media as An Alternative To Party in the Presidential Selection Process," in *Political Parties in the Eighties,* ed. Robert A. Goldwin (Washington, D.C.: American Enterprise Institute, 1980), p. 60 Polsby talks about recent changes in the nominating process as involving a "transformation of a set of decisions from deliberative to nondeliberative modes." Congress would still be a deliberative body, according to the definition of "deliberation" in Polsby's essay, but nonetheless it is interesting that the decline of deliberation in Congress to which I refer and its decline in the nominating process, mentioned by Polsby, have occurred at roughly the same time.

10. Henry Kissinger, *White House Years* (Boston: Little, Brown and Co., 1979), p. 142.

11. Remarks made at a conference, "The Role of the Legislature In Western Democracies," held June 8–10, 1979 in Surrey, England. (Washington, D.C.: American Enterprise Institute, forthcoming), session IV.

12. Theodore Lowi refers to this as "interest group liberalism" in *The End of Liberalism: Ideology, Policy, and the Crisis of Public Authority* (New York: W.W. Norton & Co., 1969), pp. 68–97.

INDEX

68673